# Kris Jamsa

# STARTING

*with*

# Microsoft®

# Visual Basic®

## Check the Web for Updates:

To check for updates or corrections relevant to this book and/or CD-ROM visit our updates page on the Web at **http://www.prima-tech.com/updates**.

## Send Us Your Comments:

To comment on this book or any other PRIMA TECH title, visit our reader response page on the Web at **http://www.prima-tech.com/comments**.

## How to Order:

For information on quantity discounts, contact the publisher: Prima Publishing, P.O. Box 1260BK, Rocklin, CA 95677-1260; (916) 787-7000. On your letterhead, include information concerning the intended use of the books and the number of books you want to purchase.

# Kris Jamsa's
# STARTING
## *with*
# Microsoft®
# Visual Basic®

**ROB FRANCIS**

Prima Tech is a division of Prima Publishing.

Prima Publishing and colophon are registered trademarks of Prima Communications, Inc. PRIMA TECH is a trademarks of Prima Communications, Inc., Roseville, California 95661.

**Publisher:** Stacy L. Hiquet

**Associate Marketing Manager:** Jennifer Breece

**Managing Editor:** Sandy Doell

**Technical Reviewer:** Greg Perry

**Production and Editorial:** Argosy

**Cover Design:** Prima Design Team

Microsoft, Windows, and Visual Basic are either registered trademarks of Microsoft Corporation in the United States and/or other countries.

*Important:* Prima Publishing cannot provide software support. Please contact the appropriate software manufacturer's technical support line or Web site for assistance.

Prima Publishing and the author have attempted throughout this book to distinguish proprietary trademarks from descriptive terms by following the capitalization style used by the manufacturer.

Information contained in this book has been obtained by Prima Publishing from sources believed to be reliable. However, because of the possibility of human or mechanical error by our sources, Prima Publishing, or others, the Publisher does not guarantee the accuracy, adequacy, or completeness of any information and is not responsible for any errors or omissions or the results obtained from use of such information. Readers should be particularly aware of the fact that the Internet is an ever-changing entity. Some facts may have changed since this book went to press.

ISBN: 0-7615-3238-2

Library of Congress Catalog Card Number: 2001086959

Printed in the United States of America.

01 02 03 04 05 II 10 9 8 7 6 5 4 3 2 1

# Dedication

To my parents, Anne and Gary, for all their support and love and especially for instilling in me the importance of education.

# Acknowledgments

Firstly, I would like to acknowledge my wife, Shahla, who threatened to play games on the computer whenever I wasn't working on the book! I think this book would have taken twice as long if not for her. I'd also like to thank my friends Blythe Walker and Ian Vink for their support and encouragement during my early stages with Visual Basic. If not for them I would never have discovered Visual Basic, intent as I was on Visual C++. I'd also like to thank my friend, Omid Dadgar, of www.arcpics.com for the use of his digital art in the book. To my immediate colleagues in alphabetical order—Shoa Aminpour, Read Currelly, Gautam Das, Desmond Pemberton-Piggott and Kouhyar Rowshan—thank you for putting up with me during the course of writing this book. Special acknowledgements to Arman Danesh and Gautam Das for their encouragement to actually write a book in the first place. Many thanks to my editor, Kris Jamsa, for all his support during this project, not to mention his patient guidance in attaining a consistent book writing style. Also many thanks to Caroline Roop, Greg Perry and Laura R. Gabler for all their friendly help throughout the entire editing process. It truly was a pleasure working with you all.

And for no reason other than promises of dreadful experiences coming my way if I didn't mention them—Mollie Sandidge, Francisco Diaz, Agazzi (I'm too cute) Diaz, Armando and Kathy Mehia, Samah Sohrab, Alex and Charlie Leith, Ethan (of The Ethan Leith Fan Club fame), Chris Lay, Savvy Him, Stuart Hall and the entire ISD department!

Thank you,

Rob Francis

# Contents at a Glance

## Part I — Basics and Fundamentals

# Part II — Interface——Look and Feel

# Part III — Advanced Concepts

# Contents

# Installing Visual Basic

If you bought this book to complement a version of Visual Basic that you have already installed, then you can skip over the rest of this lesson, which will cover the installation of Visual Basic. You can find a full Visual Basic compiler, the Visual Basic 6.0 Working Model, on the companion CD that comes with this book.

Insert the CD in the computer's CD-ROM drive and, providing you have not disabled the Windows AutoPlay feature, the initial dialog for installing Visual Basic will appear, as shown in Figure 1.1. Alternatively, if Auto-Play is turned off, then simply click your mouse on the Start button and select the Run option.

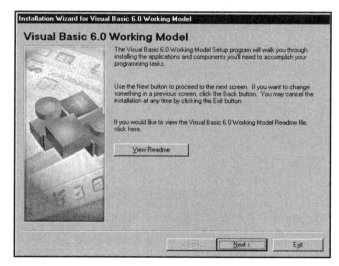

## Figure 1.1

*The initial dialog that appears when you insert the CD.*

By clicking on the View Readme button, you can view the Readme file, which is an HTML file describing known errors, bugs, and changes, as well as technical information concerning this version of Visual Basic. Click on the Next button when you are ready to continue with the installation of Visual Basic.

The next dialog is the End User License Agreement, as shown in Figure 1.2. Read through this agreement and then choose if you accept the agreement or not before clicking your mouse on the Next button.

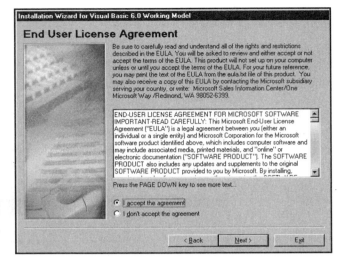

### Figure 1.2

*The End User License Agreement dialog.*

The next dialog is the Product Number and User ID, as shown in Figure 1.3. For the version of Visual Basic that comes on the CD, you will not have to supply a product number and can simply type in your name. Click your mouse on the Next button to continue.

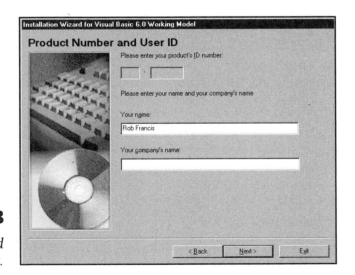

### Figure 1.3

*The Product Number and User ID dialog.*

Depending on what version of Internet Explorer you have on your computer, the Installation Wizard may next ask you to install Internet Explorer version 4.01, as shown in Figure 1.4. Be aware that after installing Internet Explorer 4.01 the Installation Wizard will require you to close all your programs before restarting the computer. If you have a version of Internet Explorer that is higher than 4.01, such as 5.0 or 5.5 for example, then it is not necessary to install Internet Explorer 4.01. Click on the Next button to continue with the installation of Internet Explorer 4.01, if necessary, following the instructions that are given.

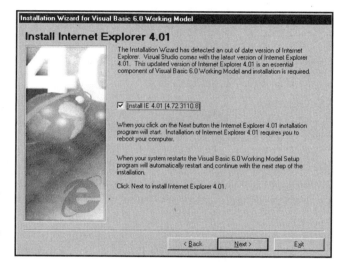

### Figure 1.4

*The Installation Wizard asks you to install Internet Explorer version 4.01.*

If you had to install Internet Explorer 4.01 and restart your computer, log on again with the same account that you used to begin the Visual Basic installation. The Installation Wizard for Visual Basic 6.0 will continue, presenting you with a dialog that informs you of the successful installation of Internet Explorer 4.01, as shown in Figure 1.5. Click your mouse on the Next button to continue.

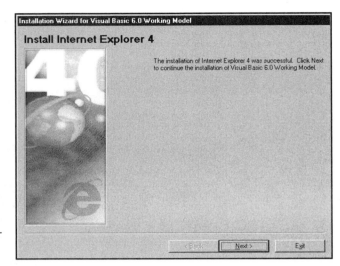

**Figure 1.5**

*The post-restart dialog after the successful installation of Internet Explorer 4.01.*

The next dialog is the Choose Common Install Folder, as shown in Figure 1.6. This section is for installing commonly used programming files, not the actual Visual Basic compiler itself. You can either accept the default installation path or enter in a different path. Click your mouse on the Next button to continue.

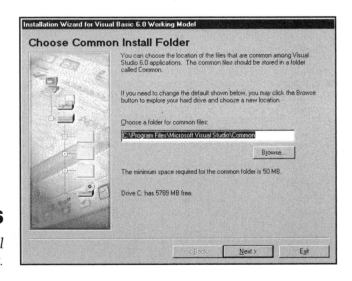

**Figure 1.6**

*The Choose Common Install Folder dialog.*

Now the actual setup process begins. The first screen that you will see in this stage is the Welcome screen, as shown in Figure 1.7. Click your mouse on the Continue button to continue with the setup of Visual Basic.

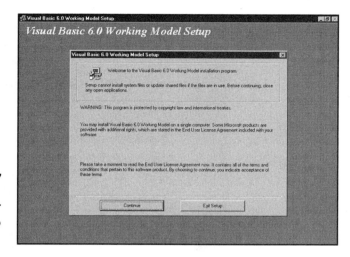

**Figure 1.7**

*The initial Welcome screen for the Visual Basic setup program.*

The next screen gives you a choice between a typical setup and a custom setup, as well as where to install the actual Visual Basic compiler files. You can either accept the default path for installing the files or select a different path. To make sure that you get everything that you can, select the custom setup by clicking your mouse on the large square button to the left of Custom, as shown in Figure 1.8.

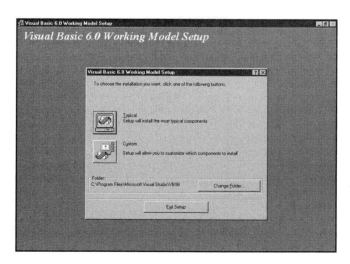

**Figure 1.8**

*Selecting between typical and custom installations.*

The next screen shows you all of the optional components that you can choose to install. Unless you have a severe shortage of space on your hard drive, you should click your mouse on the Select All button to get everything and then click your mouse on the Continue button to continue with the Visual Basic installation, as shown in Figure 1.9.

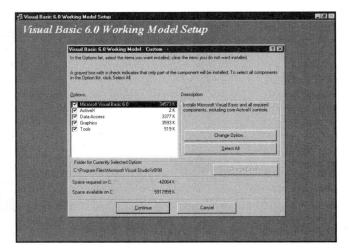

**Figure 1.9**

*Selecting all the components from the custom setup screen.*

Visual Basic setup will now start installing to your hard drive, using all the information that you have provided, giving you progress status through a progress bar, as shown in Figure 1.10.

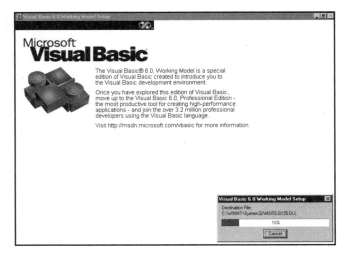

**Figure 1.10**

*Visual Basic setup's progress bar.*

After the installation of Visual Basic is complete, Visual Basic Installation Wizard will show you another screen asking you to restart the computer, as shown in Figure 1.11. Click your mouse on the Restart Windows button to restart the computer.

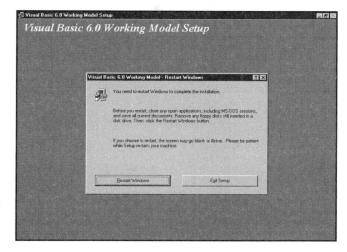

**Figure 1.11**

*Visual Basic Installation Wizard asking you to restart the computer.*

The final dialog of the Visual Basic setup asks if you want to register your copy of Visual Basic, as shown in Figure 1.12. Leave the check mark in the checkbox if you want to register or uncheck the checkbox if you do not want to register. Click your mouse on the Finish button. That's it! You have completed your installation of Visual Basic.

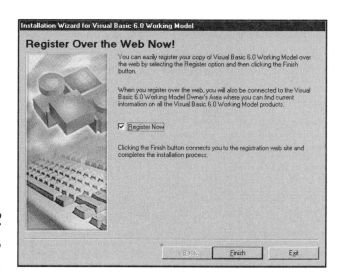

**Figure 1.12**

*The Register Over the Web Now! dialog.*

# What You Must Know

◆ An important step towards writing good programs is knowing why you use a certain feature, which then aides you in knowing when to use it and when not to use it.

◆ Design time is when you are working within the Visual Basic environment; runtime is when you are actually running a compiled version of your program.

◆ Installing a Visual Basic compiler allows you to create programs in the Visual Basic language.

# Lesson 2

---

# Creating Your First Visual Basic Program

In Lesson 1, "Installing Visual Basic," you learned how to install Visual Basic and you became familiar with the programming environment. You can now get on with the real reason you are here—to write programs! You will start with something simple of course, just to get into the swing of things, then move into more complex issues gradually so that you are not overwhelmed. Programming in Visual Basic is easy and fun, so relax and enjoy it.

In this lesson, you will create your first program using Visual Basic. By the time you finish this lesson, you will understand the following key concepts:

◆ Before you can run a program that you create or a program that you change, you must first use Visual Basic to compile the program statements, changing the statements from the textual form that you can read into the ones and zeros the computer understands. Programmers refer to your Visual Basic program statements as source code.

◆ Each Visual Basic program you create is made up of multiple files that are collectively known as a project. You must save your projects to disk to be able to access them again after closing the Visual Basic environment.

◆ Controls are prewritten modules of source code that provide functionality to your Visual Basic programs. A control's properties let you customize a control's features.

◆ There are two main elements to Visual Basic programming. The object window is where you do all your "visual" work (such as building the user interface) in Visual Basic and the code window is where you type in your source code statements.

# Starting Visual Basic

Before you can create a Visual Basic program, Visual Basic must be running. To start Visual Basic, select Microsoft Visual Basic 6.0 from your installation folder. The default location of the installation folder is Start menu Programs then in the Microsoft Visual Studio 6; however, you may have a slightly different path depending on your choices during the installation as well as the version of Visual Basic that you are using. Within the installation folder click your mouse on Visual Basic 6.0. Windows will display the Visual Basic programming environment, as well as a dialog that prompts you for project information, as shown in Figure 2.1.

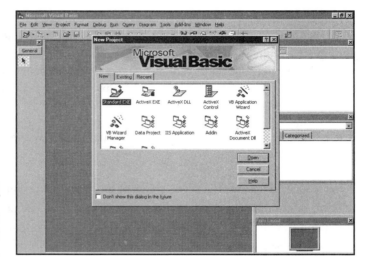

**Figure 2.1**

*The Visual Basic programming environment and New Project dialog.*

# Selecting a Project Type

Normally, when Visual Basic starts, it will display the New Project dialog previously shown in Figure 2.1 that prompts you for project information. If your screen does not contain the New Project dialog, select the File menu New option. Visual Basic, in turn, will display the New Project dialog.

In this case, because you will create an executable program (which programmers refer to as EXE files), select the Standard EXE option and then click your mouse on the Open option. As shown in Figure 2.2, Visual Basic will open your new project, displaying a new form. The form is the visual part of your program that users will see on their screen. You can think of the form as the blank canvas on which you paint your masterpiece.

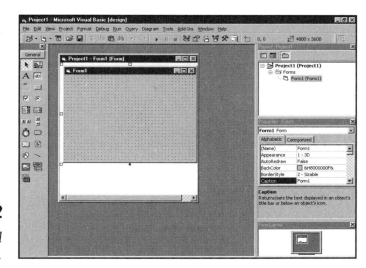

## Figure 2.2

*The new form that Visual Basic displays.*

# Working in the Visual Basic Environment

To simplify your programming tasks, Visual Basic lets your programs change the properties of various objects on the screen such as a form. For example, a form contains a *Caption* property that defines the title bar's text. There are also color properties that specify the text color or background color.

To change the form's title, you must assign new text to the *Caption* property. To start, customize your program's form by changing the *Caption* property from *Form 1* to *My First Program*. As shown in Figure 2.3, the Properties window within the Visual Basic environment contains two columns. The left column contains the property names and the right column contains the values assigned to those properties. Click your mouse in the right-hand column of the *Caption* property and use your keyboard to replace the text that is there with **My First Program**. Visual Basic will immediately reflect any changes to the *Caption* property on the title bar of the form.

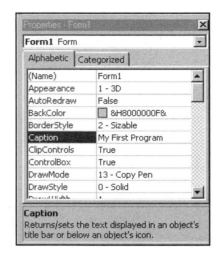

**Figure 2.3**

*Changing the Caption property.*

Next you can add some text to the form. To do this you will need to add a Label control. Controls are prewritten modules of source code that provide functionality to your Visual Basic programs. They save you from a lot of difficult and time-consuming programming and allow you to get on with what you are really trying to accomplish. The Label control looks like an uppercase A. In Figure 2.4 the Label control is the second control down in the left column.

**Figure 2.4**

*The controls panel with the Label control selected.*

To select the Label control, click your mouse on the control's icon. Visual Basic will change your mouse cursor from an arrow to a cross-hair (large plus sign) if you point somewhere within the form. Point the mouse cursor somewhere in the top left of the form but below the title bar. Hold the left mouse button down. Drag the mouse down a bit and then right so that you form a long rectangle, then release the mouse button. You have just added your first Label control.

Select the new Label control by clicking your mouse on it. Under the Properties section change the *Caption* property to **Hello, world**. A time honored tradition for first programs is to display the text "Hello, world" and you will often hear of such programs.

To run the program, simply select the Run menu Start option. Your program should look similar to Figure 2.5.

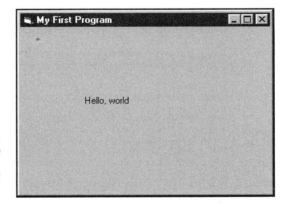

### Figure 2.5

*Displaying output from the Hello, world program.*

Congratulations! You've just created your first Visual Basic program. To exit the program, simply click your mouse on the Close button, which appears as an X in the window's top right corner, just as in any other Windows program.

# Saving Your Visual Basic Program to Disk

After creating your masterpiece you might be upset at the thought of having to start all over again simply because you failed to save your program to disk. For this reason, now would be a good time to show you how to save your project. When starting larger projects later on, you will probably find it useful to name your project and any forms, modules, or classes that you use (you will learn more about these later on) and save everything before actually starting any code or adding any controls. You will find it useful because you will often find yourself needing to save quickly or frequently later on and it is easier (actually quite transparent) if everything is organized and named from the outset. The other reason to save the program at the outset is due to the fact that your code may make references to your forms or modules and it is much more work to go back through all your code and change all references to a certain name later on than if you just name it thoughtfully at the start and save your project.

To save your current project files to disk, first select the Project menu and choose Project Properties. Visual Basic will display the Project Properties dialog as shown in Figure 2.6.

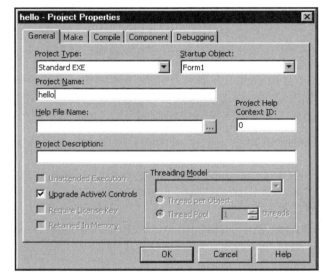

**Figure 2.6**

*The Project Properties dialog.*

Under the General tab (the default tab) you will see the Project Name field. Click your mouse in this field and replace the default name of *Project1* with **hello**. Click your mouse on the OK button and Visual Basic will save your changes and close the Project Properties dialog.

You have just renamed your project. You do not need to rename your project every time that you want to save your files, only the first time that you save a new project. If you forget how to rename your projects in future, simply refer back to this section to remind yourself. You can do this with any section actually. Do not panic if you cannot memorize all these places to click and items to change—they come with time. The book will always be there for you to quickly refresh your memory.

After renaming your project you now need to save your project files to disk. In the main Visual Basic environment, click on the File menu Save Project option. Visual Basic will display the Save File As dialog, as shown in Figure 2.7.

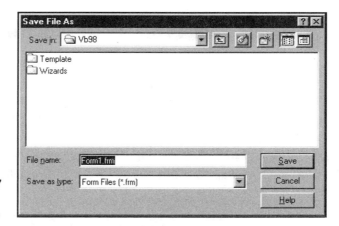

**Figure 2.7**

*The Save File As dialog.*

To better organize the projects you create, you should place each project within its own folder. Click your mouse on the Create New Folder icon and create a folder called **lesson02**. Click your mouse on the Open button to open your new folder and then follow this by clicking your mouse on the Save button. The filename default of *Form1.frm* is fine for now. In larger projects you would not use the default filenames but rather you would use a naming convention. In Lesson 5, "Understanding Subroutines and Functions," you will look more closely at naming conventions. After the Form has been saved the Save Project As dialog prompts you to save the project. Accept the default filename *hello.vbp* by clicking your mouse on the Save button again. That's it.

After you have saved your project, you do not need to do all this organizing again for each subsequent save because Visual Basic will reuse all the filename and folder options previously used for the project. All you need to do is click your mouse on the toolbar icon as in Figure 2.8 to manually save your project in future.

**Figure 2.8**

*The toolbar's Save icon.*

**Saving Your Projects Automatically**

*Visual Basic offers the option of automatically saving your project for you before you try running it. This is very useful as it can prevent you from accidentally forgetting to save your code before running something that crashes the system. Many people have lost hours of work because they compiled and ran their program without saving the project first. To set this environment variable, go to the Tools menu and select Options. Under the Environment tab, select the Save Changes radio button, as in Figure 2.9. Click your mouse on the OK button when you are finished.*

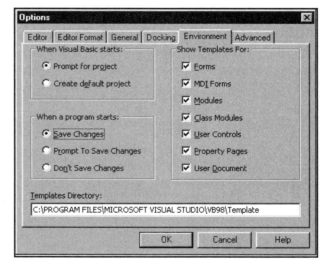

**Figure 2.9**

*The Visual Basic environment's Options dialog.*

# Loading Your Visual Basic Program from Disk

Now that you have saved your project, close it and see if everything looks alright when you open it up again. You can close your project by either selecting File menu, Remove Project or by simply clicking your mouse on the Close button in the top right corner of the window. Be careful if using the latter method that you click your mouse on the lower of the two Close buttons in the top right corner; otherwise, you could find yourself exiting from the entire Visual Basic programming environment.

To load your hello project again, there are a few choices available to you. Most of these are standard Windows options, so many of you should feel quite at home. To open the project, select the File menu, Open Project option or click your mouse on the Open Project icon on the toolbar (it looks like a yellow folder partially open and is situated to the left of the Save Project icon). Both of these methods will display a dialog with which you can navigate or browse to the project you want to open and then select the Open button.

Yet another method exists, however, that you may prefer to use. Under the File menu just above the Exit option is a list of recently used projects. Simply click your mouse on *Lesson2\hello.vbp* and your project will load. This last option is nice for two reasons. First, developers tend to work on the same project for a while before changing so there is a good chance that the project you are currently wanting to load is in this list. Secondly, you do not have to worry about the dialog that comes up with the other project loading options.

Using any of the methods above, load your *hello* project that you created and saved earlier in the lesson.

# Improving Your Program

So you have created your first program. Did you notice that there was no code on your part? That does not mean that you do not learn to program code in Visual Basic, it is merely an indication of how powerful the language is that you can achieve quite a lot with very little effort. Visual Basic has handled all the low-level, tedious work of interacting with the Windows Graphical Device Interface and input systems and allowed you to simply concentrate on what you wanted to do—display a window with text on it. You did not have to work out mathematically how many pixels wide to make your Label control. Visual Basic gives you the option to size your controls visually, which makes design very easy and quick.

You will now look at improving the program that you created earlier by making the label hidden until you click your mouse on a button.

Start off by loading up the *hello* project from earlier in the lesson if you have not already done so.

In many Windows programs, you will notice the rectangular buttons that you must click your mouse on to perform certain functions. In Visual Basic these are known as CommandButtons and they are simple controls that you can drag and drop onto your forms. You should have noticed that when you hover the mouse cursor over a control Visual Basic presents you with a small ToolTip (small rectangular box) that tells you what that control is. Click on the CommandButton control icon as in Figure 2.10 and then add the CommandButton in the same way you added the Label control earlier.

### Figure 2.10

*The CommandButton control icon with ToolTip display.*

In the Properties section for the CommandButton, change the caption to **Show me!**. If you have forgotten how to do this, refer to earlier in this lesson when you changed the caption for the Label control in the Properties section.

Now you will do some Visual Basic coding! Double-click your mouse somewhere on your form but not on the Label or CommandButton. The code window should open with the following text already given for you:

```
Private Sub Form_Load()

End Sub
```

What you want to do is hide the Label control's text until you click your mouse on the CommandButton. So you need to change the visibility property of your label. Add this line to the *Form_Load()* subroutine. It should now look something like the following:

```
Private Sub Form_Load()
    Label1.Visible = False
End Sub
```

You will notice a drop-down list appearing as you try to type in the new line of code. This is Visual Basic trying to assist you by offering all available options to you. Just keep typing until the property you want is highlighted and then press the tab key and Visual Basic will insert the full name of the property into the code for you. In your current case you only need to type the **.v** to go straight to the *Visible* property as shown in Figure 2.11.

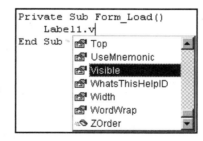

**Figure 2.11**

*The Auto List Members combo box.*

 **Toggling the Auto List Members Combo Box**

*Everyone is different. Some programmers are annoyed by certain bells and whistles that pop up while they are concentrating on writing source code. Others revel in all the fancy features that Visual Basic provides, such as the Auto List Members combo box, that causes a drop-down list to display every time that you type in the dot after an object's name.*

*You can toggle the Auto List Members combo box on or off by selecting the Tools menu, Options option with your mouse. Visual Basic will display the Options dialog. Within the Options dialog box Editor tab, click your mouse on the checkbox beside the Auto List Members field to toggle this feature on or off.*

Select the View menu, Object option, or click your mouse on the View Object button so that you can see the window with your form on it. Now double-click your mouse on the CommandButton called *Show me!* so that it takes you back to the code window. You will see some new code:

```
Private Sub Command1_Click()

End Sub
```

You will not see a detailed description of subroutines here, as this will be covered in Lesson 5, "Understanding Subroutines and Functions." For now, just accept that when you click your mouse on the *Show me!* Command-Button, any code between these two lines will be executed. You want to add a line of code to make the Label control visible. When it comes to syntax, code provides very little freedom of expression. See if you can do this on your own and then check to see if it looks exactly like the following:

```
Private Sub Command1_Click()
    Label1.Visible = True
End Sub
```

Now that the Label is visible, your *Show me!* CommandButton is no longer very useful. Be nice to your user and disable the button for them so that they know that the *Show Me!* button is no longer useful. Add a line of code to make the CommandButton's *Enabled* property *False*. It should look something like this:

```
Private Sub Command1_Click()
    Label1.Visible = True
    Command1.Enabled = False
End Sub
```

The name of your CommandButton is the Visual Basic default of *Command1*. Later in the book you will look at the importance of naming conventions and how you should give your controls meaningful names. As you are just writing a simple program, you can overlook this for the moment and concentrate on fundamentals.

Finally, you can test your program to see if all of your changes and coding work! Press F5 to compile and run the program from within the Visual Basic environment. Did your program open okay? When you click your mouse on the *Show me!* button the text, "Hello, world" should appear on your form and the CommandButton should be grayed out, as shown in Figure 2.12.

**Figure 2.12**

*Your improved program in action.*

# Creating an Executable Program

Running your programs from the Visual Basic programming environment is convenient while you are programming, but there are bound to be occasions when you would like the program to be a separate executable file so that you can run it independently or on other machines easily. To do this, you must compile the program as an executable file.

Using your mouse, select File menu, Make hello.exe, and Visual Basic will display the Make Project dialog where you can choose exactly what you want to call the executable and where you want to save it. Figure 2.13 shows an example of the Make Project dialog that Visual Basic will display.

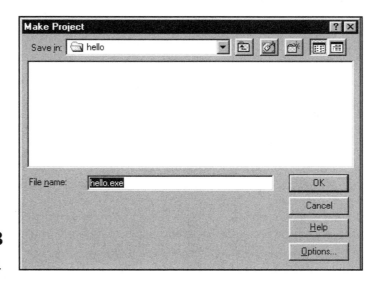

**Figure 2.13**

*The Make Project dialog.*

Type in the name of the executable you want to create (or simply accept the default) and click your mouse on the OK button. You have just created your first executable. You can double-click your mouse on that file now to run it on your computer even when the Visual Basic programming environment is not running.

# What You Must Know

The collection of related files that are required to create a Visual Basic program is known as a project, which can be either saved to disk or loaded from disk. Each new project contains a blank form to which you add controls such as Label and CommandButton. Controls not only add functionality to your Visual Basic programs but are also able to be easily customized by editing a control's properties. Although you covered some very basic source code, you will learn much more about how to manipulate source code in Lesson 3, "Using Variables and Constants." Before you continue with Lesson 3, however, make sure you understand the following key concepts:

◆ To create a new project, start Visual Basic and select a project type, such as Standard EXE, from the New Project dialog.

◆ Prior to saving your project for the first time, give your project a meaningful name by using the Project Properties dialog.

◆ To add a control to your form, such as a Label or CommandButton, select the control from the controls panel within the Visual Basic environment, then use your mouse to drag a rectangle on your form in the location you want the control added.

◆ You can customize a control using the control's properties.

◆ To connect code with a CommandButton, double-click your mouse on the control within your form. Visual Basic will bring up the code window, as well as supply you with essential wrapper code within which you can add your own code statements.

◆ To run your program in the Visual Basic environment, select the Run menu, Start option.

◆ You can create an executable program by selecting the File menu, Make project.exe option. Creating an executable program allows you to run your program outside of the Visual Basic environment.

# Lesson 3

---

# Using Variables and Constants

In Lesson 2, "Creating Your First Visual Basic Program," you learned about creating programs that use labels and buttons. In this lesson you are going to build on your programming capabilities by using variables to store information and constants to represent values that do not change while your program runs. By the time you finish this lesson, you will understand the following key concepts:

♦ You use constants in your Visual Basic source code in place of direct values. For example, rather than using the number 35, your code can refer to the more meaningful constant name *NumberOfStudents*. Constants remain unchanged as far as their value for the entire duration of the program.

♦ Using constants in your code reduces errors, saves you editing time when values change, and makes your code more readable.

♦ To declare a constant, you use the keyword *Const*.

♦ An *enumeration* is a special type of constant that lets a constant cover a range of values sequentially, as well as letting your program group constants.

♦ As your program executes, it must store different values in variables at different times. In contrast to a constant, the value a variable contains does not have to be fixed for the duration of the program.

♦ Within a Visual Basic program, you perform mathematical equations by assigning combinations of constants, variables, numerical values, and operators to a variable.

♦ Operator precedence governs the order in which equations are executed when multiple operators are involved in assigning a mathematic value to a variable.

# Understanding Constants

Within your programs, constants are like tags or labels that you can reference within your source code that contain an unchanging value. When you compile your source code, Visual Basic replaces all occurrences of these tags with a value. From the moment your compiled program starts until the time that it ends, the value of all constants within your program does not change. With constants, you change only one location in your code and not all occurrences, which is an incredible benefit to you as a programmer, especially when dealing with lengthy code.

Imagine that you have a constant called *limit* whose value is 10. Within your program you simply use the word *limit* and Visual Basic will replace this with the value 10 when it later compiles your code. Because constants have meaningful names, constants make your code clearer and much more readable than simply using numeric values throughout your code. The following code fragment creates and uses a constant named *limit*:

```
Const limit = 10
Label1.Caption = limit
```

The keyword *Const* tells Visual Basic that the name that follows is a constant. When you create constants, you should choose meaningful names that describe to another programmer who is reading your code the constant's purpose. You cannot have spaces within a constant name. If, for example, you try to name the constant *my upper limit*, Visual Basic will generate a syntax error:

```
Const my upper limit = 10          'this is wrong
```

**NOTE:** *Any code that follows an apostrophe (') on a line of Visual Basic code is considered by the compiler as a comment or remark. You will read more about comments in Lesson 5, "Understanding Subroutines and Functions."*

If you want to use a long constant name, you can use underscores or mix upper- and lowercase letters:

```
Const my_upper_limit = 10          'this is correct
Const YourUpperLimit = 20          'this is correct
```

You can also use constants within your programs to store static strings (text). Although this lesson discusses strings in a later section, you can see how useful using constants can be for strings:

```
Const myPath = "C:\Program Files\Microsoft Office\temp\"
fs.DeleteFile myPath & "tempdata.txt"
```

Instead of having to type in the long path in your code, possibly hundreds of times, you only have to type in the constant name *myPath*. Visual Basic, in turn, will substitute the constant's value within your program automatically, each time you use the constant's name. Using constants for strings also makes it easier to change the code in one place rather than having to find every instance of the string in your code.

You might feel right now that readability of code is not very important and that instead of going through all the hassle of creating constants you would rather just get a program that is functional and working. First, creating readable code is extremely important as you will come to realize when you create larger and more complex programs. Second, the use of constants gives us a single point to change a value that may be used hundreds of times throughout your code, which is extremely valuable for time saving.

You might be thinking that you could achieve the same result by using search and replace techniques on your code. While this is true, it brings us to the third reason to use constants—reducing the chance of errors creeping into your code. A scenario will show this more clearly.

Pretend you are a programmer for a big firm and that you must write a huge program. Within your code, there are 1,000 occurrences of the value 10, of which 100 are a reference to a required limit value. You chose not to use a constant and instead you just put the value 10 directly wherever you required it.

Now imagine the chaos that you would cause by replacing all occurrences of 10 in your code with, say, 15. In this case, you would ruin 900 lines of code by using search and replace! If you had used a constant for the limit, you could simply have changed the constant to equal 15 in one place without affecting any code that should not be affected:

```
Const limit = 15
```

The point is not that search and replace techniques are bad, but rather, that Visual Basic has fundamental features such as constants for a reason and that you should learn not only how to implement a feature but why and when to implement a feature. As you read through the book, this knowledge will come to you and you will soon know that there is a time and place to apply features.

To summarize the reasons you would use constants in your code:

◆ Create readable code

◆ Save time and effort when you must change a value

◆ Reduce your chance of introducing errors

**Understanding the Definition of a Constant**

*"Constants" are references to values that remain fixed for the duration of the program. Learn this definition and you are well on your way. For now, the details of how to create constants or the different variations of constants are secondary to this fundamental understanding that constants are simply names for fixed values.*

*To create a constant within your programs, you use the* Const *keyword, followed by the constant name and value:*

```
Const ConstantName = ConstantValue
```

*The following statement creates a constant called* HoursInADay*:*

```
Const HoursInADay = 24
```

# Using Enumeration to Group Values

One form of using constants that programmers often employ is enumeration, a process that lets them represent a set of related values using constants. Enumeration is basically a set of constants with a sequential (usually but not always) set of integer values. To create an enumeration in Visual Basic, you use the *Enum* keyword. The following statement, for example, groups the colors within an enumeration named *MyColor*:

```
'Enumeration example for different colors
Public Enum MyColor
    white
    red
    blue
    green
    yellow
    orange
    pink
    brown
    purple
    black
End Enum
```

As you can see, this enumeration defines a list of colors. Years ago, programmers might use values such as 0 to represent the color white, 1 to represent the color red, and so on. As you read the programmer's code, you had to memorize the numbers that corresponded to each color. Using an enumeration, however, your program can instead refer to the constant names, such as red, yellow, and blue, which makes your program much easier to read.

Within your code, you can use the enumerated names as follows:

```
Label1.Caption = green
Label2.Caption = purple
```

 *You can also declare a variable of the enumerated type, but you will look at that later in the lesson when you cover variables.*

In this example, the enumeration does not assign specific values to each color name. Rather, Visual Basic will start from 0 and then increase by 1 for each consecutive entry in the enumeration. This means that white equals 0, red equals 1, blue equals 2, and so on right down to black, which is the last entry in the enumeration and is equal to 9.

Sometimes, you will need your enumeration to start from a specific value. In these cases, all you must do is assign the value of the first enumeration and the rest will increment from this value automatically. For example, if you wanted to make white equal to 10, red equal to 11, and so on, all you would have to do is change one line in the enumeration example given earlier:

```
'Enumeration example for different colors
Public Enum MyColor
    white = 10
    red
    blue
    green
    yellow
    orange
    pink
    brown
    purple
    black
End Enum
```

This is a very small change that has a big impact on your code. To give you a better perspective on how powerful and time-saving this technique is, imagine if this was a huge project and you had 50 enumerated colors. If you had typed in white = 50, red = 51, etc. for all of the colors and then found out that you had made a mistake and it should have been white = 45, red = 46, etc. you would be in for a lot of work. But using this method of just setting the first enumeration allows you to easily change the entire set of enumerated colors with one change!

# Using Variables to Store Information

The concept of variables sometimes takes a while before it makes sense for most people when they first encounter it, yet for others it seems natural and they grasp the concept almost straight away. Regardless of which of these categories you are in or even if you are somewhere in-between, it is important for you to get a good, solid understanding of variables to be able to write even some of the simplest programs. Re-read any sections that do not make sense to you, as you will find it worth your while to learn well the skills taught in this lesson rather than moving on to other lessons with either partial understanding of variables or—heaven forbid—none at all.

 **Understanding the Definition of a Variable**

*As your program executes, a variable holds the value of an object. A variable can hold only the value of one object at any given time. In general, a variable is like a named container that can hold different values throughout the course of a program. One variable might store a student's name, while a second variable stores the student's test score.*

As your Visual Basic program executes, it uses variables holding values of objects that can change. One variable might store a user's name while a second variable may store a company's Web address. In general, a variable is simply a storage container, into which your program can place and retrieve an object's value.

Think of variables as being like a drinking glass. The glass can be empty and not hold anything. The glass can be filled with water. The glass could also be filled with milk or orange juice. At any one time the glass can be filled with water, milk, or orange juice but it cannot hold more than one glassful of any liquid or it will spill over the rim. Variables are like this. They can hold different values at different times.

To declare a variable in Visual Basic, you use the *Dim* keyword followed by the name you want to give your new variable. For example, the following declaration creates a variable named *glass*:

```
Dim glass
```

To fill the glass with water, in other words to assign a value to the variable, you use the assignment operator, which in Visual Basic is the equal sign (=). The following statement, for example, assigns the value 1 to the variable *glass*:

```
glass = 1
```

After you assign a value to a variable within your program, you can then use the variable's value. For example, the following statement assigns the value of the *glass* variable to the *Label1.Caption* property:

```
Label1.Caption = glass
```

After the program executes this statement, the *Label1* property will display the value 1 on your form. Next, assuming that your program uses the value 2 to represent milk, you could fill the glass with milk, as shown here:

```
glass = 2
```

To change *Label1* value on the form, and hence show the value that the variable *glass* contains, you would use the following assignment statement:

```
Label1.Caption = glass
```

Notice that Visual Basic *empties your glass* before filling it up with the new drink. In other words, you do not have to clear the variable before using it again because Visual Basic does this for you implicitly. If the analogy of variables being like glasses and the different values they hold being like different drinks helps you, then simply use it when working with standard integers or other variable types.

# Using Variables within Math Operations

As you have learned, variables hold object values. Within your program, each variable must store a specific type of value. One of the simplest object types is an integer. An "integer" can be any whole number (such as −3, 0, 1, 46). The range of integers in Visual Basic is from −32,768 to 32,767. It is good for you to get to know the integer type well because you will be making frequent use of it throughout this book and you will find that you will use it frequently within your own programs.

To declare variables as a specific type (in this case integer) you must specify the type within the *Dim* statement. The following statements declare three integer variables, named *a*, *b*, *c*, and then assign values to each:

```
Dim a As Integer
Dim b As Integer
Dim c As Integer
```

```
a = 5
b = 2
c = a + b
```

At this point, you may be trying to determine the value of the variable c. If you examine the statements step by step, you will find that the variable a is equal to 5 and that b is equal to 2. After the program performs the addition operation, the variable c is equal to 7.

Now this next statement is a little trickier—the statement subtracts 4 from c's current value:

```
c = c - 4
```

If you read the line above with a mathematical eye, the statement may not make sense. How can c equal itself minus 4? The trick is to think of the equal sign (the assignment operator) as meaning *gets* rather than equals. So you read the statement as c gets whatever value c currently contains minus 4. So with that in mind, what is the value of c? The value of c after the line above would be 3 (which you get by subtracting 4 from the current value of 7, or 7 − 4 = 3).

# Understanding Visual Basic's Mathematical Operators

In the previous sections, you have seen some of Visual Basic's mathematical operators—namely, the addition and subtraction operators. The following list briefly describes other operators available in Visual Basic:

| | |
|---|---|
| + | Addition |
| − | Subtraction (and negation) |
| * | Multiplication |
| / | Division |
| \ | Integer division |
| *Mod* | Remainder |
| ^ | Exponential |

The following source code example illustrates each of the operators:

```
Dim a
    a = 3 * 2        'a = 6
    a = 10 / 4       'a = 2.5
    a = 10 \ 4       'a = 2
```

```
a = 10 Mod 3      'a = 1
a = 2 ^ 3         'a = 8
```

The difference between division and integer division is that integer division truncates (chops off) anything after the decimal point. So integer division only keeps the whole numbers or integers. You must be aware that this type of division is also applied if you declare the variable as type integer. In the example above, you notice that the variable *a* is not of type integer but is in fact of type variant. Variants will be discussed later. The main thing to realize here is the difference between the two types of division operators.

The *Mod* operator often confuses programmers. Although the *Mod* operator is not used as frequently as the others, it can make your code simpler. Basically, *Mod* is the remainder of a division operation. In the example above, 10 *Mod* 3 is the same as $10 / 3 = 3$ Remainder 1.

# Understanding Operator Precedence

When you work with variables and mathematical operators, you must be aware of the fact that Visual Basic assigns a precedence to each operator, which specifies the order in which it evaluates operations. For example, consider the following statement that contains multiple operators:

```
Dim a
    a = 8 + 2 * 4 ^ 3 - 1
```

In this example, because of Visual Basic's operator precedence, the variable *a* will equal 135. That is because Visual Basic will first perform the exponential operation ($4 ^ 3 = 64$) and then the multiplication ($2 * 64 = 128$). Next, Visual Basic will perform the addition ($8 + 128 = 136$) followed by the subtraction ($136 - 1 = 135$).

Within your programs, there may be times when you want to control operator precedence. In such cases, you place parentheses around the equations you want Visual Basic to perform first. The following statement uses the same operations, but changes the order in which Visual Basic perform the operations, to produce a different result:

```
Dim a
    a = 8 + (2 * (4 ^ (3 - 1)))
```

When you place equations within parentheses, Visual Basic will always perform those operations first. In this case, *a* will equal 40:

```
a = 8 + (2 * (4 ^ (3 - 1)))
a = 8 + (2 * (4 ^ (2)))
```

```
a = 8 + (2 * (16))
a = 8 + (32)
a = 40
```

Often programmers spend hours trying to debug some strange glitch in their programs that turns out to be due to operator precedence. If you use parentheses correctly, you can always be assured of the order in which equations are evaluated.

The following list shows the natural operator precedence used in Visual Basic:

| | |
|---|---|
| ( ) | Parentheses |
| ^ | Exponential |
| – | Negation |
| * / | Multiplication and division |
| \ | Integer division |
| Mod | Remainder |
| + – | Addition and subtraction |

##  Understanding Variable Types

*Within your program, each variable must be a specific type, such as integer. When you type As (followed by a space), Visual Basic provides you with a drop-down list of all available variable types. Within Visual Basic, there are many different variable types. This book will cover the essential types. In addition to the types Visual Basic provides, you can even create your own types. If you think back to the enumeration example earlier in this lesson, you declared a variable of type myColor:*

```
Dim wall_color As myColor
```

*As you work, you will notice that Visual Basic tries to correct case-sensitivity for you. For example, if you type the following line, Visual Basic will correct the case for you:*

```
dim wall_color as mycolor
```

*Rather than introduce a long list of common types now, you will simply come across them gradually as they are introduced throughout this book. For now, simply know that your variables must be a specific type and the type specifies the set of values a variable can store and the set of operations your program can perform on the variable. For example, an integer variable can store whole numbers (numbers without a decimal point) in the range −32,678 to 32,767. Likewise, your programs can perform arithmetic operations on an integer variable. It would not make sense, for example, for your program to try a multiplication operation on a string variable that might contain a company's name.*

# Test-Driving a Variables Example

It is time to take a break from the theory and to get your hands dirty with some practical stuff. If you need, you can refer to the previous sections as you work through the example. You probably will not have to, as you will discover that you have already covered everything you will need. This section really just puts it all together so you can get an idea of how far you have come with your Visual Basic skills.

To start, what you will do is create a simple program with three different colors to choose from and a counter to keep track of the number of times a color has been chosen. To begin, open a new Visual Basic project and select a standard *EXE* project type.

Add three CommandButtons and change their *Caption* property to *Red*, *Blue*, and *Green*. Then add four label controls to your form. Change the *Caption* property of *Label1* to *Color:* and *Label3* to *Counter:* but do not worry about the other two labels. On *Label2* and *Label4*, change the *BorderStyle* property to "1—Fixed Single". The layout of your form should look something like that shown in Figure 3.1.

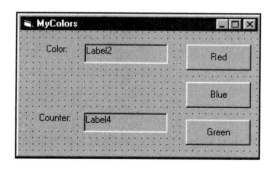

**Figure 3.1**

*Form layout within the Visual Basic environment.*

Next, double-click your mouse on your form to take you to the code window. At the very top of the window declare some constants for your three colors:

```
'These are the constants
Const red = "Red"
Const blue = "Blue"
Const green = "Green"
```

Immediately below your constants you must declare a variable. Instead of writing *Dim* to declare the variable, write *Private*. Later in this book, you will examine the *Private* keyword in detail. For now, simply understand the keyword *Private* means only code for this form can access the variable. Using the *Private* keyword, declare a variable named *counter*:

```
'This is like Dim counter
Private counter
```

Inside the subroutine for *Form_Load()* try to initialize *counter* using the assignment operator (=) by making it equal to zero (*counter* = 0). Then update *Label4* so that it is equal to *counter* (*Label4.Caption* = *counter*). Also try to set *Label2* to be equal to your constant *red* (*Label2.Caption* = *red*). Your subroutine should read as follows:

```
Private Sub Form_Load()
    'initialize and update the counter
    counter = 0
    Label4.Caption = counter

    'initialize and update the color
    Label12.Caption = red
End Sub
```

Now, all you must do is add code for the CommandButtons. From the View menu, select Object or press Shift-F7 or click your mouse on the View Object button. Then, double-click your mouse on the *Red* CommandButton to return to the code window. Within this subroutine, you will place statements that increment the counter by 1 (because the user has clicked on the color button), and you will set the current color. To do so, you must increment your counter variable by 1 and update both your *color* and *counter* labels appropriately:

```
Private Sub Command1_Click()
    'increment the counter
    counter = counter + 1
    Label4.Caption = counter

    'update the color
    Label12.Caption = red
End Sub
```

Do the same as you did for the *Red* CommandButton with both the *Blue* and *Green* CommandButtons. Make sure that you assign the correct color constant to *Label2*. The entire code window should look as follows:

```
'These are the constants
Const red = "Red"
Const blue = "Blue"
Const green = "Green"

'This is like Dim counter
Private counter


Private Sub Command1_Click()
    'increment the counter
    counter = counter + 1
    Label4.Caption = counter

    'update the color
    Label2.Caption = red
End Sub

Private Sub Command2_Click()
    'increment the counter
    counter = counter + 1
    Label4.Caption = counter

    'update the color
    Label2.Caption = blue
End Sub

Private Sub Command3_Click()
    'increment the counter
    counter = counter + 1
    Label4.Caption = counter

    'update the color
```

```
        Label2.Caption = green
End Sub

Private Sub Form_Load()
    'initialize and update the counter
    counter = 0
    Label4.Caption = counter

    'initialize and update the color
    Label2.Caption = red
End Sub
```

Compile and run the program to see the result of the code. You should see a form with three color buttons on it, as well as the current color and the counter value.

# What You Must Know

In this lesson, you have learned about constants and variables. Constants are like tags that you can substitute in your source code rather than putting in a direct value and they remain fixed for the duration of the program. Variables are like containers that can hold different values throughout the duration of your program. Variables and constants can be used together with operators for handling mathematical computations. In Lesson 4, "Understanding String Functions," a solid grounding in the string type is given combined with descriptions and an example of Visual Basic string-manipulation functions. Before you proceed to Lesson 4, however, make sure you understand the following key concepts:

◆ Constants are fixed values that never change after program compilation. Constants can be used within your Visual Basic source code to add clarity, reduce possibility of errors, and save time.

◆ In Visual Basic, constants are declared using the *Const* keyword.

◆ Enumeration is a form of constant that allows constants to be grouped. Enumeration types also allow ranges of constants to be created and modified easily.

◆ Variables hold values that are not necessarily fixed for the duration of the program. A variable can only hold one value at any particular time.

◆ Variables can be assigned constants, other variables, and direct number values that are used in conjunction with operators for mathematical equations.

◆ Visual Basic executes mathematical operators in a set order according to operator precedence. You can override operator precedence using parentheses.

# Lesson 4

---

# Understanding String Functions

In Lesson 3, "Using Variables and Constants," you learned how to create and use constants and variables within your programs. You also briefly examined strings, which let you store a sequence of characters, such as a user's name, Web site, or directory path, within double quotes. In this lesson, you will take a much closer look at strings and learn different functions for manipulating them. By the time you finish this lesson, you will understand the following key concepts:

♦ Strings are one of the most fundamental Visual Basic object types. You will use strings in almost every program.

♦ The *string* type consists of an array of characters. Visual Basic stores strings using an ordered, sequential format by which programmers can access not only the entire string but also sub-strings contained within the whole as well.

♦ String *concatenation* is the process of joining two strings where one string is appended to the end of another. Within your program, you might concatenate a string that contains a filename to a string that contains a directory name in order to create a string that contains a complete pathname.

♦ Visual Basic provides functions (small pieces of code that perform a specific operation) for string manipulation that let you break apart a string, search for and replace characters within a string, and determine string length.

♦ Case-sensitivity deals with issues relating to whether upper- or lowercase has been used for particular characters within a string. Visual Basic also provides functions for manipulating case-sensitivity in strings.

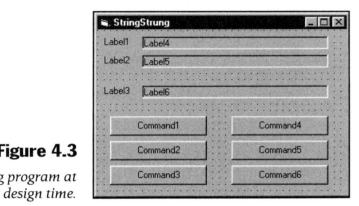

## Figure 4.3

*The* StringStrung *program at design time.*

5. Using Table 4.2, change the properties of the twelve controls that you have just added. Only the properties that require changing are mentioned, otherwise the default property values are fine.

*Table 4.2 List of some* **StringStrung** *controls and their new property values.*

| Control | Property | Value |
| --- | --- | --- |
| Label1 | Caption | *String A:* |
| Label2 | Caption | *String B:* |
| Label3 | Caption | *Result:* |
| Label4 | (Name) | *lblStringA* |
| | Caption | |
| | BorderStyle | *1—Fixed Single* |
| Label5 | (Name) | *lblStringB* |
| | Caption | |
| | BorderStyle | *1—Fixed Single* |
| Label6 | (Name) | *lblResult* |
| | Caption | |
| | BorderStyle | *1—Fixed Single* |
| CommandButton1 | (Name) | *cmdConcatAB* |
| | Caption | *Concatenate AB* |
| CommandButton2 | (Name) | *cmdLenA* |
| | Caption | *Length of A* |
| CommandButton3 | (Name) | *cmdReplaceB* |

*(continues)*

*Table 4.2 (continued)*

| Control | Property | Value |
|---|---|---|
| | Caption | *Replace l for r in B* |
| CommandButton4 | (Name) | *cmdLowerB* |
| | Caption | *Lowercase B* |
| CommandButton5 | (Name) | *cmdUpperA* |
| | Caption | *Uppercase A* |
| CommandButton6 | (Name) | *cmdLeftA* |
| | Caption | *Left 3 in A* |

At this stage of the program you have completed all the design work. Save the program to disk and then carry on with the source code for the *StringStrung* program.

Within the Visual Basic environment, double-click your mouse somewhere on the form where there is no control. Visual Basic will display the code window and provide the standard wrapper code for the *Form_Load()* subroutine. You must declare three string variables, *strA*, *strB*, and *strResult*, at the top of your code window and then assign the values to those variables within the *Form_Load()* subroutine. The variables *strA* and *strB* must then be assigned to their label counterparts. Your source code will look something like the following:

```
Private strA As String
Private strB As String

Private Sub Form_Load()
    strA = "Green"
    strB = "Berry"
    lblStringA.Caption = strA
    lblStringB.Caption = strB
End Sub
```

Next, you must add the source code for the six CommandButtons that you created earlier. In the form window, double-click your mouse on the *Concatenate AB* button. Visual Basic will display the code window and add the wrapper code for the CommandButton. Add a single line of source code to place the concatenation of *strA* and *strB* into *lblResult* as follows:

```
Private Sub cmdConcatAB_Click()
    lblResult.Caption = strA + strB
End Sub
```

Within the form window, double-click your mouse on the *Length of A* button. Visual Basic will display the code window and add the wrapper code for the CommandButton. Add a single line of source code to place the length of *strA* into *lblResult* as follows:

```
Private Sub cmdLenA_Click()
    lblResult.Caption = Len(strA)
End Sub
```

In the form window, double-click your mouse on the *Replace l for r in B* button. Visual Basic will display the code window and add the wrapper code for the CommandButton. Add a single line of source code to place the value of *strB* after replacements into *lblResult* as follows:

```
Private Sub cmdReplaceB_Click()
    lblResult.Caption = Replace(strB, "r", "l")
End Sub
```

In the form window, double-click your mouse on the *Lowercase B* button. Visual Basic will display the code window and add the wrapper code for the CommandButton. Add a single line of source code to place the value of *strB* in lowercase into *lblResult* as follows:

```
Private Sub cmdLowerB_Click()
    lblResult.Caption = LCase(strB)
End Sub
```

You will have noticed that there is a definite pattern here. See if you can add the code for the two remaining buttons. The full source code of this example program, *StringStrung*, is on the accompanying Web site, as well as the finished executable. Figure 4.4 shows the finished program in action. Please note that all of the source code for this book can be found on the accompanying Web site that is located at www.prima-tech.com/books/book/5250/945/.

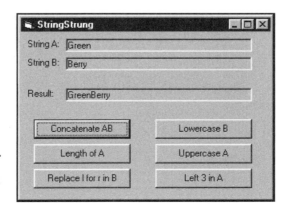

**Figure 4.4**

*The* StringStrung *program in action.*

# What You Must Know

Strings are a very important object type and are used in almost all programs. Visual Basic provides many string functions to assist programmers in string manipulation issues. Using these functions in combination with one another, you can easily create very powerful string manipulation routines within your programs. As your programs are getting larger, you must learn how to write reusable code by breaking source code into separate routines, as you will see in Lesson 5, "Understanding Subroutines and Functions." Before you continue to Lesson 5, however, make sure you understand the following key concepts:

◆ One of the most important fundamental object types for programmers is the string type, which is used in practically every application.

◆ Arrays of characters form a sequential, ordered structure known as a string, allowing programmers to access either all or part of the entire string.

◆ When two strings are joined together by appending one to the end of the other it is known as string concatenation. Visual Basic uses the operators *&* and + for string concatenation.

◆ String segmenting is achieved through use of the *Left*, *Mid*, and *Right* functions.

◆ To search for a substring within a string, Visual Basic provides the *Instr* and *InstrRev* functions.

◆ Use the function *Len* to find out the character length of any string.

◆ To replace text within a string with some other text, Visual Basic provides the *Replace* function.

◆ To deal with case-sensitivity issues, the *UCase* and *LCase* functions are very useful. The statement *Option Compare Text* can also assist in case-sensitivity issues.

# Understanding Subroutines and Functions

So far in the book you have covered enough of the basic requirements of Visual Basic to be able to create some useful programs. Although this lesson covers some important points to learn, especially if you are to progress to writing larger or more realistic programs, it also introduces quite a lot of essential ground rules to enable us to develop good coding practices right from the start. It may be tempting to be quite lax with these coding practices but one cannot stress enough the importance of being diligent and showing discipline in always using them. By the time you finish this lesson, you will understand the following key concepts:

◆ Good coding practices are methods by which your source code becomes more readable and clear to yourself or other programmers.

◆ Comments are an incredibly useful asset to all programmers, helping to clarify code that you have either never seen before or have not looked at recently.

◆ Visual Basic allows you to change the appearance of comments by changing properties such as the color, font, and size of comments. You can adhere to a comment style to further customize your comment appearance.

◆ Whitespace can enhance clarity by providing a natural breakup of code sections that allow the programmer's eyes to easily see related code at a glance.

◆ The main reason for using subroutines and functions is to create modules of reusable code. These modules also help the readability of the source code by gathering related code together.

◆ The difference between subs and functions is that functions return a value.

◆ Both subs and functions can take arguments, which allow you to pass information to these routines.

# Understanding Good Coding Practices

To learn what good coding practice is, as well as give you some insight as to how good coding practice came into being, you will look at what good coding practice is not. First, it is not about writing really good code that does some fancy "whizz-bang" tricks that make everyone go, "Oooh" and "Aaaah." Neither is it about writing the program cleverly so that nobody without your cryptic variable key or some other strange technique will ever be able to decipher your spaghetti code in less than four years. Good coding practice is not about trying to use the same variable name as many times as is humanly possible within your program relying on nothing but scope (you will cover scope in detail later in this lesson) to form the boundaries.

Good coding practices are methods to clarify to yourself or anyone else what is going on in your code, not only for the present but in future. Imagine in two years time when you've forgotten all the little idiosyncrasies that you took for granted while originally coding the program. Or, to put the shoe on the other foot, wouldn't you appreciate starting out in your new job and finding that you had inherited code with which you could clearly see what was going on? Sure you would—just the same as everyone else.

# Taking a Look at the "ZapSoft Company" Experience

Imagine the following scenario: You are the senior recruiting officer at ZapSoft, a large programming company. Your company develops customized software to meet the demands of large enterprise corporations. Your clients are often spread out internationally with offices in major cities throughout the world. For ongoing support and additions to previously written software, ZapSoft also has offices internationally. From a long list of hopefuls, you have narrowed it down to two possible candidates for employment at ZapSoft.

Mack is a brilliant programmer. You look through his papers and see that he is self-taught and has been coding since he was eight—a natural programmer who knows nothing else. He has been programming for decades. His previously written programs all look very polished and slick. They run fast and efficiently. You notice that he has always worked solo in his programming career. You ask to see some of the source code for the simplest of demonstration programs he has presented. Although you are a pretty good programmer yourself and have worked at ZapSoft in a programming position before being promoted to senior recruiting officer, you can barely follow the source code that is presented to you.

Josh is a decent programmer. He has a formal education in computers with a bachelor's degree. He has worked in two companies previously doing a mixture of group and solo projects. His programs are not as flashy as Mack's but they are solid and efficient nonetheless and demonstrate knowledge of many powerful features. Josh shows you the source code for one of the programs at your request. Excellent structure and well-organized code that is easily and clearly readable greets you from the screen.

Even though Mack is the better of the two programmers, ZapSoft requires programmers that can work in a team and write code that others in the company can easily look at later to make modifications to. If Mack had been employed and had continued programming as he always had, he may have written a brilliant program for one of ZapSoft's clients who pays over a million dollars for it. But then Mack gets a better offer and leaves ZapSoft and that particular client that is using Mack's program requires some modifications due to new tax laws or something. ZapSoft would now have to rewrite the program at their own great expense.

You congratulate Josh on his new position in ZapSoft.

## Understanding the Value of Comments

Putting comments in your code is one of the most useful things you can do for good coding practices. Even if you program in a very unorthodox style, if you comment your code thoroughly someone else will be able to understand what is going on. Putting comments into your Visual Basic code is extremely easy. All you must do is put an apostrophe at the start of the line. Anything you type on that line after the apostrophe is ignored by the Visual Basic compiler.

```
'This is a comment.
```

"Comments" are also referred to by programmers as "remarks." You might come across this alternate term in programming articles or books, not to mention hearing the term used by a colleague.

## Adding More Green (the Visual Basic Comment Color) to Your Programs

Visual Basic by default makes your comments appear in a green color. Though this can be changed, there is no real need to do so. The main idea here is that your comments are clearly visible and separate from lines of code. For some people colored text is difficult to read, but after a while almost everyone finds it beneficial having the program's comments in a different color to the code. For those people who find reading green text difficult, go to the Tools menu and select Options as in Figure 5.1.

**Figure 5.1**

*Selecting Options from the Tools menu.*

When the Options dialog opens, select the Editor Format tab, and under the Code Colors section, select Comment Text from the listbox as in Figure 5.2.

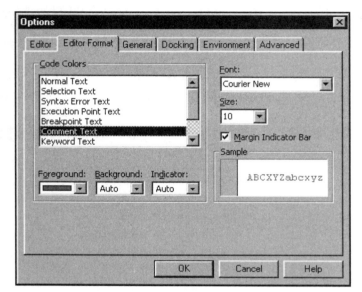

**Figure 5.2**

*Changing the comment color in the Options dialog.*

Under Foreground is a drop-down combo box with a choice of possible colors for you to choose from. You could also change the font and font size or font properties for sections other than comments, but you probably will never need to.

# Commenting by Block

You can easily comment out entire blocks of code in Visual Basic. A block of code is similar to a paragraph in a book, only instead of sentences you have multiple lines of code. Imagine if you had to individually comment out fifty lines of code and then later when you have fixed the bug or added some code or something you have to go back and uncomment each of those fifty lines! Commenting out entire blocks of code is something that many programmers do on a regular basis. Later, if you need to, you can just as easily uncomment those blocks of code.

# Taking a Look at Comment Styles

When you are creating your comments, try to be a little imaginative and form some sort of style that stays the same throughout each program if not all your programs. When you talk about the use of style with comments, what you mean is the extra borders that you use to signify areas of code more clearly. Although you will see the so called "classic style" throughout this book and also in any of the source code at www.prima-tech.com/books/book/5250/945/, please feel free to use another style if you so desire. The ideas below are there not only for you to choose a style from but also to help you along with your imagination in thinking of other styles. Do not concern yourself with the names of the styles as there is no formal comment style names. These names are just made up to display the different styles with some comment in them:

```
' " " " " " " " " " " " " " " " " " " " " " "
'  THE  CURVY  STYLE
' " " " " " " " " " " " " " " " " " " " " " "
'========================================
'  THE  CLASSIC  STYLE
'========================================
' * * * * * * * * * * * * * * * * * * * * * * * * * * * * *
'  THE  STAR  STYLE
' * * * * * * * * * * * * * * * * * * * * * * * * * * * * *
' < < < < < < < < < < < < < < < < < < < < < < < < < < < < < <
'  THE  ARROW  STYLE
' > > > > > > > > > > > > > > > > > > > > > > > > > > > > > >
' . . . . . . . . . . . . . . . . . . . . . . . . . . . . . .
'  THE  DOTTY  STYLE
' . . . . . . . . . . . . . . . . . . . . . . . . . . . . . .
' _____
'  THE  UNDERLINE  STYLE
' _____
'########################################
'  THE  SHARP  STYLE
'########################################
'++++++++++++++++++++++++++++++++++++++++
'  THE  PLUS  STYLE
'++++++++++++++++++++++++++++++++++++++++
' OOOOOOOOOOOOOOOOOOOOOOOOOOOOOOOOOOOOOOO
'  THE  CIRCLE  STYLE
' OOOOOOOOOOOOOOOOOOOOOOOOOOOOOOOOOOOOOOO
```

# Using Whitespace to Make Your Code Easier to Read

You can also use whitespace in your program code to make things more readable. Whitespace is really just the blank lines between code although it comes from the whitespace rivers that are caused when text is justified in books. If you are working on your code and write a comment of what you are doing and then supply some code, put in some whitespace before writing the comment for what the next section of code does. This helps to easily draw your eye to sections of related code as well as the associated comment. Often it helps to keep a bit of extra whitespace between different subs and functions, which brings us to the topic of building reusable routines.

 **A Good Time for Comments**

*Rather than writing comments after you complete the entire code for a program, try to get into the habit of writing comments while you are actually writing the code. By doing this you not only help to clearly cement your intentions while you program, but you also ensure that you don't fall into the trap of never actually getting around to writing comments. Commenting your code as you write is much easier than trying to comment a program that you wrote six months ago.*

# Building Reusable Routines

When you program you often find code that is repetitious so you end up having to either type the same thing over and over again or do a lot of copying and pasting. Either way your program gets very bloated with the same code. However, you can use what are known as subroutines or functions to store a section of your code separately and then simply refer to this routine whenever you must run that code.

As a simple example to help clarify things, imagine that you have five variables that must be initialized and then assigned values, then initialized again and assigned different values, etc. The code might look something similar to the following:

```
'==================================
'No routines or reusable code
'==================================
'declare variables
Private strA As String
Private strB As String
Private strC As String
Private int1 As Integer
```

```
Private lng1 As Long

'=================================
' This is the only routine in the
'entire program so everything is
'here in a linear order.
'=================================
Private Sub Form_Load()
    'initialize all the variables
    strA = ""
    strB = ""
    strC = ""
    int1 = 0
    lng1 = 0

    'assign some values
    strA = "Monday"
    strB = "Tuesday"
    strC = "Wednesday"

    'initialize all the variables
    strA = ""
    strB = ""
    strC = ""
    int1 = 0
    lng1 = 0

    'assign some values
    strA = "Peter"
    strB = "Susan"
    int1 = 465

    'initialize all the variables
    strA = ""
    strB = ""
    strC = ""
```

```
    int1 = 0
    lng1 = 0

    'assign some values
    strC = "What a wonderful world."
    int1 = 23
    lng1 = 89762989
End Sub
```

Now look at the same code when you use a subroutine or as it is known in Visual Basic, a sub, to extract the reusable code.

```
'=================================
'Using a sub for reusable code
'=================================
'declare variables
Private strA As String
Private strB As String
Private strC As String
Private int1 As Integer
Private lng1 As Long


'=================================
' Initialize all the variables
'=================================
Private Sub InitAll()
    strA = ""
    strB = ""
    strC = ""
    int1 = 0
    lng1 = 0
End Sub


'=================================
' This is the start routine
'=================================
```

```
Private Sub Form_Load()
    InitAll

    'assign some values
    strA = "Monday"
    strB = "Tuesday"
    strC = "Wednesday"

    InitAll

    'assign some values
    strA = "Peter"
    strB = "Susan"
    int1 = 465

    InitAll

    'assign some values
    strC = "What a wonderful world."
    int1 = 23
    lng1 = 89762989
End Sub
```

Did you notice the difference between the two pieces of code? In the second piece of code, you used a sub called *InitAll*. Whenever you wanted to initialize all of your five variables you simply called this sub. Using subs and functions helps programmers in more than just tidying up code. It allows you to have a single point to make changes for code that is used multiple times, which is extremely useful for cutting back on the chances of errors occurring.

Take a closer look at how you construct your own sub. First, you provide the keyword *Private* or *Public* (these will be discussed later in the book) followed by the keyword *Sub*.

```
Private Sub
```

Next, you add the name of your sub. You cannot name every sub the same thing or you would have ambiguity. The name must be unique so as not to confuse either yourself or the Visual Basic compiler.

```
Private Sub MyNewSub
```

At this point you can simply hit return and Visual Basic will complete the basic structure for you.

```
Private Sub MyNewSub()

End Sub
```

 **Understanding Other Forms of Reusable Code**

*Using subroutines and functions are not the only method that Visual Basic provides programmers when it comes to writing reusable code. In Lesson 12, "Using Forms and Modules," you will learn how to create entire sections of code into reusable modules that you can easily add to other programs for functionality. This concept of reusable code being cross program is incredibly useful, as you can have many different subroutines and functions that are all related or perhaps dependent on each other in one module, as well as the ability to simply drop in error free, fully tested functionality.*

*Although not covered in this book, advanced Visual Basic techniques include further reusable code options such as creating COM and DLL objects. These are basically separate libraries of routines that are stored as a file and can be accessed by multiple programs.*

*As you can see, Visual Basic allows many methods for reusable code creation.*

# Understanding the Difference between Subs and Functions

Now that you know how to create your own subs what do you need functions for? What's the difference between the two? Up until now you have only looked at subs. Functions are almost exactly the same only there is one distinguishing feature that separates the two—functions return a value.

The following example shows you how a function returns the value for the addition of two variables. Even though the example is simple, the idea here is for you to see the concepts being used clearly without being obscured in complex code that you do not yet understand.

```
'=================================
' Function Example
'=================================

'declare variables
Private a As Integer
Private b As Integer


'=================================
' Returns the sum of a and b
'=================================
Private Function AddMe() As Integer
    AddMe = a + b
End Function


'=================================
' This is the start routine
'=================================
Private Sub Form_Load()
Dim c As Integer
    a = 7
    b = 2
    c = AddMe
End Sub
```

In this example, the variables *a* and *b* are assigned the values 7 and 2 respectively. Then you see a funny line where *c*, which is an integer, is assigned a function! How can this be? An integer cannot hold a function! But if you look at what the function returns you see that it is an integer and so your variable *c* equals 9.

So, constructing a function is almost the same as a sub except for three points. First, you use the keyword *Function* instead of *Sub*. Note that this keyword is used in two places—both at the start and end of the routine. Secondly, you add the keyword *As* followed by the variable type that you want your function to return.

```
Private Function MyNewFunction() As String

End Function
```

The third difference is that you must return a value by using the name of your function and assigning the value you want returned to it.

```
Private Function MyNewFunction() As String
    MyNewFunction = "I am a programmer."
End Function
```

# Using Arguments in Subs and Functions

You have covered a lot already in this lesson, but the trickiest section has been saved for last. You should now have a fairly good idea of how to create your own subs and functions. You know that a function is just like a sub except that it returns a value. Did you notice that so far both your subs and functions have all had empty parentheses after their unique name? The parentheses that follow the name of a sub or function are for passing arguments.

Although you touched on this subject earlier it is important enough to look at again. Arguments—and you are not talking about angry disputes here either—are variables or values that are passed to either a sub or a function in order for that piece of routine to make use of the information. Arguments are also known as parameters, so do not be surprised if you see a reference to either of these terms in various books or knowledge articles.

The following example shows a function that returns the square of a value. For those of you who are a little rusty on your math, the square of a number is when the number is multiplied by itself. Therefore, $3^2 = 3 * 3 = 9$.

```
Private Function SquareMe(ByVal i As Integer) As Integer
    SquareMe = i * i
End Function
```

Using this new function you can now square any integer that you want simply by changing the argument that is passed.

```
Private Sub Form_Load()
Dim a As Integer
    a = SquareMe(3)      'a = 9
    a = SquareMe(7)      'a = 49
    a = SquareMe(25)     'a = 625
End Sub
```

Did you notice when you create a sub or function that you use the keyword *By Val*? *By Val* is short for *By Value*, and any argument passed using this keyword cannot be changed. However, you could also use *ByRef*, which means *By Reference*. Declaring an argument to be *ByRef* means that the sub or function can actually change the value of the argument passed.

# What You Must Know

In this lesson, you have learned about subroutines and functions. Good coding practices include putting comments into your code, using whitespace, and using a consistent style throughout your code. Subroutines and functions allow you to segment code into modules that can be reused. Lesson 6, "Making Decisions within Your Programs," will introduce you to conditional programming, which lets your programs make decisions, and then branch into different areas depending on whether conditions are met or not. Before you continue on to Lesson 6, however, make sure you understand the following key concepts:

◆ Source code becomes more readable and clear by consistent use of good coding practices.

◆ For clarity of code, both for yourself and others who might have to read your code, comments are a tremendous asset. Good use of comments can save you a lot of work trying to discern what code is actually trying to do.

◆ Comments in the Visual Basic environment are green in color by default. However, you can change the color and other properties of comments to customize their appearance. Use of a consistent comment style further assists in providing easier code readability.

◆ Use whitespace to visually separate segments of code from each other. Whitespace can enhance source code clarity and improve readability.

◆ Reusable code is the main reason for using subroutines and functions. The same source code can be executed multiple times with reusable code, saving time, effort, and space, as well as reducing the chance of errors.

◆ Functions and subs are very similar except that functions return a value.

◆ Information in the form of values can be passed to subs and functions as arguments. Arguments are not compulsory—that is, they can be made optional—and multiple arguments can be used.

```
Select Case variable
Case value1
     Line 1 of code
     Line 2 of code
       . . .
     Line n of code
Case value2
     Line 1 of code
     Line 2 of code
       . . .
     Line n of code
  . . .
  . . .
  . . .
Case valuen
     Line 1 of code
     Line 2 of code
       . . .
     Line n of code
End Select
```

As an example of this, take another look at the color problem that you have been studying this lesson but this time as it would appear using a *Select Case* structure.

```
'What color did the user select?
Select Case color
Case green
     Label1.Caption = "Color is green."
Case blue
     Label1.Caption = "Color is blue."
Case white
     Label1.Caption = "Color is white."
Case yellow
     Label1.Caption = "Color is yellow."
Case red
     Label1.Caption = "Color is red."
Case Else
```

```
        Label1.Caption = "Color unknown"
End If
```

The short form of this allows you to use a colon immediately after the case value followed by a line of code. So the end result would be:

```
'What color did the user select?
Select Case color
Case green: Label1.Caption = "Color is green."
Case blue: Label1.Caption = "Color is blue."
Case white: Label1.Caption = "Color is white."
Case yellow: Label1.Caption = "Color is yellow."
Case red: Label1.Caption = "Color is red."
Case Else: Label1.Caption = "Color unknown"
End If
```

As you can see, the *Select Case* structure is very tidy and readable. You will probably find that you use the *Select Case* structure quite a lot when programming in Visual Basic because it is so useful. Did you notice the way the *Select Case* structure makes use of the *Else* conditional? As with the *ElseIf* statement, if you are going to use the *Case Else* conditional, it must come last as seen in the earlier examples.

# Understanding *Is*, *To*, and Comparison Operators

You probably think that you know all about how useful the *Select Case* structure is, don't you? Well, let me break this to you gently—it's even more useful than you thought! *Select Case* structures can support ranges, which is extremely useful for programmers. The comparison operators will be covered first, then followed by a brief explanation of how to use them with the *Is* and *To* keywords.

*Table 6.1 The comparison operators.*

| Operator | Meaning |
| --- | --- |
| = | Equal to |
| <> | Not equal to |
| < | Less than |
| > | Greater than |
| <= | Less than or equal to |
| >= | Greater than or equal to |

The *Is* keyword is used before these operators followed by a value. The *To* keyword is used between two values to form a range. An example will help clarify this.

```
Select Case mynumber
Case Is < 10:     'This is a small number
Case 10 To 998:  'This is a medium number
Case Is >= 999:  'This is a big number
End Select
```

You will never need to use the "Is =" combination because in this circumstance you would simply put in the value directly as was seen in earlier examples (e.g. Case red **not** Case Is = red).

A more realistic example of the kind that you might actually use in a program would be covering ranges of test result scores. Imagine that you were working with a team on some elaborate program that tested the user and then presented the result. Instead of just giving the raw percentage value, think of how you could use what you have learned in this lesson to also add a more personalized touch to the results, based on the range in which the user scored. It might look something like the following:

```
'Show test result comment
Select Case finalscore
Case 0: lblResult = "You didn't score but keep trying."
Case Is < 10: lblResult = "You got some right!"
Case 10 To 25: lblResult = "You've almost got a quarter."
Case 26 To 49: lblResult = "Almost there. Just a few more."
Case 50: lblResult = "You've passed!"
Case 51 To 69: lblResult = "Not bad at all."
Case 70 To 89: lblResult = "Very good. Nice score."
Case 90 To 99: lblResult = "Excellent result!"
Case 100: lblResult = "Perfect! Congratulations."
End Select
```

Of course, you may have different comments, add flashing graphics, or do a myriad other things, but you can see how the technique for using ranges has saved us from writing out 101 different *If-Then* statements or having a *Select Case* structure with 101 different *Case* statements contained inside.

## Success HINT: Understanding Default Control Properties

*In the previous example, the Label is called* lblResult *and different strings have been assigned to the* lblResult *Caption property without actually specifying the keyword* Caption. *The reason you are able to do this is because Visual Basic has a default property for every control. Therefore, if you do not specify any property, Visual Basic will assume that you mean the default property. The default property for a Label control is, of course, the* Caption *property.*

# Building the *MiniCalc* Example Program

All of the example programs so far have been rather simple. In reality though, you have learned quite a lot of powerful commands. For this example you are going to call on all the skills that you have covered so far and create a fully functional calculator program. You will not worry about memory, exponentials, trigonometric functionality, or other features, but you will just create a simple calculator.

1. Open a new Visual Basic project and name the form **frmCalc** and the project **MiniCalc**.

2. Change the frmCalc's caption to **MiniCalc**.

3. Add a Label control and call it **lblDisplay**.

4. Change the Label control's BackColor property to be white by selecting the Palette tab and clicking your mouse on the white box from the color selection.

5. Add sixteen CommandButtons and arrange them and change their captions so that the form resembles Figure 6.1.

6. Name the CommandButtons accordingly by using Table 6.2.

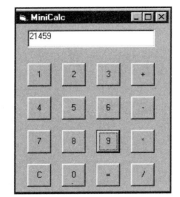

## Figure 6.1

*MiniCalc in action.*

*Table 6.2* MiniCalc's *CommandButtons and their captions.*

| (Name) | Caption |
|---|---|
| cmd1 | 1 |
| cmd2 | 2 |
| cmd3 | 3 |
| cmd4 | 4 |
| cmd5 | 5 |
| cmd6 | 6 |
| cmd7 | 7 |
| cmd8 | 8 |
| cmd9 | 9 |
| cmd0 | 0 |
| cmdC | C |
| cmdEquals | = |
| cmdAdd | + |
| cmdSubtract | − |
| cmdMultiply | * |
| cmdDivide | / |

You have completed the design stage of the MiniCalc form. All you have to do now is add the source code for functionality. The complete code is at www.prima-tech.com/books/book/5250/945/ for you to compare or reference.

```
'=================================================
'=================================================
' MINICALC - By Rob Francis
'
'This program is a fully functional working
'calculator handling addition, subtraction,
'multiplication and division.
'=================================================
'=================================================

Option Explicit

'Define global constants
Const none = ""

'Declare global variables
Private num1
Private num2
Private operator


'=================================================
'NUMBER BUTTON SUBS
'=================================================
Private Sub cmd0_Click()
    NewNumber 0
End Sub

Private Sub cmd1_Click()
    NewNumber 1
End Sub

Private Sub cmd2_Click()
    NewNumber 2
End Sub
```

```
Private Sub cmd3_Click()
    NewNumber 3
End Sub

Private Sub cmd4_Click()
    NewNumber 4
End Sub

Private Sub cmd5_Click()
    NewNumber 5
End Sub

Private Sub cmd6_Click()
    NewNumber 6
End Sub

Private Sub cmd7_Click()
    NewNumber 7
End Sub

Private Sub cmd8_Click()
    NewNumber 8
End Sub

Private Sub cmd9_Click()
    NewNumber 9
End Sub

Private Sub NewNumber(ByVal i As Integer)
    If operator = none Then
        num1 = (num1 * 10) + I
        lblDisplay = num1
    Else
        num2 = (num2 * 10) + I
        lblDisplay = num2
    End If
```

```
End Sub




'================================================
'OPERATOR SUBS
'================================================
Private Sub cmdAdd_Click()
    operator = "+"
End Sub


Private Sub cmdDivide_Click()
    operator = "/"
End Sub


Private Sub cmdMultiply_Click()
    operator = "*"
End Sub


Private Sub cmdSubtract_Click()
    operator = "-"
End Sub




'================================================
'EQUALS BUTTON SUB
'================================================
Private Sub cmdEquals_Click()
    'evaluate the result and display it
    Select Case operator
    Case "+": lblDisplay = num1 + num2
    Case "-": lblDisplay = num1 - num2
    Case "*": lblDisplay = num1 * num2
    Case "/": lblDisplay = num1 / num2
    End Select
```

```
    'prepare the global operators for further
    'calculating by the user
    operator = none
    num1 = lblDisplay
    num2 = 0
End Sub




'==============================================
'C BUTTON SUB
'==============================================
Private Sub cmdC_Click()
    'initialize the global variables
    num1 = 0
    num2 = 0
    operator = none
    lblDisplay = ""
End Sub




'==============================================
'START OF PROGRAM
'==============================================
Private Sub Form_Load()
    cmdC_Click
End Sub
```

 **Understanding Boolean Logic**

*A useful thing to know when dealing with conditional programming is boolean logic. When something is said to be boolean, then that means it has two possible states. This could mean that an item is true or false, one or zero, on or off, etc. Visual Basic provides a type known as boolean that you can use for true or false. This allows you to do more with your conditional programming by using variations on whether a condition is true or false. Actually, all conditions are implied to be equal to True unless stated explicitly otherwise.*

```
1. If (i > 7) Then . . .
2. If (i > 7) = True Then . . .
3. If (i > 7) = False Then . . .
```

*In the example code above, lines 1 and 2 are the same with the explicit equality to* True *making no difference to the implicit version. However, line 3 requires the opposite of lines 1 and 2 before the condition is met.*

*Boolean logic is simply further flexibility when dealing with booleans. Remember that all conditions are implicitly boolean if not explicitly so. If you have multiple conditions that all must be met before you can do something, then use the* And, Or, *and* Not *keywords to apply boolean logic within your Visual Basic conditional source code. And means that both conditions must be met, Or means that either condition must be met, and Not means that a particular condition is not met.*

```
If (i > 7) And (i < 10) Then . . .
```

*In the conditional expression above, the value of i would have to be either 8 or 9 for the resultant code to be executed. This use of boolean logic is another form of creating ranges of values within our conditions. You can have multiple boolean logic keywords on a single line but the complexity increases.*

```
If ((i > 7) And (i < 10) And Not (i = 9)) Or (i = 5) Then . . .
```

*In the above line of code, i could equal either 5 or 8 for the condition to be met.*

# What You Must Know

In this lesson, you have learned about conditional programming. Conditional programming allows your source code to traverse different paths depending on whether conditions are met. Visual Basic provides the *If-Then* statement to cater to conditional programming needs. The *Select Case* structure is another form of using conditional programming that makes use of multiple conditions and handles ranges. In Lesson 7, "Using Message Boxes," you will learn all about how to present message boxes to the user from within your program, as well as a method for getting user input. Before you continue with Lesson 7, however, make sure you understand the following key concepts:

◆ You can place conditions within your source code to allow programs to execute different lines of code depending on whether conditions are met or not.

◆ Conditional programming is mostly through use of the *If-Then* statement within Visual Basic.

◆ To create a block of code that is to be handled if a condition is met, the *End If* command is used to show where an *If-Then* statement ends. The *End If* command allows for multiple lines of code to be subjected to a single condition.

◆ Alternative options for circumstances when conditions are not met are provided for by Visual Basic in the form of *Else* and *ElseIf*.

◆ A variable can be compared against many different possible conditions using the *Select Case* structure. If none of the explicit cases is met, the *Case Else* option can be used.

◆ Ranges of values can also be easily used in *Select Case* structures through use of the *Is* and *To* commands and also the comparison operators.

# Lesson 7

# Using Message Boxes

In Lesson 6, "Making Decisions within Your Programs," you learned about conditional programming and some of the different methods and options that Visual Basic makes available to you to achieve this. In this lesson, you will be introduced to message boxes. Message boxes are usually small dialogs that appear on your screen whenever you encounter an error or must confirm something. By the time you finish this lesson, you will understand the following key concepts:

◆ Message boxes are used to present the user with information. The information being presented can range from critical errors and warnings to confirming whether a new folder should be created.

◆ Windows, including message boxes, can be modal or modeless, which affects the ability of other windows to be the active window. When a window is modal, it can be system modal and it can also be application modal.

◆ Visual Basic allows easy creation of message boxes through the use of the *MsgBox* command.

◆ The *MsgBox* command can take five arguments: *Prompt, Buttons, Title, HelpFile*, and *Context*. Only the *Prompt* argument is compulsory, all the others are optional.

◆ The *MsgBox* is a function that returns a value. This return value can be one of five possible return values and indicates the button selected by the user.

◆ The *InputBox* function is similar to the *MsgBox* function although it has a different appearance and slightly different arguments. Using *InputBox*, it is possible to easily obtain input directly from the user.

```
Private Sub Form_Load()
    MsgBox "Alert! RAID disk 4 is dead!", vbCritical + _
    vbApplicationModal + vbSystemModal, "Critical error"
End Sub
```

**Figure 7.9**

*A message box displaying the critical icon.*

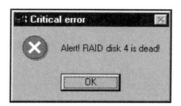

 **Making Arguments More Readable**

*Earlier in the book you learned the importance of good coding practices. When you are using subroutines or functions that can take multiple arguments, such as MsgBox, trying to work out how many commas to put in to skip optional arguments or trying to read the code later can be difficult.*

*You can name arguments explicitly, which not only assists greatly for readability but also allows programmers to do away with counting out commas for skipped arguments. You can also place the arguments in whatever order you want when you explicitly name them.*

*To explicitly name an argument, simply type in the name of the argument followed by a colon and equals sign. The following example shows how to call up a message box with just a prompt and title.*

```
MsgBox Title:="Programming Language", Prompt:="Visual Basic"
```

*The following example shows the same MsgBox command without using named arguments but relying on arguments being in proper order and having the correct number of commas to separate empty arguments:*

```
MsgBox "Visual Basic", , "Programming Language"
```

# Getting User Input

There may be times when you must not only put up a message box for the user on their screen but also get back some information from the user. In these cases there is a special message box provided by Visual Basic known as an *InputBox*. An *InputBox* command takes slightly different arguments to a *MsgBox* command. However, if you leave out all the optional arguments and simply supply a string to display the two types of message boxes, they appear to be very similar.

Create a new project and type the following into the code window:

```
Private Sub Form_Load()
    MsgBox "Hello, world"
    InputBox "Hello, world"
End Sub
```

Press F5 to run the code but when prompted just click your mouse on Cancel to not bother saving the project or form.

In their simplest code form the *MsgBox* and *InputBox* may appear similar but, as seen in Figure 7.10 and Figure 7.11, you'll note that their output is quite different.

**Figure 7.10**

*The MsgBox result.*

**Figure 7.11**

*The InputBox result.*

The *InputBox* is used just like the *MsgBox* except that instead of prompting the user to simply click the mouse on a button, the input box is used to prompt the user for some text. The return value of *InputBox* is the string entered by the user. If the user clicks the mouse on the Cancel button instead of the OK button then the string that is returned is empty or zero-length ("").

So what else is different about the *InputBox*? Besides the basic look and feel, the *InputBox* takes some different arguments than the *MsgBox*. You do not have a choice of buttons or icons. You cannot make it modal. Take a look at the syntax of the *InputBox*:

*resultant_string* = InputBox(*prompt* [, *title*] [, *default*] [, *xpos*] [, *ypos*] [, *helpfile*, *context*])

Most of the arguments are so similar to *MsgBox* that you can practically skip over them. The prompt is the string you want to display. The title is the string for the title bar. The help file and context arguments are the same, not only in the *MsgBox* function, but many other functions as well and will be covered later in the book. This leaves really just two major argument differences: The default text in the text box and the *x* and *y* positions of the *InputBox*. The *x* position is how far from the left side of the screen to place the *InputBox* while the *y* position is how far from the top of the screen. A brief example should make everything clearer, and then you can try out your own variations and experiment with this yourself.

```
Private Sub Form_Load()
Dim username As String
    username = InputBox("Please type your name below.", "Username", _
    "Jane Doe", 120, 200)
End Sub
```

Try entering this code into a new project, and then compile and run it using the F5 key. You should get a result similar to that in Figure 7.12.

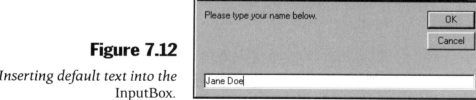

**Figure 7.12**

*Inserting default text into the* InputBox.

# What You Must Know

Message boxes allow you to easily present information to the user directly from your program. Highly customizable, message boxes can be created to suit a particular need through alteration of properties and displayable icons and buttons. You can use a form of message box that can actually receive data from the user known in Visual Basic as an input box. In Lesson 8, "Using Text Boxes," you will learn even more ways that Visual Basic enables you to get user input, as well as create your own input forms. Before you continue with Lesson 8, however, make sure you understand the following key concepts:

◆ You can present information, such as errors, confirmations, or questions, to the user directly from your program by using message boxes.

◆ Modal windows prevent the user from selecting other windows within the program if application modal settings are applied, or selecting windows of other programs if system modal settings are applied. Modeless windows place no such restriction upon the user.

◆ The Visual Basic command *MsgBox* allows you to easily create message boxes from within your own programs.

◆ The arguments that are taken by *MsgBox* are *Prompt*, *Buttons*, *Title*, *HelpFile*, and *Context*. Applying different options and combinations of arguments allows you to customize your message boxes. Only the *Prompt* argument is mandatory.

◆ You can use the *MsgBox* as a function that returns a value. The return value indicates which button in the message box the user clicked the mouse on. There are five return values possible.

◆ Similar in many ways to the *MsgBox* command, *InputBox* gives the Visual Basic programmer a simple way to get input from the user by presenting a message box. The *InputBox* function returns a string.

# Lesson 8

---

# Using Text Boxes

In Lesson 7, "Using Message Boxes," you learned how to present information to the user in the form of a message box. You also learned how to get input from the user through the *InputBox* command. In this lesson, you will take this one step further by learning how to get user input within forms of your own design. By the time you finish this lesson, you will understand the following key concepts:

- ◆ Using text boxes you can get user input directly from your own forms, allowing you to customize the look and feel presented to your users to a greater extent than is possible using the *InputBox* command.

- ◆ The TextBox control can be sized and placed on your form to fit your requirements. Multiple TextBox controls can be placed on the same form.

- ◆ Text boxes can be single or multiline and can be limited to a maximum number of characters. When the multiline option is used you can also select to use scrollbars.

- ◆ When obtaining passwords, text boxes allow the display to be masked with a character of your choice while allowing your source code to easily work with the real input string.

- ◆ Through the *Text* property, it is possible to either get or set the current value of a TextBox control. User input is retrieved through this method.

- ◆ The RichTextBox control allows you to get past some of the limitations of the TextBox control. RichTextBox controls allow multiple fonts, colors, sizes, and styles and are not limited to a 64K buffer size.

## Introducing Text Boxes

Text boxes are used all the time when programming because they take a lot of the work out of getting user input. They are almost like a mini editor program, such as NotePad, except that you can specify to an extent how they look and behave as well as keep them within your own program. So you can use this versatile control to easily add a one line entry box for different options in your programs or just as easily create a large multiline editor with scrollbars for simple documents, batch files, and other needs. A basic text box looks like Figure 8.1.

**Figure 8.1**

*A basic text box.*

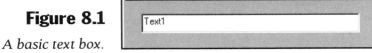

Users can edit these boxes simply by clicking the mouse in the box and typing, exactly as they do with most Windows programs. If you combine your knowledge of the Label control with text boxes you can easily create a prompt just above or to the left of the text box indicating what type of entry is expected, as in Figure 8.2.

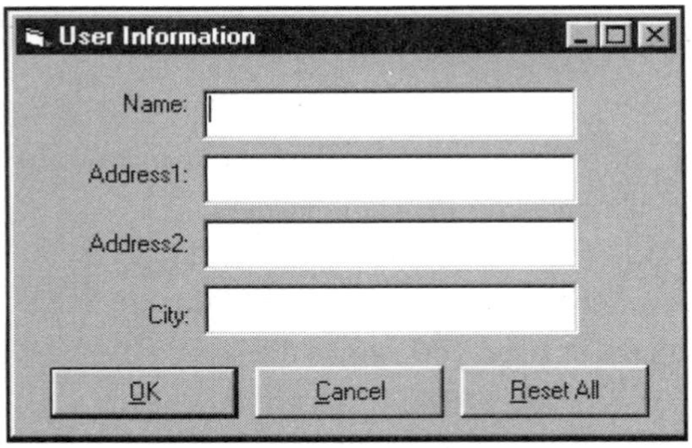

**Figure 8.2**

*Combining Label and TextBox controls.*

This gives your programs a much more professional feel. You might have encountered dialogs with a similar look and feel to them before, only now you will be writing them yourself. You're on your way!

# Creating Text Boxes

The text boxes that you use in Visual Basic are created by selecting the TextBox control then dragging the rectangular size on the form in the same manner as you do the Label control. The control for TextBox looks like Figure 8.3.

**Figure 8.3**

*The TextBox control.*

# Sizing a Text Box

After you have added the TextBox you may want to resize it. You do this by simply selecting the TextBox that you want to resize by clicking on it with the mouse then pointing to the edge of the TextBox where one of the tiny blue squares are, as seen in Figure 8.4.

**Figure 8.4**

*Resizing a TextBox control using the blue squares.*

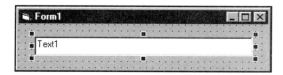

The blue squares in the corners allow you the freedom of sizing in both the vertical and horizontal planes. However, all the blue squares that are not situated in a corner are for sizing on one plane only. This is very handy if you want to adjust the length of a text box without changing the height at all or vice versa. So simply click your mouse and drag the TextBox until it is the size you want.

Sometimes, however, you may want to change the size of the TextBox at runtime rather than design time. Or you may want to find out the height or width of the TextBox for use in your code. The TextBox control has the properties *Height* and *Width* that allow you to do exactly this from within your code. The following code shows a simple example of how to get the current size value of a TextBox and also how to set the size to something else:

```
Private Sub Form_Load()
Dim old_height As Integer
Dim old_width As Integer

    'get the current size
    old_height = Text1.Height
    old_width = Text1.Width

    'set the new size
    Text1.Height = 30
    Text1.Width = 95
End Sub
```

Now that you know how to change the TextBox's Height and Width properties at runtime, you probably realized that you can also directly edit these same properties at design time under the Properties section. Figure 8.5 shows this more clearly.

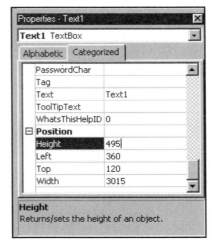

**Figure 8.5**

*Changing a TextBox's Height property directly at design time.*

## Placing a Text Box

You decide on the placement of the TextBox when you first drag a rectangle of it on your form. After this you must either use the mouse or keyboard to alter the TextBox control's position or placement at design time. Figure 8.6 shows what it would look like if you were to use the mouse to drag a TextBox a little to the right and down a bit. You can see the gray outline, which shows you the resultant placement.

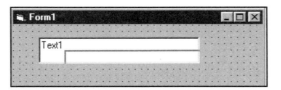

**Figure 8.6**

*The gray outline showing TextBox placement.*

To use the keyboard to achieve your TextBox placement, or any other control for that matter, simply click your mouse on the control and then, holding down the Ctrl button, use the arrow buttons on the keyboard to reposition the control. If you are using a grid you will notice that the movement occurs in grid intervals.

## Copying a Text Box

You may sometimes find yourself in a situation where you must create a number of identically sized TextBoxes. If you have had to spend quite some time getting a TextBox to just the right size, you do not want to have to do the same thing for fifteen other TextBox controls! In these cases you can simply copy the original TextBox and paste copies on the form. You will probably end up getting a message box pop up on your screen similar to the one in Figure 8.7.

**Figure 8.7**

*Multiple instance of control dialog.*

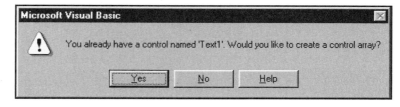

In the advanced section of this book you will take a look at arrays and how you can utilize control arrays, but for now simply click your mouse on the No button. You can paste as many copies of the TextBox control as you like. When you have spent time setting up the spacing and alignment of a group of TextBox controls of which you require an identical copy, then copy the whole group of TextBox controls in one shot. By dragging the mouse from the top left of the form to the bottom right so that all the controls are selected, you can then simply copy and paste the same as you did with the single TextBox control.

It may be worth mentioning that you can use this technique with practically any control. Also of note is the fact that the controls do not all have to be of the same type. For instance, you may do a group selection of two TextBoxes, a Label, and an Image control and then copy and paste this whole mixed group.

# Understanding Text Box Naming Conventions

Do not forget your Visual Basic naming conventions. For a TextBox control, the default names are Text1, Text2, Text3, etc. However, if you are actually writing some real code for a program you should write something more meaningful, such as txtResult, txtResponse, txtName, etc. The name of the TextBox control should be changed prior to doing any code for the control because otherwise you must go back through all your code to make changes. You specify the name of the TextBox through the (Name) property under the Properties section. If you are using the Alphabetic tab, then this property is right at the very top of the list.

# Controlling Text Box Appearance

Your TextBox controls can take on a different look and feel depending on the settings you apply to a control's properties. As with many things in Visual Basic, you will find that the skills you learn for this object and its properties will apply to many other objects as well.

## Appearance (3-D vs. Flat)

The *Appearance* property will set whether the border around the TextBox has a 3-D look to it or just a flat 2-D look. The default is to have a 3-D appearance.

## BorderStyle

This property sets the TextBox to either have no border or to have one. Note that if the *Appearance* property is set to 3-D then even if there is no border set in the *BorderStyle* property you will still see some form of 3-D border. Setting the Appearance to Flat and the *BorderStyle* to None allows a TextBox to *blend in* with the form that it is on. Of course, you must also select the background color, which you will cover shortly.

## Alignment

The *Alignment* property allows you to specify if you want the text in the TextBox control to be left- or right-aligned or possibly even centered. It is important to realize that text alignment within the TextBox control only takes effect when the multiline property is True.

## Font

You can easily set the font to be used for text in your TextBox by editing the *Font* property. Font details will not be gone into here as this is covered in Part II of the book, "Interface—Look and Feel," in a lesson of its own. One point worth noting about fonts and TextBox controls is that there can only be one font used at any particular time per TextBox control. This limitation will be addressed later in this lesson. The default font is MS Sans Serif in a regular style and 8 point size.

## ForeColor and BackColor

There are two properties that affect the color used in the TextBox control. The *ForeColor* property sets the color of the text, while the *BackColor* property sets the canvas upon which the text is written or displayed. If you want to change either of these, you use the drop-down menu for these properties. The drop-down menu provides you with two different methods of selecting a color. The Palette tab allows you to simply click your mouse on the color that you want from the available selection and is very easy. The System tab appears to have fewer colors but is really a method of selecting colors that the users have set for their system so your program has the ability to blend in with a user's color preferences. Figure 8.8 and Figure 8.9 show the two color selection tabs.

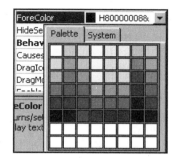

### Figure 8.8

*The Palette tab for color selection.*

### Figure 8.9

*The System tab for color selection.*

# Getting User Input

Text boxes can easily be used for getting user input from within your programs. Although you have covered the *InputBox* method, this can be somewhat limiting. As mentioned in the introduction to this lesson, you can easily couple TextBox and Label controls together to form an intuitive display for user input.

You know already how to create a TextBox control and also how to alter its appearance to suit your needs. However, what do you do when a user enters input into a TextBox? How do you find out what they entered? From within your Visual Basic code you can work with the properties of a TextBox control quite easily.

```
'initialize the TextBox control
txtFirstName.Text = ""


'get the user input
Dim strUserName1 As String
strUserName1 = txtFirstName.Text


'set the TextBox control
txtFirstName.Text = "Harry"
```

You can use these types of commands easily from many different places within your code. For example, you may only get the input when the user clicks the mouse on the OK button or put back the previous values if the user clicks the mouse on the Cancel button. If the user clicks the mouse on the Reset All button you might initialize all the TextBox controls to be empty again. The possibilities are many and are really up to you.

# Limiting Text Box Length

Sometimes you want to limit the length that the user can input into your text box. Why would you ever want to do this? One example that occurs often in practice is that the data being received from the user is for a database with set lengths for its fields. In these cases you can do either of two things. First, you could let the user enter as much as they want and then put up a message box telling them that the limit is such and such and truncate their input string afterwards. Or as a second and preferred method, you could set the *MaxLength* property to a value such as 10. This would alert the user immediately to the fact that there is a limit imposed upon the input length because it does not allow excess characters to be entered.

The other side to this coin is that the common TextBox control is limited to 64K of text. So even if you set the *MaxLength* to some ludicrously large number, you will still be limited to 64K. Later in this lesson you will take a look at how to overcome this limit in case you are designing something that might require more than 64K, such as a text editor.

# Using a Text Box for Passwords

One thing that Visual Basic makes very easy for you is to use TextBox controls for getting passwords from users. Imagine if you wrote a program that required only authorized people to be able to run it because it accessed sensitive data for the company. In these cases, the first thing you might do is to prompt the user for the program password. There are many other situations when you might need the user to enter a password.

Currently, if the user typed the password into one of your text boxes, she would see the text that she typed in on-screen and so could anyone looking over her shoulder. That wouldn't be very secure now, would it? So how do you change the text in the TextBox to be hidden? Easy! All you have to do is type in a character, such as *, in the *PasswordChar* property of the TextBox. This character will be displayed instead of the actual text input by the user.

What happens to your program code? Every time you copy the input from the user out of one of these password TextBox controls aren't you going to just get a string of the same character? Nothing needs to happen to your code as a result of using the *PasswordChar* property. Visual Basic handles everything for you and although the user simply sees a long line of the same character on the screen, behind the scenes your program code is passed the actual values typed in by the user. So if your user typed in "welcome" for her password, she would see something like "*******" while your code would receive the text *"welcome"*.

## Selecting Text through Code

*You may need to select the text or part of the text through code for the user. Although you can get by without ever having to learn this more advanced technique, selecting text through code can relieve the user from having to manually select text and change it. The properties SelLength, SelStart, and SelText are the key properties that you will deal with when handling selected text.*

*To retrieve the currently selected text, simply use the SelText property.*

```
Dim foo As String
    foo = Text1.SelText
```

*To retrieve the length of the selected text, the property SelLength is used. To retrieve the starting position of the selected text, use the SelStart property. You can also replace the currently selected text with something else by assigning a string to the SelText property. To select the entire text in a TextBox control, simply assign the value 0 to SelStart and then assign the length of the Text property to the SelLength property.*

```
Text1.SelStart = 0
Text1.SelLength = Len(Text1.Text)
```

*Playing around with these three properties, you will easily be able to handle all of your text selection needs.*

# Controlling the Text Box

At runtime you must often control the TextBox. Visual Basic provides you with properties for doing exactly that.

## *Enabled*

If you wish to have a TextBox visible but obviously disabled until the user has selected a certain object or some other task has been completed first, then you can use the *Enable* property. The *Enable* property is a boolean type, which was covered earlier in the book. So the only ways to use this control would be one of the following:

```
Text1.Enabled = True
Text1.Enabled = False
```

## Locked

You can also lock a TextBox control. This is useful if you want to toggle the TextBox between allowing and not allowing user input. It is also useful as a read-only field in your program in cases where a Label control would be too restrictive for your needs. Usually, you would set the *Locked* property to *True* at design time as there is no visual difference to the user; however, if you want to dynamically change the *Locked* property at runtime, the following commands would be used:

```
Text1.Locked = True
Text1.Locked = False
```

## Visible

The *Visible* property you have used for other controls earlier in the book, so you should already be familiar with it. If you want your TextBox control to be completely hidden from the user, you simply set the *Visible* property to *False*. You might also want to have the TextBox visible at first but then after the user has entered some input you either hide it completely or make it disabled. By now, you already know the pattern of how to set the *Visible* property at runtime.

```
Text1.Visible = True
Text1.Visible = False
```

You have probably noticed that all of these properties have been of boolean type and so take either *True* or *False* for a value.

# Creating a Multiple Line Text Box

Most of what you have dealt with so far is very useful for small one line TextBox controls, but you want to have a small editor program that can handle multiple lines of text. Visual Basic once again makes this a snap for you by giving you the *MultiLine* property. The *MultiLine* property is simply a boolean. If you want a multiple line TextBox then set the *MultiLine* property to *True*—otherwise, set it to *False*. This can only be done at design time and cannot be changed at runtime.

Remember to make your TextBox size a bit larger so that the user can actually see multiple lines in the TextBox. While this is not compulsory, there may be times when you only want the user to see one line at a time of a multiple line TextBox—it is something you must think about. Otherwise, in larger projects you might need to rework entire forms because you didn't allocate a large enough amount of space for the TextBox. This all comes down to planning and designing your projects, which will come with experience.

# Using Scrollbars to Reveal Text Box Text

Now that you can create a multiple line TextBox, you may require scrollbars so that the user can still access the information if the length or height of the data entered is more than one screen.

The TextBox has a property called *Scrollbars* that will automatically handle all the hard work for you. In some programming languages, the programmer needs to write a lot of handler code to be able to implement scrollbars, but Visual Basic takes care of all this for you and makes a nice job of it too. The *Scrollbars* property can take one of four possible values: *None*, *Horizontal*, *Vertical*, or *Both*. The default is to have no scrollbars, so if you want them you must remember to set them yourself.

Scrollbars can only be set at design time and you cannot change this property from within your code.

# Understanding the RichTextBox Control

Although the TextBox control is simple and easy to use, there are limitations to it that, at times, are unacceptable. In these cases, you should consider using a RichTextBox control. A RichTextBox control is like a big brother to the TextBox control. It maintains almost all of the functionality of a TextBox control, including some additional features, but without some of the limitations.

One of the most noticeable features of a RichTextBox control is the fact that you can have multiple fonts simultaneously when displaying text. You can have different font sizes, colors, and styles. You can also have indents, hanging indents, and bulleted lists, making the RichTextBox control a very attractive prospect to Visual Basic programmers.

The TextBox control is limited to a 64K buffer size that can impose an unacceptable limit upon text editing programs written by Visual Basic programmers. You can use the RichTextBox control in these cases to overcome this limitation, as it does not apply to RichTextBox controls.

 **Advanced RichTextBox Features**

*Although it is beyond the scope of this lesson, the RichTextBox control has many uncovered features that you may want to explore. Some of these features will be covered in later lessons that are dedicated to that topic, such as printing or OLE.*

*Using the OLE control you can drag and drop Word documents or other such files to your RichTextBox, including graphics files such as bitmaps. These capabilities can greatly enhance the look and usability of your program.*

*The RichTextBox control deals mostly with text, and as such it would be nice if it could handle loading text files from disk and then saving them back again later. Actually, the RichTextBox has these features too, but you won't really cover this until much later in the book when you learn about storing and retrieving information by using files.*

# Creating a RichTextBox

To create a RichTextBox control, you must first add the appropriate component to your Visual Basic environment's control panel. To add a component, from the Visual Basic environment select Project menu, Components. Visual Basic will display the Components dialog as shown in Figure 8.10.

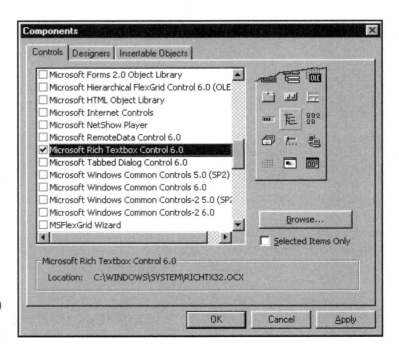

### Figure 8.10

*The Components dialog.*

Within the component list under the Controls tab, click your mouse in the checkbox beside the Microsoft Rich Textbox Control 6.0 so that there is a check mark present. Click your mouse on the OK button to close the Components dialog box.

On the control panel within your Visual Basic environment, you will now see the RichTextBox control icon, as in Figure 8.11.

### Figure 8.11

*The RichTextBox control icon.*

You can now select the RichTextBox control to add to your form in exactly the same manner as you add any other control to your form.

## What You Must Know

You have now covered some very different methods of obtaining user input. TextBoxes give you more options than the *InputBox* command, allowing much greater customization. The TextBox control not only has a wide set of visual properties that can be altered but also provides many functional features such as password masking, enabling, locking, and more. In Lesson 9, "Using List Boxes," you will learn how to display lists of information visually, as well as how to manipulate those lists from within your programs. Before you continue with Lesson 9, however, make sure you understand the following key concepts:

◆ With greater customization options than the *InputBox* command, text boxes allow you to get user input from the user directly from your own forms.

◆ When adding a TextBox control to your form, you can set both the size and the placement to suit your needs. You can have more than one TextBox control on a single form.

◆ You can limit the maximum length of a TextBox control regardless of whether it is a single or multiline configuration. Scrollbars and text alignment can be used with multiline text boxes.

◆ The TextBox control can easily accommodate masking the display for passwords to prevent the actual text from being shown on screen. The actual text is easily obtained through source code, however.

◆ Getting user input from a TextBox control is largely based on the *Text* property. The *Text* property can be both retrieved for the current value and assigned to provide a default value.

◆ To get past some of the TextBox control's limitations, use a RichTextBox control instead. RichTextBox controls are not limited to a 64K buffer and also have enhancements such as multiple fonts, colors, sizes, and styles.

# Lesson 9

# Using List Boxes

Y ou have learned quite a lot about getting user input in recent lessons using a variety of different controls and methods. In this lesson, you will learn about displaying user input or other information using the ListBox control and how to use the ListBox control within your own programs. By the time you finish this lesson, you will understand the following key concepts:

◆ ListBoxes allow you to present to the user a list of items from which they can select one or more.

◆ Scrollbars are automatically provided for you with the ListBox control whenever the current list is more than can be displayed at once.

◆ ListBoxes can dynamically have items added or removed from the list and also easily provide you with the current number of items in the list.

◆ Visual Basic will take care of sorting the list alphabetically if you set the *Sorted* property to *True*; however, you must not insert items to a particular index for Visual Basic to maintain the integrity of the sort order.

◆ Columns in a ListBox control are snaked, wrapping from the bottom of one column to the top of the next and continuing in this manner. Using columns in a ListBox causes the scrollbar to switch from vertical to horizontal.

◆ You can have different forms of multiselection with ListBox controls. Multiselection enables the user to select more than one item at a time. Checkboxes present another form of multi-selection.

◆ With similar features to a ListBox control, a ComboBox control offers some variations in display and user interaction.

# Introducing the ListBox Control

Imagine if you had a list of two hundred items that you would like the user to be able to select from. It would be unreasonable and rather impractical to try to create a button for each item on your form. You could use a TextBox control to store all the items but would then be left to do all the work of sorting, adding, and removing items yourself through source code. Visual Basic provides a control known as a ListBox that allows lists of items to be displayed easily and that contains simple methods for manipulating the items such as adding, deleting, and sorting. Figure 9.1 shows a simple ListBox control.

### Figure 9.1

*A simple ListBox control.*

ListBox controls are very good for dynamic data, that is, data that changes. If you were writing a program for a network administrator, you could easily find yourself having to list all the users or computers in the network. Data, such as users and computers, change with time so a ListBox is perfect for handling this, as it can easily be altered from source code. Anything that requires a list of objects that might change is a good candidate for using with a ListBox control.

A ListBox control will automatically provide scrollbars if the list is longer than what can currently be displayed. So unlike other controls, such as a TextBox control, you do not have to do anything for scrollbar support and functionality.

# Creating a List Box

To create a list box, all you must do is add the ListBox control to your form in the same manner as you have added all the controls previously covered in this book. The ListBox control icon is shown in Figure 9.2.

### Figure 9.2

*The ListBox control icon.*

You can size and place the ListBox control in the same manner as you did with the TextBox control.

# Adding Items to a List Box

Adding items to a list box through source code is a relatively straightforward matter. If your *ListBox* object is called *List1*, then adding an item to the list would look like the following:

```
List1.AddItem "Red"
```

You can also add items using variables rather than literal strings.

```
Dim s As String
    s = "Blue"
    List1.AddItem s
```

 **Inserting Items into a List Box**

*Using the AddItem method with a single argument is the safest and easiest way to add items to a list box. However, you can also add items by inserting them into a particular position within the list. To insert an item into the list you must indicate the index number where you want the item to be added. The first item in a ListBox control is index 0.*

*Look at the simple list of colors in Figure 9.1 and the order that they are in. The item Red would be index 0, Blue 1, Green 2, and Yellow 3. Think of the single line of source code required to insert an item called Orange between the items Blue and Green. Pretend that the ListBox object is called List1. You would end up with a line as follows:*

```
List1.AddItem "Orange", 2
```

*The ListBox would, after adding the new Orange item, appear as shown in Figure 9.3.*

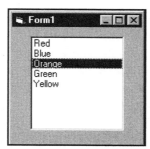

**Figure 9.3**

*The ListBox after inserting the item Orange.*

# Deleting Items from a List Box

The ListBox property *RemoveItem* is used to remove or delete a single item from the list. However, deleting an item from a ListBox control is not as simple as adding an item because you must know the index number of the item that you are deleting. The following line of source code would remove the second item in the list. (Recall that the index starts at 0.)

```
List1.RemoveItem 1
```

Using the *RemoveItem* to clear the list entirely is not a very efficient way of doing things. Deleting hundreds or thousands of items one line at a time could also cause unnecessary delays for the user. Visual Basic provides you with another property of the ListBox called *Clear*. The *Clear* property will remove all items in the ListBox and does not take any arguments.

```
List1.Clear
```

# Counting Items in a List Box

Obtaining the number of items in a ListBox control is made extremely easy by using the *ListCount* property. The following code shows how to get the total number of items in a ListBox control and then display this in a Label control called *lblTotal* for the user's benefit.

```
lblTotal.Caption = "Total: " & List1.ListCount
```

# Using Advanced List Box Features

You have now covered all the basic features of using a list box within your own programs. The sections that follow cover more advanced features that are more useful to those programmers that have definite requirements.

# Sorting a List Box

Sorting the items in a list box alphabetically is very simple. The *Sorted* property is a boolean so it will take either *True* or *False*. You cannot change the *Sorted* property of a list box through source code at runtime. To set your list box to be automatically sorted alphabetically, assign *True* to the *Sorted* property of your list box using the Properties section at design time as shown in Figure 9.4.

**Figure 9.4**

*Changing the Sorted property of a list box.*

The trick with using the sorting routine is not to insert items using an index number but to simply add them to the list and let Visual Basic take care of the insertion point. If you fail to do this, Visual Basic may not be able to properly sort any subsequent items.

The default value of the *Sorted* property for a ListBox is *False*, so if you want your ListBox sorted you must remember to set this property yourself.

# Defining Columns within a List Box

A ListBox control can be divided into columns. These are not individual or related columns linked by rows, as many programmers first believe, but "snake" columns that wrap around when they get to the bottom of a column and start again at the top of the next column. The most well-known application that uses snake columns is Windows Explorer when the View option is set to List.

If the *Columns* property is set to 0, which is the default value, then there is only a single column with a vertical scrollbar. When the *Columns* property of a ListBox control is set to a value of 1 or greater, then the scrollbar changes to a horizontal scrollbar. Figures 9.5 and 9.6 show the difference between these two options.

**Figure 9.5**

*The* Columns *property when set to 0.*

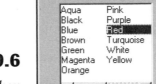

**Figure 9.6**

*The* Columns *property when set to 2.*

 **Working with Related List Box Columns**

*Although the ListBox control only has snaked columns, there are many occasions when you might need related columns. Related columns are where the items in the first column have a relation across each row with the items in any other column. These types of columns are available in a list box type of control known as a ListView. The ListView control is a much more feature-rich list box than the standard ListBox control.*

*To try the ListView control, you must add the component Microsoft Windows Common Controls 6.0 using the Project menu Components option. Adding components was covered earlier in this book.*

*Although a detailed discussion of this control is beyond the scope of this success hint, the brief requirements will be given for setting up multiple columns.*

*Right-click your mouse on your ListView object to bring up its Properties dialog. The* View *property needs to be set to lvwReport. Under the Column Headers tab, use the Insert Column button to add as many columns as you require. Figure 9.7 shows you what a ListView control with multiple related columns looks like, although the ListView control can have many different types of appearance and is highly customizable.*

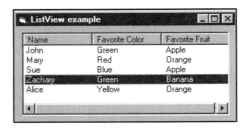

**Figure 9.7**

*A ListView control with multiple related columns.*

*The ListView control is far more complex than the standard ListBox control and is recommended for programmers who have covered all the fundamentals and are confident with Visual Basic.*

# Selecting Multiple List Box Items

Most of the time, ListBox controls are used for selecting single items from a list. You can set ListBox controls to accept multiple selections, however, by using the ListBox control's *MultiSelect* property. The default value of the *MultiSelect* property is *0*, which is for selecting single items only. Setting the *MultiSelect* property value to *1* puts the ListBox into simple mode for multiselection, and setting the *MultiSelect* property value to *2* puts the ListBox into extended mode for multiselection.

In simple mode, multiselection consists of mouse clicks and pressing the spacebar to toggle between selecting and deselecting items in the list. Using the arrow keys on the keyboard will move the focus to different items.

In extended mode, multiselection can do everything that simple mode can do but with extended features. The extended features allow the user to hold the Shift key down to select a range of items in the list. Holding down the Ctrl key allows you to deselect items from the range.

To find out easily how many items have been selected, use the *SelCount* property of the ListBox. This property simply returns the number of items that are currently selected.

# Using Checkboxes in a List Box

You can use checkboxes next to the individual items within a list box by setting the *Style* property to *1—Checkbox*. The default value of the *Style* property is *0—Standard*, which does not use checkboxes.

If you use checkboxes in your list box then you can no longer use the *MultiSelect* property with any value other than 0. This is because the checkbox is a different form of multiselection. Figure 9.8 shows an example of using checkboxes in a ListBox control.

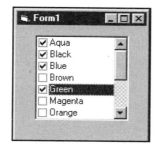

**Figure 9.8**

*Using checkboxes in a ListBox.*

You can use the *SelCount* property with checkboxes as well, to find out quickly how many items have been selected. To find out if a particular item has been selected, you must use the *Selected* property along with the index of the item that you are checking. The *Selected* property returns a boolean value—*True* if the item is selected and *False* otherwise. The following code shows how to check if the first item in the list has been selected.

```
If List1.Selected(i) Then MsgBox "First item selected!"
```

 **Finding All Selected Items**

*In the next lesson, "Using Loops to Repeat One or More Instructions," you will cover lots of techniques for creating loops in your code, as well as get a thorough description of what loops are for and how to utilize them. One of the loops you will learn about is the For...Next loop. This loop is perfect for finding all the selected items in a ListBox, especially if the content of the ListBox is not static. Look at the following code, which shows how to find all the selected items in a ListBox and presents a MsgBox telling you each time it finds one such item. You, of course, may do whatever you want when you find a selected item. The object of this success hint is merely to show you how to find them.*

```
For i = 0 To List1.ListCount − 1
    If List1.Selected(i) Then MsgBox List1.List(i)
Next
```

*In the next lesson, you will see more examples of loops in combination with List-Box controls.*

# Using the ComboBox Control

Another form of list box is the ComboBox control. The ComboBox is very similar to the ListBox control in many ways and has many of the same properties. What is fundamentally different is that while a ListBox maintains a set size on the form to display the list, the ComboBox usually only shows the current selection unless the drop-down menu is activated displaying the list from which the user can choose. Figure 9.9 shows a ComboBox on a form and Figure 9.10 shows the same ComboBox with the drop-down menu activated by clicking the down arrow to open the ComboBox.

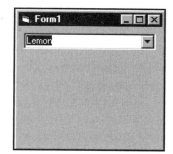

**Figure 9.9**

*A ComboBox on a form.*

**Figure 9.10**

*A ComboBox with the drop-down menu activated.*

ComboBox controls can have different styles. The *Style* property of the ComboBox control specifies which of three possible styles to use. The default style is the Dropdown Combo, which is a combination of a ListBox and a TextBox allowing the user to either select from the list or type directly into the text field. The Dropdown List style is the same as the Dropdown combo except that the user cannot type directly into the text field and must select a choice from the list. The remaining style is the Simple Combo, which does not have a drop-down menu but rather a fixed size list. When using a Simple Combo style, the user can either select from the list or type directly into the text field. Figure 9.11 shows a Simple Combo style ComboBox.

**Figure 9.11**

*A Simple Combo style ComboBox.*

# What You Must Know

The ListBox control gives you an easy method of presenting dynamic or static lists of information to the user. A ListBox can be used for either single or multiple selections. Features such as sorting, columns, checkboxes, and more make the ListBox a very useful control for Visual Basic programmers. In Lesson 10, "Using Loops to Repeat One or More Instructions," you will learn how to create loops within your programs, as well as what loops are and when you should apply them. Loops can not only save you a lot of work but can get around some problems that would be almost impossible to solve otherwise. Before you continue with Lesson 10, however, make sure you understand the following key concepts:

◆ A list of items can be displayed to the user through use of the ListBox control, which allows single or multiple selections to be made.

◆ The ListBox control will automatically provide scrollbars if the amount of data in the list exceeds the amount that can currently be displayed.

◆ ListBoxes can be either static or dynamic, with items able to be added and removed at runtime. The ListBox control keeps track of the number of items currently in the list at any given time and has this information readily available to the program.

◆ Alphabetically sorting the list in a ListBox control can be automated for you by Visual Basic. When sorting is done by Visual Basic, new items that are added to the list must not be inserted by index number.

◆ The ListBox control can have *snake* columns that wrap from bottom to top with each successive column. Scrollbars switch from vertical to horizontal when columns are used.

◆ ListBox controls allow multiselection in different forms including checkboxes.

◆ A ComboBox control offers similar features to a ListBox control with some variations in display and user interaction.

# Lesson 10

---

# Using Loops to Repeat One or More Instructions

In Lesson 9, "Using List Boxes," you learned how to present information in the form of a list to the user and also how to dynamically modify that list. In this lesson, you will learn about loops, the different methods of applying loops and how to use loops to solve problems dealing with repetitive tasks being applied to dynamic lists, such as those stored in ListBox controls. Loops can be applied in many areas of programming and are an extremely powerful technique. By the time you finish this lesson, you will understand the following key concepts:

◆ Loops are a form of reusable code and allow you to repeatedly execute the same block of code within your programs.

◆ Programming effort and lines of code can both be greatly saved through the use of loops.

◆ The *For-Next* loop is most useful when you have a definite start and end value and is probably the most commonly used loop.

◆ The *For Each-Next* loop is for dealing with groups of items that you may not know the exact number of. The *For Each-Next* loop is used mostly with arrays, collections, and Active Directory objects.

◆ The *Do-Loop* can use the *While* or *Until* keywords. The *Do-Loop* can have its condition at the end of the loop to ensure that the contents of the loop are executed at least once. The *Do-Loop* is especially useful for looping an indefinite number of times before a condition is met.

◆ Avoid endless loops by checking your source code carefully.

◆ Random numbers can be easily generated by Visual Basic using the *Rnd* function. Use the *Randomize* command to change the seed used by *Rnd* based on the current time.

# Introducing Loops

The word loops might bring to mind different images of circles, colorful hoops, or other objects that when followed for long enough bring you back where you started. This is not far off the mark when you think of loops in Visual Basic. A loop allows you to repeatedly execute a block of code until a certain condition is met. Executing a block of code repeatedly may not at first appear to be such an amazing feat to accomplish. You can already write reusable code in the form of a sub or function. Take a look at a scenario and then think about how you can solve it using the skills that you currently have. You will see more clearly why there is a need for loops in programming, and by the end of this lesson you will have lots of ideas about where you could use loops in your own programs and the potentialities that loops open up to you.

Imagine that you have to write a simple program that displays a ListBox control with a list of names of all the employees in a large company. A data-entry clerk will enter in all the names for you so the list will be dynamic. The company boss wants to be able to select multiple names from the list and then click her mouse on a button that will add all the selected names to a second ListBox to be able to see the shortlist of selected names.

At first glance, you feel that you could write this program using all the Visual Basic skills that you have learned so far in this book. You could have a form with two ListBox controls on it. You could have a TextBox control to allow the data entry clerk to enter in the names. You could have a button to add the names to the first ListBox. The first ListBox could be set to be multiselection to allow the company boss to select multiple names. You know how many items are in the list using the *ListCount* property. You create a sub that takes an integer for an argument representing the index of a list item. The sub then checks if this item in the first ListBox has been selected, copying the name to the second ListBox if the result is *True*. Hey! You have learned quite a lot already!

Now comes the difficult part. When you wrote the program you could not have known ahead of time how many entries would be in the dynamic list. There is no way to call the sub the exact amount of times. The *ListCount* property can tell you how many items are in the ListBox, but you cannot use this information to solve the problem. Think about this scenario problem yourself before moving on to the next section.

The solution to the scenario problem would be to use a loop. A loop would allow you to repeatedly call the sub, passing it a different argument each time. After the loop has executed its block of code *ListCount* times, it stops and your program code continues.

Loops in general can save you a lot of programming effort and lines of code. A loop of three lines of source code could be the equivalent of one thousand or more lines of source code had the loop not been used. If changes to limits or conditions are required, the use of loops allows you to make the change in one place as opposed to changing multiple lines of source code. Changing multiple lines of source code can be tedious and also leads to errors creeping in through typos and other user mistakes.

There are different variations of loops available to Visual Basic programmers, and you will learn which types of loops are more suitable under certain conditions than others. At times, choosing between different loop variations comes down to preference and source code readability.

# Using the *For-Next* Loop to Repeat Instructions a Specific Number of Times

If you know how many times a loop needs to occur, then using a *For-Next* loop is often a good choice. Whenever you are dealing with an object that has a count of all its items available, such as a ListBox, then you can use this count in your *For-Next* loop.

Basically, a *For-Next* loop relies on a counter that is usually incremented on each loop to reach an end value. This counter is simply a variable. The syntax of the *For-Next* loop is as follows:

**For** *counter = start* **To** *end*
...
**Next**

To create a *For-Next* loop that loops ten times and displays a *MsgBox* on each iteration of the loop, your source code would look something similar to the following:

```
Private Sub Form_Load()
Dim i As Integer
    For i = 1 To 10
        MsgBox "This is loop number " & i
    Next
End Sub
```

To increment the counter by more than one each iteration of the loop, Visual Basic provides the keyword *Step* for use with *For-Next* loops. At the end of the first line of a *For-Next* loop, place the keyword *Step* followed by the amount to increment the counter by.

To create a *For-Next* loop that loops from 1 to 10 in steps of 2 and displays the result of each iteration of the loop in a ListBox, do the following:

1. Open a new project in Visual Basic. Place a ListBox on the form. Add the following source code:

   ```
   Private Sub Form_Load()
   Dim loopnum As Integer
       loopnum = 0
       For i = 1 To 10 Step 2
           loopnum = loopnum + 1
   ```

```
      List1.AddItem "Loop: " & loopnum & "   Counter: " & i
  Next
End Sub
```

2. Click on the Run menu Start command to see the result of your program, which should be similar to what is shown in Figure 10.1.

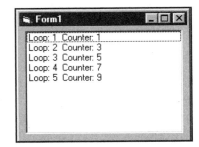

**Figure 10.1**

*Incrementing a loop with a step of 2.*

Loops do not have to increase their counters all the time either. Using the *Step* keyword, you can also decrease the counter in a loop. To decrease the counter in a loop, modify the value following the *Step* keyword to be a negative number. Modify one line of the previous example, altering the program to decrement from 10 to 1 with a step of −1. The result should appear as shown in Figure 10.2.

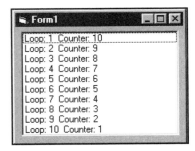

**Figure 10.2**

*Decreasing the counter in a loop.*

To achieve the results in Figure 10.2, you must change the line of code from

```
For i = 1 To 10 Step 2
```

to

```
For i = 10 To −1 Step −1
```

## Success HINT: Using Timers as Loops

*Although not covered in this lesson, Timers are objects provided by Visual Basic that allow you to execute a block of code every n milliseconds (thousandth of a second). The interval between Timer loops is variable and you can change this if you require. The fundamental difference between Timers and other loops is that a Timer loop relinquishes control to the program until the time interval is reached. You will learn more about Timers and their usage in Lesson 11, "Working with Timers, Time, and Dates."*

# Using the *For Each-Next* Loop

There are times when you do not know exactly how many items are in a group or collection of items. At these times, it is often useful to consider using a *For Each-Next* loop. Unlike a *For-Next* loop that has a definite start and end value and reiterates through the loop a set number of times, a *For Each-Next* loop reiterates through the loop once for every item in a given group. The syntax of the *For Each-Next* loop is as follows:

**For Each** *item* **In** *group*
…
**Next**

Imagine if there was no method given to you by Visual Basic for obtaining the number of items in a ListBox control. It would not be possible to use a *For-Next* loop because you would have to guess what the end value would be. Using a *For Each-Next* loop, you would be able to reiterate through the loop once for each item in the List-Box. Fortunately for you, Visual Basic does provide a method for obtaining the number of items in a ListBox control, but this is not the case with all object types. It is important to be aware of the *For Each-Next* loop so that you can use it when the need arises.

There are restrictions as to when the *For Each-Next* loop can be applied in Visual Basic. You cannot use the *For Each-Next* loop on user-defined types when using arrays, as only arrays of type *Variant* are eligible. When using collections with the *For Each-Next* loop, you can have items of type *Variant*, as well as items of types listed in the Object Browser and generic object types. Arrays and collections are discussed in detail in Lesson 27, "Using Arrays and Collections."

The *For Each-Next* loop is also used frequently with Active Directory objects and allows you to loop through an unknown number of shares, computers, users, and more. Active Directory is discussed in detail in Part III, "Advanced Concepts," along with examples of using a *For Each-Next* loop.

Although the *For Each-Next* loop is used in conjunction with more advanced objects, you only need to be aware of it at this stage and can incorporate the *For Each-Next* loop into your own programs later. The *For Each-Next* loop is mentioned in this lesson for completeness, although it could have been left until you cover the more advanced objects and sections of this book.

# Understanding the *Do-Loop* Family

A *Do-Loop* can be used when you want to loop an indefinite number of times before a certain condition is met. Not unlike the *If-Then* statement, the *Do-Loop* is a form of conditional programming. You supply a set of criteria or conditions that are either met or not. The conditions, as explained earlier in the book, are actually boolean and return either *True* or *False*. You can use multiple conditions and link them together using boolean logic.

There are four variations of the *Do-Loop* family, each of which is very similar to the others. The four variations are as follows:

- ◆ *Do While…Loop*

- ◆ *Do-Loop While*

- ◆ *Do Until…Loop*

- ◆ *Do-Loop Until*

The syntax of a *Do While…Loop* is as follows:

**Do While** *condition*
…
**Loop**

 **Variable Declaration Shortcut**

*When you are declaring variables to use in your subroutines and functions, you can declare multiple variables on a single line using a single Dim keyword by separating each of the variables by a comma. So the syntax would be:*

*Dim* variable1, variable2, …,variablen

*Variables declared in this manner are of type Variant. Be aware that excessive use of the variable declaration shortcut can diminish the readability of your code.*

*However, if you feel that the readability of your code is still clear, then by all means use the variable declaration shortcut. You will certainly see the shortcut used in other people's source code so it is good for you to be aware of.*

Look at an example of a multi-conditional *Do While…Loop* and think about whether you could duplicate this feat using a *For-Next* loop or any other Visual Basic commands that you have covered so far in this book. The example code continues looping while the value of *i* is less than 10 and *j* is less than 15.

```
Private Sub Form_Load()
Dim i, j
    i = 3
    j = 3
    Do While (i < 10) And (j < 15)
        i = i + 1
        j = j + 2
    Loop
    MsgBox i & "    " & j
    End
End Sub
```

The syntax of a *Do While…Loop* is as follows:

**Do**

…

**Loop While** *condition*

The difference between a *Do While…Loop* structure and a *Do-Loop While* structure is simply that the latter loop will always execute at least once. Other than a *Do-Loop While* structure always executing at least once, the two loops are the same. The following example shows the difference between a *Do While…Loop* structure and a *Do-Loop While* structure.

```
Private Sub Form_Load()
Dim i
    i = 10
    Do While i < 10
        MsgBox "The value of i is: " & i
    Loop
End Sub
```

The message box would never get displayed using a *Do While...Loop*. However, if the same example were to use a *Do-Loop While* structure, you can be sure that the contents of the loop will be executed at least once and the message box would be displayed.

```
Private Sub Form_Load()
Dim i
    i = 10
    Do
        MsgBox "The value of i is: " & i
    Loop While i < 10
End Sub
```

The *Do Until...Loop* has the following syntax:

**Do Until** *condition*

…

**Loop**

Very similar to a *Do While...Loop*, a *Do Until...Loop* works in exactly the same way except that the loop continues as long as the condition is equal to *False*. When the condition is *True*, the loop terminates. You could emulate any of the *Do* loops that use the keyword *While* with an equivalent Do loop that uses the keyword *Until*, by explicitly making the condition equal to *False*. You can achieve the reverse emulation by explicitly making the condition equal to *False* after swapping the keyword *Until* with the keyword *While*, as well.

The *Do-Loop Until* is the same as a *Do Until...Loop* except that it will always execute the contents of the loop at least once. The syntax of the *Do-Loop Until* is as follows:

**Do**

…

**Loop Until** *condition*

 **Avoiding Endless Loops**

*When you use loops you must be careful that the exit condition is not impossible to achieve. Imagine if you had a loop that continued until the user selected the color red from a selection of colors provided. If red was not actually in the selection of colors provided then the loop will be endless and the program would be unable to continue. By testing and examining your code carefully, you can avoid endless loops from occurring in your programs. The following is an example of an endless loop:*

```
i = 10
Do
    MsgBox "I'm in an endless loop!"
Loop While i > 1
```

# Generating Random Numbers

Whenever you are writing Visual Basic programs you never know when you might need to have the computer generate random numbers for you to use. In the *Loopy* example that follows, you will be making use of loops to generate lots of random numbers, so it seems appropriate that you learn how to create random numbers in Visual Basic before then.

The keyword *Rnd* returns a random number in Visual Basic. The number *Rnd* returns is greater than or equal to zero but less than one. You can pass a number as an argument to *Rnd*, but you will not usually do this.

You can produce random integers in a range if you know the maximum and minimum values of the range. Use the following formula, where max is a variable representing the maximum value and min is a variable representing the minimum value:

```
Int((Rnd * (max - (min + 1))) + min)
```

To further randomize the numbers returned by the *Rnd* function, use the command *Randomize* before calling *Rnd*. You call *Randomize* to set the seed that *Rnd* uses based on the current system time. *Randomize* does not take any arguments. Using *Randomize* once when your program launches is sufficient to cause the values returned by *Rnd* to not be identical each time your program is run.

# Looking at the *Loopy* Example

In this example, you are going to create a program that has three ListBox controls. You will populate the first ListBox with 100 random numbers using a loop. In the second ListBox, you will use a loop to copy all of the items in the first ListBox and add 7 to their value. In the third ListBox, you will use a loop to copy all the items from the second ListBox and sort them numerically. Note that if the third ListBox is sorted alphabetically using the *Sorted* property, then a number such as 1111 would come before 23 even though it is higher. Although a ListBox can easily be sorted alphabetically by Visual Basic, using loops you can sort a ListBox using different criteria. Figure 10.3 shows the *Loopy* program in action.

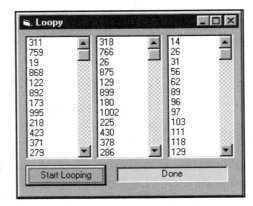

**Figure 10.3**

The Loopy *program in action.*

1. Open a new project in Visual Basic.

2. Name the project **Loopy** and name the form **frmLoopy**.

3. Add three ListBox controls to your form similar to Figure 10.3.

4. Add a CommandButton and change the name to **cmdStart** and the *Caption* property to **Start Looping**.

5. Add a label similar to the one shown in Figure 10.3. Change the name to **lblStatus** and the *Caption* property to be blank. Change the Alignment property to be **2—Center**. Change the BackColor property to be a lighter gray using the Palette tab. Set the BorderStyle property to be **1—Fixed Single**.

You have now completed the form design. Move on to the source code by double-clicking your mouse somewhere on the form but not on any of the controls. Edit the wrapper source code that Visual Basic provides by inserting the *Randomize* command.

```
Private Sub Form_Load()
    'set the seed for the random numbers
    Randomize
End Sub
```

From the Object window in the Visual Basic environment, double-click your mouse on the CommandButton, *cmdStart*. Add code to clear the three lists and then add code to call three different subs for our loops.

```
Private Sub cmdStart_Click()
    'clear all the lists
    List1.Clear
    List2.Clear
    List3.Clear

    'start the loops
    GoLoop1
    GoLoop2
    GoLoop3
End Sub
```

Create a subroutine and call it *GoLoop1*. This subroutine will fill List1 with random numbers.

```
Private Sub GoLoop1()
Dim i
    For i = 1 To 100
        List1.AddItem Int(Rnd * 1000)
    Next
End Sub
```

Create a subroutine and call it *GoLoop2*. This subroutine will fill List2 with the numbers in List1 after adding seven to their value. *GoLoop2* will also copy each item in List2 into List3.

```
Private Sub GoLoop2()
Dim i
    For i = 1 To List1.ListCount
        List2.AddItem List1.List(i - 1) + 7
        List3.AddItem List2.List(i - 1)
    Next
    DoEvents
End Sub
```

Create a subroutine and call it *GoLoop3*. This subroutine will sort the items in List3 numerically and use the Label control, *lblStatus*, to give the user feedback.

```
Private Sub GoLoop3()
Dim SORTING As Boolean
Dim i
```

```
Dim buffer As Integer
    SORTING = True
    i = 0
    lblStatus.Caption = "Sorting..."
    Do While SORTING
        If Int(List3.List(i + 1)) < Int(List3.List(i)) Then
            buffer = Int(List3.List(i + 1))
            List3.RemoveItem i + 1
            List3.AddItem buffer, i
            i = 0
        Else
            i = i + 1
        End If
        If List3.ListCount = i + 1 Then SORTING = False
        DoEvents
    Loop
    lblStatus.Caption = "Done"
End Sub
```

Select Start from the Run menu to see the *Loopy* program in action. Refer to the source code for the *Loopy* program at www.prima-tech.com/books/book/5250/945/ if you have any difficulties.

# What You Must Know

Loops are a very powerful programming tool that can save you effort and lines of source code. There are many different variations of loops in Visual Basic. Using loops, you can work through large lists or groups of items with relative ease. In Lesson 11, "Working with Timers, Time, and Dates," you will learn how to create loops based on time rather than values, as well as how to handle time and date issues using Visual Basic. Before you continue with Lesson 11, however, make sure you understand the following key concepts:

◆ You can repeatedly execute the same block of code within your programs using loops. Loops are a form of reusable code.

◆ Loops can save you from writing a lot of source code, as well as save you a lot of programming effort.

◆ There are many different types of loops in Visual Basic, each for a particular purpose.

◆ When you have a definite start and end value, the *For-Next* loop is the most useful. The *For-Next* loop is probably the most commonly used loop.

◆ Dealing with groups of items, especially arrays and collections, that you may not know the exact number of, is the specialty of the *For Each-Next* loop.

◆ There are four different loops in the *Do-Loop* family. When the condition is at the end of a *Do-Loop* the contents of the loop are always executed at least once. A *Do-Loop* will iterate indefinitely until the loop condition is met.

◆ Carefully check your source code to avoid endless loops occurring in your programs.

◆ You can easily generate random numbers in your programs using the *Rnd* function. The seed used by the *Rnd* function can be set based on the system time by using the *Randomize* command without any arguments.

# Lesson 11

---

# Working with Timers, Time, and Dates

In Lesson 10, "Using Loops to Repeat One or More Instructions," you learned how to repeat code a definite and indefinite number of times, using a variety of loop structures. In this lesson, you will learn a different type of loop that is based not on numbers but on time and time intervals. You will also learn how to deal with time and date aspects from within your Visual Basic programs. By the time you finish this lesson, you will understand the following key concepts:

- ◆ Timers are controls that you can add to your forms. The position or size of Timers on your form does not matter, as they are always invisible at runtime.

- ◆ Timers are like loops that deal with the passing of time rather than loops that iterate a certain number of times.

- ◆ Time intervals are measured in milliseconds with a maximum possible interval of about 65 seconds.

- ◆ Visual Basic is an event-driven language. When a preset circumstance is met an event is issued by Visual Basic to execute the code, if any, for that event. The Timer control only has the Timer event.

- ◆ Timers can decrease CPU usage when your program requires an indefinite loop while waiting for some external condition to be met.

- ◆ The Time and Date functions can be used on their own or using specific formatting.

```
        EXITNOW = True
End Sub


'===============================================
'Start button to commence looping
'===============================================
Private Sub cmdStartLoop_Click()
        Timer1.Enabled = True
End Sub


'===============================================
'Program start
'===============================================
Private Sub Form_Load()
        EXITNOW = False
End Sub


'===============================================
'Timer loop
'===============================================
Private Sub Timer1_Timer()
        If EXITNOW = True Then
                Timer1.Enabled = False
        Else
                DoEvents
        End If
End Sub
```

7. Run *LoopTest2* and monitor the CPU usage.

8. Click your mouse on the Start Loop button and watch the CPU usage. Wait for at least thirty seconds to get a good estimate of CPU performance.

9. Click your mouse on the Exit Loop button. Using a Timer control for looping indefinitely until a condition is true has a negligible effect on CPU usage. The results of *LoopTest2* are shown in Figure 11.6.

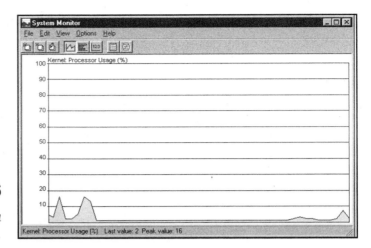

**Figure 11.6**

*CPU usage trends when running LoopTest2.*

 **Giving Your Programs a Snappy Feel**

*When a program uses 100% of the CPU for a prolonged period of time, the computer appears very sluggish and slow to the user and the whole system crawls. Making use of Timer controls to decrease the CPU usage of your programs' loops will give your users a more responsive feel when using your programs.*

*Timer controls cannot replace all other loops but they are excellent when your program must periodically check for a condition while looping indefinitely or when your program requires a delay.*

# Working with Time and Dates

There are many occasions when your programs may require handling time and dates. Visual Basic makes handling both of these very simple. To obtain the current system time, you use the *Time* function. To obtain the current system date, you use the *Date* function.

```
Dim myTime, myDate
myTime = Time '4:27:26 PM
myDate = Date '9/1/00
```

You can change the format of the time and date that is returned from these functions by using the *Format* function. The *Format* function will take an expression such as those returned by the *Time* and *Date* functions as its first argument. For the second argument you specify the format you want. For time, the format is dealing with hours (h), minutes (m), seconds (s), and whether to use AM or PM (AMPM). You must specify the format within quotes as a string. The following are some examples of changing the time and date formats:

```
myTime = Format(Time, "hh:mm:ss")        '16:27:26
myTime = Format(Time, "h:mm:ss AMPM")    '4:27:26 PM
myTime = Format(Time, "h:mm")            '16:27
myDate = Format(Date, "dddd, mmm d yyyy")    'Friday, Sep 1 2000
myDate = Format(Date, "ddd, mmmm dd, yyyy")  'Fri, September 01, 2000
```

When working with time and dates, your program may require more interaction with the user, such as having the user select a particular date. Visual Basic has a control known as the DateTimePicker control that accommodates you in user input matters. You must add the component from the Project menu Components option dialog, as you learned earlier in the book. The component to add is called *Microsoft Windows Common Controls-2 6.0*. The DateTimePicker control has a ToolTip of *DTPicker* when you point your mouse over it.

By changing the DateTimePicker control's *Format* property, you can set the format to be for time, date in short form, date in long form, or custom format. Figure 11.7 shows the DateTimePicker control in action.

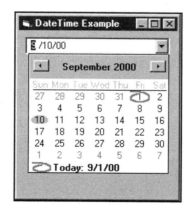

**Figure 11.7**

*The DateTimePicker control in action.*

 **Additional Time and Date Functions**

*In the advanced section of this book, you will learn about Windows API functions and how they are used in Visual Basic. Although it is not possible to explain Windows API functions in any depth here, you can refer back to some of these time functions later if you are really keen to work with advanced time and date functions. A list of some of these Windows API calls is shown in Table 11.1.*

*Table 11.1 Windows API time and date functions for advanced functionality.*

| | |
|---|---|
| *EnumCalendarInfo* | *GetTimeFormat* |
| *EnumDateFormats* | *GetTimerResolution* |
| *EnumTimeFormats* | *GetTimeZoneInformation* |
| *GetCurrentTime* | *SetLocalTime* |
| *GetLocalTime* | *SetSystemTime* |
| *GetMessageTime* | *SetSystemTimeAdjustment* |
| *GetSystemTime* | *SetTimeZoneInformation* |
| *GetSystemTimeAdjustment* | *SystemTimeToTzSpecificLocalTime* |
| *GetTickCount* | |

# What You Must Know

Timer controls are like loops that deal with time that passes. The time interval used by the Timer control can be set anywhere within a preset range. You can easily obtain the current time and date using Visual Basic's *Time* and *Date* functions, as well as customize the output format. In Lesson 12, "Using Forms and Modules," you will learn how and why to segment your code into modules, as well as covering multiple forms within your programs. Before you continue with Lesson 12, however, make sure you understand the following key concepts:

◆ You can add Timer controls to your forms, although their size and position have no relevance as they are not visible at runtime.

◆ Rather than dealing with the number of iterations of a loop, Timers deal with the passage of time to govern looping.

◆ Timers use time intervals that can be set as high as 65 seconds. Time intervals determine the length of time that passes before the Timer code is executed again.

◆ Event-driven languages such as Visual Basic allow code to be executed only when a certain condition is met. The *Timer* event is the only event of the Timer control.

◆ The CPU usage of your programs can be decreased through use of a Timer control in certain circumstances.

◆ Visual Basic provides the *Time* and *Date* functions that you can use within your programs. You can customize the format of the *Time* and *Date* functions.

◆ When your programs require user input of time or dates, then you can use the DateTimePicker control to easily add a visual interface for your users.

# Lesson 12

# Using Forms and Modules

So far in this book, all the programs you have written have used only a single form to display your controls and objects in. In this lesson, you will learn how to create programs that use multiple forms so that you can have different display interfaces to present to the user. You will also learn how to create reusable files of related source code in the form of subroutines and functions, known as modules. By the time you finish this lesson, you will understand the following key concepts:

◆ By separating out the different sections of code, both forms and modules have a very important effect on programs for readability and code access.

◆ The difference between forms and modules is that forms also contain a graphical aspect that your program can display to the user, while modules do not.

◆ Your programs can contain multiple forms and modules.

◆ Use the Project menu to add or remove forms and modules.

◆ Only subroutines and functions within the form or module can access objects declared as *Private*. However, any subroutines or functions can access objects declared as *Public*.

◆ You can switch between forms using the *Show* and *Hide* methods.

◆ Forms can be disabled through use of the *Enabled* property.

◆ Correctly named modules and explicit calls in combination can enhance code readability.

◆ Forms and modules can be written to be reusable. Reusable forms and modules can save time and effort on the part of a Visual Basic programmer, allowing prewritten and tested functionality to be quickly added to programs.

The final result shows that in the module *ListBoxSort*, the subroutine *AscNumerical* exists, which takes a *List-Box* as an argument and sorts it numerically in ascending order. Other routines you might expect in this module are *DescNumerically*, *AscAlphabetically*, and *DescAlphabetically*. The point is that the module name clearly describes the purpose being served and, together with explicit calls, makes your code much more readable.

# Reusing Forms and Modules

Forms and modules can be thought of as reusable code. Although you might at first think that a form is specific to a program, there are forms that could be used in many programs. Examples of this type of form might be an improved message box, a user selection dialog, or a special progress bar. There are many other examples and reasons where related code can be placed into separate modules and forms.

One of the key reasons for writing reusable modules and forms is that the code is already written and thoroughly tested by you, saving you a lot of time reinventing the wheel or rewriting code as the case may be. In the case of reusing forms, you also benefit from the graphical components having already been designed by you.

To be able to use forms and modules in multiple programs, you must write the code carefully. If you are writing a module that references subroutines, functions, global variables, or constants that are declared elsewhere in the program, you should either rewrite the code so that the module is self-contained or, failing that, make a reference to the dependencies at the top of the module in the form of a comment.

One very good method of writing code, with the intention of the code being reusable, is to not directly access remote variables but rather to use parameters or arguments in your subroutines and functions. In this manner, you can pass different variables to the same routines, making those routines not only reusable within the program but also reusable between programs.

Pretend that you wrote a wonderful program called *MyMath* in Visual Basic. *MyMath* uses multiple modules to handle all the different mathematical requirements. You are now wanting to write a new program called *Fun-Math* in which you would like to use the same module for sorting that you wrote for *MyMath*. The sorting module is called *Sorting.bas*.

Remember that you are just pretending that you have these programs. To use the *Sorting.bas* module in your new *FunMath* program, you must go to the project folder for *MyMath* and copy the file *Sorting.bas* and paste it into the project folder for *FunMath*. Next, you must add the *Sorting.bas* module into your *FunMath* project by selecting the Project menu Add Module option from within your Visual Basic environment. Visual Basic will present the Add Module dialog. Within the Add Module dialog, you must select the Existing tab and then browse to your *FunMath* folder to add the module *Sorting.bas*, as shown in Figure 12.6.

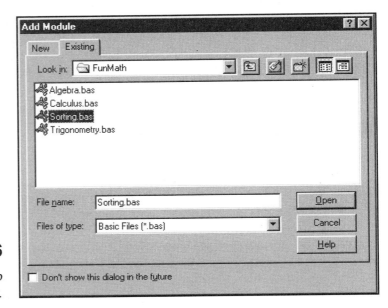

**Figure 12.6**

*Adding an existing module to a project.*

After you select the module you want to add, in this case *Sorting.bas,* click your mouse on the Open button and Visual Basic will add the module to your project.

Modules and forms can also be removed from projects if they are no longer required by your program. To remove a module or form, make it the currently active window by selecting it with your mouse and then select the Project menu, Remove option. The Remove option is accompanied by the name of the form or module that Visual Basic will remove. If the name of the form or module next to the Remove option is not the same as the name of the form or module you want to remove, then stop and go back. Make sure the currently active window is the form or module you want Visual Basic to remove, before trying again.

# What You Must Know

Forms and modules are similar in many ways except for the fact that forms include a graphical component. You can have multiple forms and modules in your Visual Basic projects. Multiple forms allow you to present the user with different interfaces and visual options. Multiple modules allow you to segregate related source code into separate sections making your program easier to read and manage. In Lesson 13, "Understanding Classes," you will learn how to create a more complex type of module that is used as *a* user-defined variable definition. Before you continue with Lesson 13, however, make sure you understand the following key concepts:

◆ By using forms and modules to separate out the different code sections, readability, and code access of programs is improved.

◆ Although very similar in many respects, forms contain a graphical component which modules lack.

◆ Your programs can contain multiple forms and modules.

◆ You can add or remove forms and modules through the Project menu.

◆ Objects declared as *Public* can be accessed by any subroutine or function in any form or module. However, objects declared as *Private* are limited to the form or module in which they are declared.

◆ You can switch between forms using the *Show* and *Hide* methods.

◆ Through use of the *Enabled* property, forms can be disabled.

◆ Explicit calls and well-named modules in combination can enhance code readability.

◆ Reusable forms and modules can save you time and effort. If written correctly, reusable forms and modules allow prewritten and tested functionality to be quickly added to your programs.

# Lesson 13

# Understanding Classes

In Lesson 12, "Using Forms and Modules," you learned how to segment related code into separate files. You also learned earlier about creating your own enumerated types that you can declare variables as. In this lesson, you will learn how to create a special, custom type known as a class, which is stored as a separate file, the same way that a module is. By the time you finish this lesson, you will understand the following key concepts:

◆ User-defined types are easily created but are subject to relying on the programmer's memory for any limitations or special conditions involving the individual items contained.

◆ User-defined types offer direct access to variables contained within them.

◆ Classes are a special type of module that offer much more functionality than the basic user-defined types.

◆ Classes offer indirect access to variables contained within them.

◆ Scope is important within class modules to determine what parts of the class can be seen or accessed from external code.

◆ Classes are designed to be reusable across projects and between programmers. When well written for reusability, classes are an efficient way of adding instant functionality to Visual Basic programs.

◆ When creating a class, you must use the *Property* keyword along with the *Get* or *Let* keyword to make the basic property access routines.

◆ Methods within classes are simply procedures that can access the class's property variables directly and save time and lines of code on the part of the programmer.

◆ The Class Builder Utility Wizard offers a nice method to quickly create all the code necessary for the basic class functionality.

◆ When using a class in your programs you must declare variables of type class using the *New* keyword to create a new instance of the class.

◆ Embellishing class routines is what really separates the class from user-defined types, allowing you to honor limitations or create complex dependencies during property access.

# Introducing Classes

If you have ever programmed in C++ then you will be quite familiar with classes and how they work. Visual Basic programmers have only been able to enjoy the benefits of classes since Visual Basic 6 was released, so classes are still new in Visual Basic, relatively speaking.

A class is a special kind of module. Classes are stored as separate files the same as standard modules, except that they have a *.cls* extension rather than a *.bas* extension. You can add multiple class modules to your projects and you can reuse class modules in different projects.

You will shortly learn about creating user-defined types (UDTs) in Visual Basic. A user-defined type is a set of variables that you can reference as a single variable. A class is fundamentally a user-defined object with a set of variables that you can also reference as a single variable. The difference then between a user-defined type and a class is that the user-defined type gives direct access to the set of variables contained within whereas a class offers indirect access to the set of variables within by way of methods and routines that screen the access first. There are many other differences between classes and user-defined types; however, you only need to know that classes are far superior to user-defined types in the flexibility and wealth of options available. Although many people at first do not see the difference between a class and a user-defined type, when you actually use the full set of features that a class module has to offer the difference becomes much clearer.

Classes can do much more than simply screen access to a set of variables. Classes can contain properties, methods, and events, making them more closely associated with a control than with user-defined types.

# Creating User-Defined Types

User-defined types can be made use of both inside classes and outside of them. You could create a user-defined type in a module or form. To create a user-defined type, declare the user-defined type with the keyword *Private* or *Public* followed by the keyword *Type* and the name of the new type you are creating. For example, you might want to make a user-defined type to describe a game character's attributes.

```
'Declare a game character type
```

```
Private Type ACharacter
    Name As String
    Strength As Integer
    HitPoints As Integer
    ArmorClass As Integer
    Magical As Boolean
End Type
```

After you create your user-defined type, you can declare variables of this type. Variables of user-defined types are declared in the same manner as any other form of variables are declared.

```
Dim Barbarian As ACharacter
```

You can assign values to any of a user-defined type's properties in the same manner as any of a standard type's properties. When you place a dot after the variable name for any variable of user-defined type, the Auto List Members droplist will be displayed by Visual Basic, as shown in Figure 13.1.

**Figure 13.1**

*The Auto List Members droplist for the user-defined type* ACharacter.

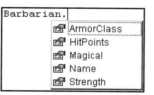

You can assign values to any of the user-defined type's properties or retrieve the current property values in the same manner as you would the properties of a control. The following example code shows some assigning and retrieving of property values for user-defined types.

```
Dim Barbarian As ACharacter
Dim chName As String
    Barbarian.Name = "Conan"
    Barbarian.Strength = 90
    Barbarian.ArmorClass = 10
    chName = Barbarian.Name
    If Barbarian.Magical = True Then MsgBox "A wizard!"
```

Although user-defined types can be useful, they rely on the programmer to remember what their limitations are, what special restrictions apply to them, and what is required for error checking. For example, if the user-defined type *ACharacter* had a maximum limit of 500 for the *Strength* property, there would be nothing to stop your program from assigning a value higher than 500 to the *Strength* property. In large projects or when working with a team, protecting the access to a user-defined type becomes an issue. This is where a class module provides a superior solution for Visual Basic programmers.

# Understanding Scope within Classes

Although previously covered in this book, using keywords such as *Private* or *Public* is very important when dealing with classes because they determine the scope of all variables, user-defined types, functions, and subroutines declared within the class. Any global variables declared in a class module that are declared using the *Private* keyword can only be seen by the subroutines and functions within the class module. Only subroutines and functions that you want the class to display should be declared using the *Public* keyword.

# Building Reusable Classes

Classes by design are for using between projects or even between programmers. A class should be a self-contained module with no external dependencies if possible. When you create a class, you should remember that you are writing reusable code and take great care to make the class as functional and well documented as you can. Writing a class well means that you will probably use that class again because you can rely on its functionality and stability. Always test class modules thoroughly by assigning them to a variable and trying all the properties and methods available. Assign very high, very low, or incorrect values to class properties to see how your class handles them.

To reuse a class module, you must follow almost the same steps as for reusing a standard module. The only difference is that you will be copying a *.cls* file rather than a *.bas* file and that you must select the Project menu Add Class Module instead of the Project menu, Add Module. As you have already learned in the previous lesson, select the Existing tab and then navigate to the folder and file you want.

# Creating Classes

To manually create a class module, select the Project menu, Add Class Module option. Visual Basic will display the Add Class Module dialog, as shown in Figure 13.2.

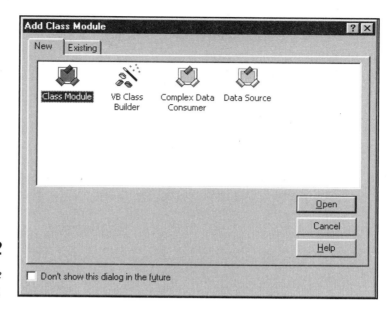

**Figure 13.2**

*The Add Class Module dialog.*

Within the Add Class Module dialog, select the Class Module icon and click your mouse on the Open button. Visual Basic will add a new class module to your project.

Now that you have a new class module in your project, you must decide exactly what you expect from the class before you can attempt any form of implementation. For purposes of comparison, you will implement a more advanced *ACharacter* type than the user-defined type you were working with earlier.

Change the *Name* property of your new class module to *ACharacter*. The name that you assign to a class is the same name that you reference the class with when declaring a variable of that type.

At the top of the *ACharacter* Code window, declare all the properties that you want in the *ACharacter* class type, however, add a prefix such as *m* to each of the variable names. You declare the variables with a prefix to the names you would normally use to assist in hiding these variables from direct access and to avoid confusion when referencing them. Make sure that you declare the variables using the *Private* keyword so that access to these variables is limited to code within the class module, as shown:

```
'Declare the variables as private
Private mName As String
Private mStrength As Integer
Private mHitPoints As Integer
Private mArmorClass As Integer
Private mMagical As Boolean
```

For each of these variables you must create a routine to handle the property for external access. Creating a routine for handling the properties for external access is very similar to creating a function. Take a look at a Property routine for retrieving the value of the *mName* property first, and then read about all the points of importance afterwards, before looking at the code for the rest of the properties.

```
Public Property Get Name() As String
    Name = mName
End Property
```

To allow external code to see the property you must declare the routine as *Public*. After the *Public* keyword, you must use the *Property* keyword to tell the Visual Basic compiler that this is a property. When you are writing routines for retrieving the value of a property, you must follow the *Property* keyword with the keyword *Get* and then the name of the property, as you want it to be seen when accessing it from external code.

Similar to a function, you must declare what type the routine will return by using the *As* keyword followed by the type. Also similar to a function is the method of assigning a return value by making something equal the name of the routine. The same way that you close a subroutine or function by following the keyword *End* with the keyword describing the routine type, close *Property* routines with the command *End Property*.

All of the *Private* variables you declare in a class require a *Property Get* procedure so that they can be accessed by code external to the class module, as shown:

```
Public Property Get Strength() As Integer
    Strength = mStrength
End Property

Public Property Get HitPoints() As Integer
    HitPoints = mHitPoints
End Property

Public Property Get ArmorClass() As Integer
    ArmorClass = mArmorClass
End Property

Public Property Get Magical() As Boolean
    Magical = mMagical
End Property
```

You are now able to access all of the *ACharacter* class's properties indirectly to retrieve the current value of those properties. To set the values of the *ACharacter* class's properties, you must now write *Public* routines that can be accessed from code external to the class module. These routines for setting properties within classes are very similar to the routines for getting values of properties within classes. However, where a *Property Get* routine resembles a function, a *Property Let* routine resembles a subroutine. Recall that a subroutine does not return a value. To receive the new value that is to be assigned to the property, use an argument of the same type as the property being changed. Use the keyword *Let* rather than *Get* to let the property equal a new value, as shown:

```
Public Property Let Name(ByVal vData As String)
    mName = vData
End Property

Public Property Let Strength(ByVal vData As Integer)
    mStrength = vData
End Property

Public Property Let HitPoints(ByVal vData As Integer)
    mHitPoints = vData
End Property

Public Property Let ArmorClass(ByVal vData As Integer)
    mArmorClass = vData
End Property

Public Property Let Magical(ByVal vData As Boolean)
    mMagical = vData
End Property
```

## Creating Methods within Classes

You can also provide methods within your classes to make it easy to deal with common tasks concerning the class properties. A method is simply a subroutine or function that is declared using the *Public* keyword within a class. Methods can save you having to do a lot of extra code every time that you want to use a common routine. For example, rather than having to explicitly set each property to be reset to minimal values wherever you must clear character values within your code, it is much easier to create a method that does all the explicit calls for you within the class itself.

```
Public Sub Clear()
    mvarcName = ""
    mvarStrength = 0
    mvarHitPoints = 0
    mvarArmorClass = 0
    mvarMagical = False
End Sub
```

You can create many different methods within your classes depending on what you require. The more complex a class is, the greater the need usually for methods to implement common tasks.

# Creating Classes Using the Class Builder Wizard

If you have the Professional or Enterprise versions of Visual Basic then you can also use the Class Builder Utility to create the class for you. Open a new project. From within the Visual Basic environment, select the Add-Ins menu and see if there is already an entry for Class Builder Utility. If the Add-Ins menu Class Builder Utility option exists then select it with your mouse, otherwise select the Add-Ins menu Add-In Manager option. Visual Basic will open the Add-In Manager dialog. Within the Add-In Manager dialog select VB 6 Class Builder Utility from the list and check the Loaded/Unloaded checkbox and the Load on Startup checkbox in the Load Behavior frame, as shown in Figure 13.3.

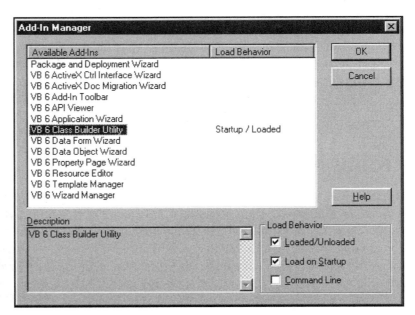

**Figure 13.3**

*Adding the Class Builder Utility add-in component.*

Click your mouse on the OK button to add the Class Builder Utility add-in component. Select the Add-Ins menu Class Builder Utility option. Visual Basic will display the Class Builder dialog, as shown in Figure 13.4.

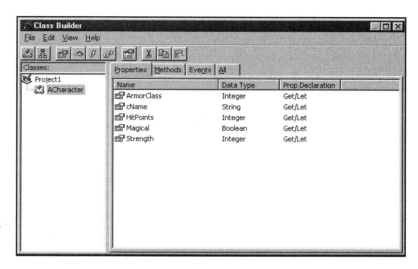

**Figure 13.4**

*The Class Builder dialog.*

From the Class Builder dialog, select the File menu New and then Class option. Visual Basic will present the Class Module Builder dialog. For the name of your class, type in *ACharacter* in the Name field and then click your mouse on the OK button. Select File menu, New and then Property option. Visual Basic will display the Property Builder dialog, as shown in Figure 13.5.

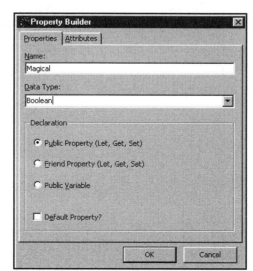

**Figure 13.5**

*The Property Builder dialog.*

**Understanding Class Builder Utility Limitations**

*When you use the Class Builder Utility Wizard for creating your class, be aware that there are limitations to what it can handle. Notably, there are certain words that the Class Builder Utility will not accept, such as Name. In these cases, you can either rename the property or manually edit the name later. Notice that although the Class Builder Utility does not handle a property being called Name, you were able to successfully create a property called Name earlier in this lesson when you created a class manually.*

*Although you have yet to come across them, beware of collections within collections, as the Class Builder Utility chokes on these and produces code that is not adequate at all for handling complex types such as these. There are times when it pays to be able to know how to manually create classes in Visual Basic and not rely too much on the Class Builder Utility Wizard.*

Enter in the name of a class property and specify the property type. Repeat these steps to add additional properties to your class. When you have completed adding all the properties for your class, select the File menu, Update Project option and then close the Class Builder dialog. Visual Basic will create your new class and add it to your project. Double-clicking your mouse on the new class will display the class module code window, as shown in Figure 13.6.

**Figure 13.6**

*The result of creating a class using the Class Builder Utility.*

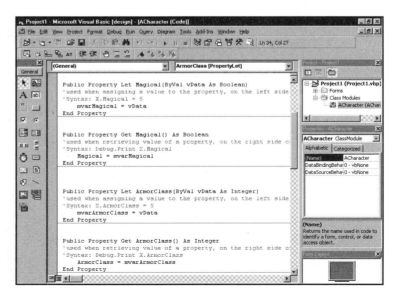

**Understanding Advanced Class Features**

*Although it is beyond the scope of this lesson or even this book for beginners in Visual Basic, there are many other advanced features of classes that can be utilized. Some of the key concepts that you can look into on your own are adding events within your classes, declaring objects as Friendly, and basing new classes on existing classes. These are not beginner concepts and are more suited for advanced Visual Basic programmers or programmers who are versed in C++.*

# Using Classes

Using classes from your code is very simple, which is why many programmers take such pains in making sure that their reusable classes are well written. Firstly, you must declare a variable as a new instance of your class, as follows:

```
Dim mc As New ACharacter
```

The keyword *New* tells the Visual Basic compiler to create a new instance of your class. Having multiple instances of the *ACharacter* class allows you to have multiple characters at the same time. To assign values to a class property, simply use the property routine the class provides you with, the same as when you are assigning to properties of controls or other objects.

```
mc.Name = "Conan"
```

Retrieving the value of class properties is also the same as you have learned earlier in the book for other objects.

```
Label1.Caption = mc.Strength
```

To use a class method, simply follow the variable name with a dot and then the name of the method, as follows:

```
mc.Clear
```

# Embellishing Class Routines

At the moment, you have had to put in a considerable amount of work to create a class as opposed to creating a simple user-defined type. By simply assigning whatever is passed as an argument to each property variable, the class does not actually achieve anything more than the user-defined type did. By embellishing the routines within a class module, you can screen all attempts to alter the actual variables that comprise the properties.

Think of the *Strength* property in the *ACharacter* type. If the maximum value that the *Strength* property should ever reach is 500, there would be no way to control any code that attempts to assign a higher value, such as 600, to the *Strength* property if a user-defined type were used. However, you can embellish a class to perform limit checking of upper bounds very easily. The *Strength* property in the *ACharacter* class would appear similar to the following code:

```
Public Property Let Strength(ByVal vData As Integer)
    If vData > 500 Then
        mStrength = 500
    Else
        mStrength = vData
    End If
End Property
```

Even when values higher than 500 are assigned to the *Strength* property, the class handles the argument passed and imposes the upper boundary limitation without causing errors. A user-defined type cannot match such graceful functionality as a class displays in this regard.

Embellishing routines within class modules is not limited to containing arguments within boundaries. You can create complex dependencies upon other properties that can change how a routine handles an argument. For example, say you want the characters that have an *ArmorClass* of 21 or higher to no longer be magical. You could modify the routine for *ArmorClass* as follows:

```
Public Property Let ArmorClass(ByVal vData As Integer)
    mArmorClass = vData
    If mArmorClass >= 21 Then mMagical = False
End Property
```

 ## Understanding the *Static* Keyword

*When you are using classes, you can often come across times when you must keep track of an item or value within a subroutine or function but require the variable to remain, even when the routine is exited by your code. You might be tempted to use a global variable, a variable declared outside of any routines at the top of your module.*

*An alternative and preferable option is to use the keyword* Static *to declare variables within your methods, subroutines, and functions instead of the keyword*

Dim. *These variables will remain for the duration of the program and are only accessible within the routine in which they are declared.*

*Without getting into detail, a static variable (declared with* Static) *or a local variable (declared with* Dim) *are much more preferable in your program than a global variable for the compiler and your Visual Basic program's performance.*

# What You Must Know

User-defined types allows you to access a cluster of related variables as a single variable. Class modules allow you to protect the direct access of variables contained within by presenting properties and methods. Embellishing class routines lets you screen all access to properties for highly customizable options. In Lesson 14, "Creating and Displaying Graphics," you will move beyond the fundamentals of Visual Basic and begin your journey of the user interface elements that are extremely important in transforming programs from being dull and awkward to use into being visually pleasing and polished. Before you continue with Lesson 14, however, make sure you understand the following key concepts:

◆ User-defined types are a convenient method of grouping variables together to be accessed by a single variable; however, they rely on the programmer to remember all the limitations and special conditions that apply to all the items within the user-defined type.

◆ User-defined types offer direct access to variables contained within them.

◆ User-defined types do not offer as much functionality or options as the special module type known as classes.

◆ Classes offer indirect access to variables contained within them.

◆ Scope determines which properties or methods can be seen by code that is external to the class module.

◆ Reusable classes save work and add functionality both across projects and between programmers and should be written with care.

◆ Use of the *Property* keyword in combination with either the *Let* or *Get* keywords forms the basic routines for property access when creating a class.

◆ Methods are subroutines or functions within the class module that are declared with the *Public* keyword. Methods can save time and lines of code by accessing internal variables directly for the programmer.

◆ The Class Builder Utility Wizard can quickly create all the code necessary for the basic class functionality but is only available to Professional or Enterprise Edition Visual Basic users.

◆ The keyword *New* is used when declaring variables of a class type. Using the *New* keyword creates a new instance of the class.

◆ Embellishing class routines allows classes to protect property variables from being assigned values beyond their limits and also make use of other elements to determine a course of action. Embellishing class routines gives classes functionality that cannot be matched by user-defined types alone.

# Part II

# Interface — Look and Feel

# Lesson 14

# Creating and Displaying Graphics

U p until this point in the book, you have covered fundamental programming skills with Visual Basic. However, to keep up with current user demands, many programs require a good use of graphics to add visual eye-candy. In this lesson, you will learn how to add graphics to your programs and also how to easily manipulate those graphics. By the time you finish this lesson, you will understand the following key concepts:

◆ Using a *With-End With* block, you are able to access members that have long references by simply placing a dot before the member you are accessing. *With-End With* blocks are very useful when dealing with graphics because you often require many properties and settings to be adjusted for a particular graphical object.

◆ Visual Basic uses an (x, y) coordinate system to determine the position of a given point within a form or other container such as a PictureBox or Frame. The x-axis relates to the horizontal position and the y-axis relates to the vertical position.

◆ Visual Basic uses colors in the format of a long integer representing an *RGB* (Red Green Blue) value. There are color constants available and two functions—*RGB* and *QBColor*—that you should use when dealing with colors.

◆ Primitive graphics in Visual Basic include points, lines, and circles, which can easily create arcs, ellipses, pattern filled boxes, and more, as well as using different colors.

◆ The properties *DrawMode*, *DrawStyle*, and *DrawWidth* are all related to each other and affect the output of the graphics methods and the Line and Shape controls.

◆ Visual Basic makes use of *CurrentX* and *CurrentY* properties in forms and other objects, which can make determining position much easier for programmers. *CurrentX* and *CurrentY* can be explicitly set.

◆ The Line control allows you to work with lines at design time, which is much easier than having to use the primitive *Line* method in your code and compile the program first to see what the result looks like.

◆ The Shape control lets you easily create rectangles, squares, ovals, circles, rounded rectangles, and rounded squares. You can customize properties for border, color, fill style, and more to attain different effects.

# Using the *With-End With* Block

As you start to work with graphics and objects that support graphics, you will find that accessing items can be a long procedure and a lot of tedious typing. Using a *With-End With* block allows you to specify to Visual Basic that you are working with a particular object and that anything starting with a dot should be dealt with as though it is directly preceded by this particular object.

Imagine that you have a TextBox control called *txtGraphicalCommentary* on a form called *frmFamousPaintings*. From source code, making changes to the text box is tedious and also a lot of unnecessary work for the compiler to have to follow all the references.

```
frmFamousPaintings.txtGraphicalCommentary.Text = "Mona Lisa"
frmFamousPaintings.txtGraphicalCommentary.Alignment = 2
frmFamousPaintings.txtGraphicalCommentary.BackColor = &HC0E0FF
frmFamousPaintings.txtGraphicalCommentary.ForeColor = &H800080
frmFamousPaintings.txtGraphicalCommentary.Visible = True
```

However, by using a *With-End With* block, the Visual Basic compiler only needs to reference your object once, making your code more efficient and you do not have to type as much, making your code smaller and more readable. By using a *With-End With* block you also only have to make changes to a reference in one place rather than several places.

```
With frmFamousPaintings.txtGraphicalCommentary
    .Text = "Mona Lisa"
    .Alignment = 2
    .BackColor = &HC0E0FF
    .ForeColor = &H800080
    .Visible = True
End With
```

*With-End With* blocks are useful in Visual Basic whenever you have long object names to reference, whether they are graphical or not.

# Understanding Coordinates in Visual Basic

Regardless of the type of screen measurement units that you use, each form in Visual Basic uses a set coordinate system that increases from left to right and from top to bottom. The coordinate system in Visual Basic is based on an x- and y-axis, where the x-axis determines the position of any particular point on the horizontal (left to right) and the y-axis determines the position of any particular point on the vertical (top to bottom).

Any objects or points that you need to reference within a form must use this coordinate system, which therefore makes understanding the coordinate system important for positioning and manipulating graphics.

There are many different possible units of measurement that Visual Basic handles, although you will probably find that the units you most commonly use will be twips, points, and pixels. The default measurement unit in Visual Basic is twips. The *ScaleMode* property of forms and objects determines the measurement unit that they should use. Table 14.1 shows the possible measurement units and also gives a brief description of each.

*Table 14.1 Measurement units in Visual Basic.*

| *ScaleMode* Constants | Description |
| --- | --- |
| *vbUser* | Custom |
| *vbTwips* | 1/1440th of an inch |
| *vbPoints* | 1/72nd of an inch |
| *vbPixels* | Smallest viewable unit of monitor resolution |
| *vbCharacters* | 120 twips horizontally and 240 twips vertically |
| *vbInches* | An inch |
| *vbMillimeters* | A millimeter |
| *vbCentimeter* | A centimeter |

Imagine a form whose dimensions are 5670 twips wide and 2535 twips high. If you were to add a rectangle in this form, the corner coordinates of the rectangle would appear something similar to Figure 14.1, with the x-coordinate given first and then the y-coordinate, with a comma separating the two.

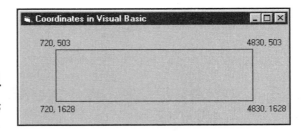

**Figure 14.1**

*A display of coordinates on a form.*

# Assigning Colors within Visual Basic

There are different formats for storing and working out specific colors using numerical formats. When working with graphics in Visual Basic it is important to have some understanding of how you can obtain colors so that you can attain the effect you desire.

Visual Basic provides color constants that you can use anywhere in your own program code, as shown in Table 14.2.

*Table 14.2 The Visual Basic color constants.*

| Color Constant | Actual Value |
| --- | --- |
| *vbBlack* | *&H0* |
| *vbBlue* | *&HFF0000* |
| *vbCyan* | *&HFFFF00* |
| *vbGreen* | *&HFF00* |
| *vbMagenta* | *&HFF00FF* |
| *vbRed* | *&HFF* |
| *vbYellow* | *&HFFFF* |
| *vbWhite* | *&HFFFFFF* |

## *RGB*

RGB stands for Red Green Blue and is a standard for specifying colors in a numerical format. Visual Basic provides an *RGB* function that you can use to make specifying RGB values very simple. The *RGB* function returns a long integer value so you should assign it to a variable of type Long. The more red you want in a particular color, the higher the value you assign to red. The same principle applies to green and blue. The syntax of the *RGB* function is:

**RGB**(red, green, blue)

To get a red color you could specify something similar to:

```
lngColor = RGB(255, 0, 0)
```

By opening up the Microsoft Paint program, you can see the RGB color values easily by selecting the Colors menu, Edit Colors option. Microsoft Paint will open the Edit Colors dialog. Click your mouse on the Define Custom Colors button, and Microsoft Paint will extend the Edit Colors dialog to show you a color range including RGB values, as shown in Figure 14.2.

**Figure 14.2**

*Getting RGB values from the Edit Colors dialog.*

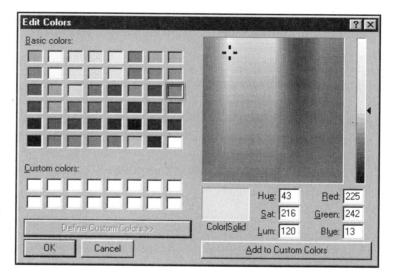

## QBColor

The *QBColor* function is really more for support of older versions of Basic and simply converts these colors into a long integer representing the RGB color value. The syntax of the *QBColor* function is as follows:

**QBColor**(color)

The argument color can be anything from 0 to 15, as shown in Table 14.3.

*Table 14.3 The QBColor values.*

| Color | Value | Color | Value |
|---|---|---|---|
| Black | 0 | Gray | 8 |
| Blue | 1 | Light Blue | 9 |
| Green | 2 | Light Green | 10 |
| Cyan | 3 | Light Cyan | 11 |
| Red | 4 | Light Red | 12 |
| Magenta | 5 | Light Magenta | 13 |
| Yellow | 6 | Light Yellow | 14 |
| White | 7 | Bright White | 15 |

# Creating Primitive Graphics

Although graphics may bring to mind beautifully rendered landscapes, monsters in labyrinth-like dungeons, or some other incredible image, graphics in their primitive form are the building blocks for the more commonly seen graphics of today.

## *Point* and *PSet*

Every graphic that you see on a computer can be broken down to a series of joined pixels. Pixels are the individual dots on the screen. A point, in Visual Basic, is a unit of measurement consisting of $1/72^{nd}$ of an inch. Often the terms pixel and point are interchanged by Visual Basic programmers and used loosely; however, there is a difference.

To retrieve the color value of a particular point, you must use the *Point* function and pass the arguments for the x and y coordinates of the point you want, as shown in the following example:

myColor = Point(10, 20)

To change the color value of a particular point, you can use the *PSet* method. The *PSet* method has the following syntax:

object.**PSet** [Step] (x, y), [color]

The *PSet* method requires the x- and y-coordinates, however, both of the items in square brackets (Step and color) are optional. When you do not supply *PSet* with a color argument, *PSet* uses the current *ForeColor* property's value. To change the point at coordinates (10, 20) to red, you would type a command similar to the following:

```
Form1.PSet (10, 20), vbRed
```

 **Primitive Graphics and Refresh**

*When you are using any of the primitive graphics techniques, such as PSet, Line, Circle, or Print, a refresh of the container will wipe them all clear. For this reason, you should not use any of these techniques within the Form_Load() procedure. By creating a subroutine that handles the display using primitive graphics calls and methods, you can easily recall this subroutine after every refresh. To call your primitive graphics subroutine automatically, place a call to it in the Form_Paint() event.*

*For example, if your subroutine was called PrimitiveGFX(), then you would add the following code to your program:*

```
Private Sub Form_Paint()
     PrimitiveGFX
End Sub
```

*The other method you can take to have your primitive graphics automatically redrawn is to set the AutoRefresh property of your form to True. Although setting the AutoRefresh property to True is easier, you can run into complications or compatibility problems later on; for example, when using a resizing control that insists that the AutoRefresh property is set to False. Being aware of both methods should see you through almost any situation.*

## Line

To draw a line between two points, you could either use loops and lots of *PSet* calls or you could make life easier on yourself and use the *Line* method. The *Line* method has the following syntax:

object.**Line** [Step] (x1, y1) − [Step] (x2, y2), [color], [B][F]

At first, the *Line* method looks rather daunting, but it is actually very straightforward after you use it a few times. The only compulsory arguments are the actual coordinates, so a simple *Line* method might look similar to the following:

```
Form1.Line (100, 600) — (800, 1200)
```

The first set of coordinates specifies the point from which to start the line and the second set of coordinates specifies the point to which the line is to be drawn. As with the *PSet* method, you can specify a color based on any of the color constants in Table 14.2. or pass any long integer color value explicitly based on RGB values.

The *Line* method will also enable you to easily draw boxes simply by passing a B in the third argument. When you specify to the *Line* method that you want a box drawn, the *Line* method will take the two coordinates given and treat them as opposite corners of the box. So the first set of coordinates will represent the top left corner of the box, and the second set of coordinates will represent the bottom right corner of the box.

You can fill the boxes that are drawn with the *Line* method by specifying BF in the third argument. You cannot specify F on its own without the B because the *Line* method will only fill boxes. By modifying the form's properties, such as *DrawMode*, *DrawStyle*, *DrawWidth*, and *FillStyle*, you can customize the look of the box that you create with the *Line* method. You will cover all of these properties in more detail later in this lesson.

 **Using the *Step* Keyword**

*The primitive graphics techniques such as PSet, Line, and Circle can all optionally take the keyword Step as an argument. The Step keyword indicates that rather than giving exact coordinates of where you want a point, you are giving relative distances from the previous coordinates.*

*Take the Line method, for example, and assign it coordinates (50, 200) to (350, 200), as shown:*

```
Form1.Line (50, 200) — (350, 200)
```

*To now redraw an identical line at another location you would have to calculate the exact coordinates of where the line is drawn to again, as shown:*

```
Form1.Line (165, 310) — (465, 310)
```

*However, by using the Step keyword you can easily accomplish the same results without having to recalculate final coordinates.*

```
Form1.Line (50, 200) — Step(150, 0)
```

```
Form1.Line (165, 310) - Step(150, 0)
```

*The Step keyword makes it easier for you to work with relative distance rather than exact coordinates.*

## Circle

The *Circle* method allows you to easily create circles, arcs, and ellipses. The syntax for the *Circle* method is as follows:

object.**Circle** [Step](x, y), radius, [color], [start], [end], [aspect]

The compulsory arguments for the *Circle* method are the coordinates and the radius. All the other arguments are optional. A simple *Circle* method looks similar to the following:

```
Form1.Circle (1500, 1500), 250
```

The color argument for the *Circle* method is exactly the same as for the *PSet* and *Line* methods. When drawing arcs, you can specify the start and end points in radians using the start and end arguments. Both start and end arguments have a range of $-2\pi$ to $2\pi$ (roughly $-6.28$ to $6.28$).

To form an ellipse, change the aspect argument to a value other than 1.0, which is the default and forms a circle. Values smaller than 1.0 form an ellipse that is longer in the x-axis, while values greater than 1.0 form an ellipse that is longer in the y-axis.

A more complex example of the *Circle* method is shown in Figure 14.3, and the source code can be found at www.prima-tech.com/books/book/5250/945/.

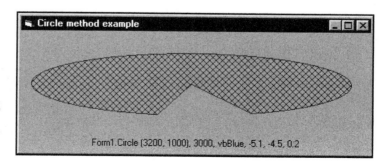

**Figure 14.3**

*A complex example of the Circle method.*

## Printing Text Directly

*Although using a Label control is simple and often of great convenience to Visual Basic programmers, there is another method of displaying text on a form. By using the command* Print *and following it with the string you want to display on the form, Visual Basic will output the text directly onto the form in the same manner as primitive graphics. The following line of code shows how to output the current x- and y-coordinates of a form using the* Print *command:*

```
Print "Pos: " & Form1.CurrentX & ", " & Form1.CurrentY
```

*The* Print *command does not have all the features and options of a Label control; however, it is very useful when you are debugging your program or just want to output some text quickly. You cannot move text that has been output by the* Print *command. The output from the* Print *command goes to the* CurrentX *and* CurrentY *positions of the form.*

## *Cls*

To clear the screen of any primitive graphics drawn or any text displayed by the *Print* command, simply use the *Cls* method. Using *Cls* on its own causes Visual Basic to assume that you are referring to the current form. However, you could use *Cls* to clear a PictureBox as well as a form. You can improve your code readability and remove ambiguity by explicitly typing the object prior to the *Cls* method, as shown:

```
Form1.Cls
Picture1.Cls
```

## Understanding the Limitations of Primitive Graphics

*Although the primitive graphics command set provided by Visual Basic contains useful functions that you might use frequently in your programs, be aware that they cannot be used within a With-End With block.*

## DrawMode, DrawStyle, and DrawWidth

In the properties for a form and also other objects, you will find *DrawMode*, *DrawStyle*, and *DrawWidth*, which each affect the output of various drawing techniques including the Line and Shape controls. The *DrawWidth* property can be set to anything in the range of 1 to 32,767. The *DrawWidth* property sets the thickness of the point being drawn. The *DrawStyle* property allows you to select whether you want to draw solid lines, dashes, dots, or other combinations, as shown in Table 14.4.

*Table 14.4* DrawStyle *options.*

| Constant | Style |
|---|---|
| *vbSolid* (default) | Solid |
| *vbDash* | Dash |
| *vbDot* | Dot |
| *vbDashDot* | Dash-Dot |
| *vbDashDotDot* | Dash-Dot-Dot |
| *vbInvisible* | Invisible or Transparent |
| *vbInsideSolid* | Inside Solid |

The *DrawStyle* options involving dashes and dots are drawn as a solid if *DrawWidth* is set to a value greater than 1.

*DrawMode* allows you to change the mode of drawing. The default mode is *vbCopyPen*, which uses the color specified in the *ForeColor* property. However, you can choose from 16 different possible modes that you can see in the drop-down combo box next to the *DrawMode* property. Setting *DrawMode* to *vbInvert* is commonly made use of because it guarantees that whatever you are drawing will be seen regardless of what the background color is. So if you were drawing a white circle onto a white background, the result would be a black circle. Experiment with the different *DrawMode* values to see what effect they have. The most important point is that you become aware that the *DrawMode* property exists.

# Locating Yourself Using *CurrentX* and *CurrentY*

When you use primitive graphics techniques Visual Basic makes use of what are known as the *CurrentX* and *CurrentY* properties. These two properties maintain a set of coordinates that many methods can make use of. Pretend that you want to draw a series of ten lines with each subsequent line starting from the point where the previous line will finish. You could accomplish this task easily by setting the start coordinates for your *Line* method calls to use *CurrentX* and *CurrentY*, as shown:

```
Private Sub Form_Click()
```

```
Dim i As Integer
    'set the starting point
    Form1.CurrentX = 250
    Form1.CurrentY = 500

    'draw ten lines using a different color for clarity
    For i = 1 To 10
        Form1.Line Step(0, 0)-Step(400, 0), QBColor(i)
    Next
End Sub
```

The result of this code is shown in Figure 14.4, and the code itself is available at www.prima-tech.com/books/book/5250/945/ for you to experiment with yourself.

**Figure 14.4**

*Drawing lines based on* CurrentX *and* CurrentY.

Notice that the following two lines are identical, except that by using the *Step* keyword you can save yourself some typing because the Step keyword makes use of the *CurrentX* and *CurrentY* values behind the scenes.

```
Form1.Line Step(0, 0)-Step(400, 0), QBColor(i)
Form1.Line (Form1.CurrentX, Form1.CurrentY)-Step(400, 0), QBColor(i)
```

When you use the primitive graphics methods, Visual Basic will set the value of the *CurrentX* and *CurrentY* according to the method, as shown in Table 14.5.

**Table 14.5 *Values that* CurrentX *and* CurrentY *are set to.***

| Method | Values that *CurrentX* and *CurrentY* Are Set To |
| --- | --- |
| Circle | The center point of the circle |
| Line | The last point of the line |
| PSet | The point changed by *PSet* |
| Print | The start of the next line |
| Cls | 0, 0 |

# Understanding Line Control

To work with graphical lines at design time rather than only at runtime, Visual Basic provides you with the Line control. The Line control is similar to the *Line* command in Visual Basic's primitive graphics command set. The Line control allows you to add lines to your form, PictureBox, or Frame without having to write any code. Although the Line control is easier to use than the *Line* method, it is not as powerful and lacks some of the features and flexibility of the primitive *Line* method. The Line control icon can be found with the other controls in the Visual Basic environment's control panel and appears as shown in Figure 14.5.

**Figure 14.5**

*The Line control icon.*

Unlike many other controls, you cannot use the *Move* method to move a Line control at runtime. To move a Line control you must change its coordinates by assigning different values to x1, x2, y1, or y2. The Line control, unlike the *Line* method, is unaffected by a refresh and the *AutoRefresh* property can be set to *False* without adverse effects.

# Understanding Shape Control

Visual Basic provides you with easy shape functionality through the Shape control. By adding a Shape control to your project, you can specify different shapes, fill colors, and fill patterns. The Shape control icon appears on your Visual Basic control panel, as shown in Figure 14.6.

**Figure 14.6**

*The Shape control icon.*

After adding a Shape control to your project, you can set the *Shape* property of the Shape control to one of six different shapes, as shown in Table 14.6.

*Table 14.6 The various shape styles available in the Shape control.*

| Shape | Constant |
| --- | --- |
| Rectangle | *vbShapeRectangle* |
| Square | *vbShapeSquare* |
| Oval | *vbShapeOval* |
| Circle | *vbShapeCircle* |
| Rounded Rectangle | *vbShapeRoundedRectangle* |
| Rounded Square | *vbShapeRoundedSquare* |

You can set the pattern to fill the Shape by specifying one of the values in Table 14.7 for the *FillStyle* property of the Shape control.

*Table 14.7 The various* FillStyle *options and their constants.*

| FillStyle | Constant |
| --- | --- |
| Solid | *vbFSSolid* |
| Transparent (Default) | *vbFSTransparent* |
| Horizontal Line | *vbFSHorizontalLine* |
| Vertical Line | *vbFSVerticalLine* |
| Upward Diagonal | *vbFSUpwardDiagonal* |
| Downward Diagonal | *vbFSDownwardDiagonal* |
| Cross | *vbFSCross* |
| Diagonal Cross | *vbFSDiagonalCross* |

Figure 14.7 shows all of the *Shape* options and uses a mixture of *FillStyle* options.

**Figure 14.7**

*An example of the various shapes and fill styles.*

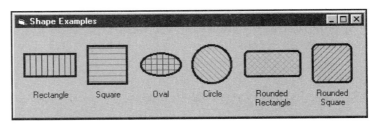

You can set the properties *BorderWidth*, *BorderStyle*, and *BorderColor* to further customize your shapes.

# Looking at the Palette Power Example

Although the example program Palette Power uses some as yet uncovered skills and techniques, it is a good example of how you can use the skills learned in this lesson and apply them in a practical situation. Palette Power is simply for example purposes and as you progress with Visual Basic you will learn more advanced methods for graphic manipulation. Palette Power allows you to load in a bitmap graphic file or an entire folder of bitmap files and then using skills such as *RGB*, *Point*, *PSet*, and *Line*, which you have just been learning about, duplicates the first graphic using the closest match it can find from the given palette. Palette matching is really an advanced technique that you would only use when trying to optimize speed or maintain graphic appearance under limited screen resolutions. You can run Palette Power from the companion Web site for this book at www.prima-tech.com/books/book/5250/945/ and browse through the source code, but just remember to ignore any new commands for the moment, as you will learn about those shortly.

# What You Must Know

Visual Basic uses a coordinate system for determining the position or location of any particular point. The primitive graphics methods *Point*, *PSet*, *Line*, and *Circle* can be quite powerful and offer many possibilities to programmers. Higher end controls such as the Line control and the Shape control make drawing graphics even easier for Visual Basic programmers. In Lesson 15, "Using Icons, Picture Boxes, and Image Controls," you will look more deeply into Visual Basic graphic techniques and learn some different methods for displaying graphics in your own programs. Before you continue with Lesson 15, however, make sure you understand the following key concepts:

◆ To access items that have long references by simply placing a dot before the item you are accessing, use a *With-End With* block. Due to the fact that programmers must often set multiple settings and properties for any given graphical object, *With-End With* blocks are very useful when dealing with graphics.

◆ The coordinate system used by Visual Basic works on an x-axis for the horizontal position and y-axis for the vertical position.

◆ Colors in Visual Basic are in the form of a long integer that represents an RGB value. The functions *RGB* and *QBColor* both return the format Visual Basic requires, as does the set of color constants available.

◆ Primitive graphics techniques allow you to draw points, lines, circles, boxes, triangles, arcs, ellipses, and other shapes through code.

◆ *DrawMode*, *DrawStyle*, and *DrawWidth* are all properties that affect the output of drawing techniques including the Line and Shape controls.

◆ The properties *CurrentX* and *CurrentY* allow you to easily set or get the next point to draw, which can make programming graphics much easier.

◆ Although the *Line* method is more powerful, the Line control is visible at design time and allows you to position lines much more easily without needing to compile your Visual Basic program to verify results. Also, the Line control will not disappear after a refresh.

◆ The Shape control is extremely useful for creating rectangles, squares, ovals, circles, rounded rectangles, and rounded squares, which can all be customized by you in terms of fill styles, colors, and borders.

# Lesson 15

---

# Using Icons, Picture Boxes, and Image Controls

In Lesson 14, "Creating and Displaying Graphics," you learned how to use Visual Basic's primitive graphics methods, as well as the Line and Shape controls to add a graphical element to your programs. In this lesson, you will learn how to work with icons and how to display and manipulate graphics using the PictureBox control and the Image control. By the time you finish this lesson, you will understand the following key concepts:

◆ You can assign a different icon to individual forms within a project and select from these forms to allocate an icon for the program itself to use.

◆ A PictureBox control is very versatile and feature-filled, allowing you to easily add pictures from a variety of graphic formats into your programs. The PictureBox control's *Picture* property contains the picture, which is clipped by Visual Basic unless the *AutoSize* property is set to *True*.

◆ An Image control is a cut-down version of the PictureBox control, allowing faster display, graphic stretching, and less resource usage.

◆ Hot spots can be easily created in your programs by adding empty Image controls that do not contain a picture on top of a larger PictureBox control or Image control that does. The Image control's *Click* event should be used for executing specific hot spot code.

◆ The *PaintPicture* method is a powerful drawing method in Visual Basic allowing many options such as positioning, clipping, flipping, wallpapering or tiling, compressing, enlarging, and advanced bitwise operations.

◆ Visual Basic uses the keyword *Me* to refer to the current form.

◆ Frame controls provide clear divisions and sections visually for the user and also allow programmers to move a set of objects without breaking their relevant position to each other.

◆ OptionButton controls provide users with a clear selection to choose from. OptionButton controls are most often placed within Frame controls for grouping purposes and can be textual or graphical.

◆ You can create keyboard shortcuts by placing an ampersand sign before a character. Visual Basic will underline that character, which can be used, together with the Alt key, to activate the shortcut.

◆ The Format menu can be used to make alignment of multiple controls in various ways much simpler for Visual Basic programmers. Control alignment is an important factor in user-interface design.

◆ By using a Timer control, you can flip through a sequence of images to form an animation and by altering the Timer control's *Interval* property, you can adjust the animation speed.

# Changing the Program Icon

Icons are the small graphical pictures that you associate with every file and folder. When you create a Visual Basic program it has a very plain icon. Within the Visual Basic environment, select the *Icon* property of a form in the Properties section. Click your mouse on the button with three dots on it. Visual Basic will display the Load Icon dialog box, as shown in Figure 15.1.

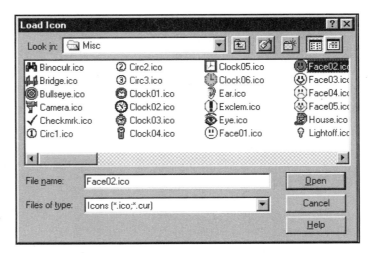

**Figure 15.1**

*The Load Icon dialog box.*

Navigate to an icon file on your hard drive, select the icon file, and click your mouse on the Open button. Visual Basic loads the icon file into your project and applies this icon to the form. When your project contains only one form, your application will use the same icon. However, if your project contains multiple forms that each associates with a different icon you must select which form's icon to use for the application.

Select the Project menu Properties option and, from the Project properties dialog box that Visual Basic displays as a result of your action, click your mouse on the Make tab. Within the Application frame is a selection for the title and icon of the application. Use the drop-down combo box next to the icon selection to choose from your list of forms, as shown in Figure 15.2.

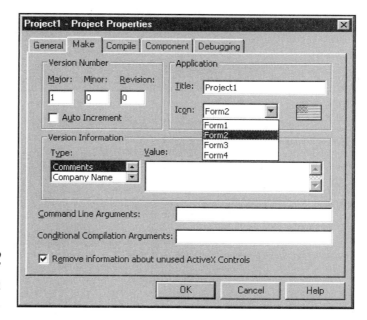

**Figure 15.2**

*Selecting the application icon from multiple forms.*

# Using the PictureBox Control

Visual Basic makes it easy to add graphics to your programs through use of the PictureBox control, whose icon is shown in Figure 15.3.

**Figure 15.3**

*The PictureBox control's icon.*

A PictureBox control can handle bitmaps, JPEGs, GIFs, icons, and metafiles (including enhanced metafiles). If the size of the graphic that you load into a PictureBox control is greater than what the PictureBox control can display, then Visual Basic will clip the graphic to fit the displayable area. Although clipping graphics can be useful, you can have a PictureBox control resize automatically to accommodate graphics by setting the *AutoSize* property to *True*.

To load a picture into a PictureBox control at design time, in the Properties section within the Visual Basic environment select the *Picture* property and then click your mouse on the button with three dots. Visual Basic will display the Load Picture dialog box, from which you can navigate through your files, as shown in Figure 15.4.

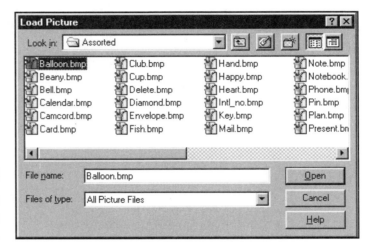

**Figure 15.4**

*Selecting a picture to load using the Load Picture dialog box.*

A PictureBox control is similar to a form in the sense that it is a type of container able to support many other controls such as a Label control. A PictureBox can therefore support combinations of graphics, text, and other miscellaneous controls at the same time, which leaves room for many possibilities.

# Using the Image Control

You can add an Image control to your form for easy handling of graphics. The icon for an Image control is shown in Figure 15.5.

**Figure 15.5**

*The Image control's icon.*

An Image control can handle the same graphic formats as a PictureBox control. The difference between the Image control and the PictureBox control is that the Image control uses less system resources, is faster to display graphics, and has the ability to stretch a graphic. The Image control is like a cut-down version of the PictureBox control and does not have as many options or features. Use an Image control in your programs where possible unless you must use features in the PictureBox control that are not in the Image control.

Image controls are very good for quickly creating hot spots within larger graphics. To achieve this effect, load your large picture into an Image control and then place smaller Image controls on top of the first. You can edit the smaller Image controls' *ToolTips* property to give some indication to users that the mouse is hovering over a hot spot. Each of the smaller Image controls has a *Click* event, which you can use for executing code specific to that hot spot.

# Using the *PaintPicture* Method

The *PaintPicture* method allows you to draw a graphic directly and specify the exact position at which to draw it. Your programs can save a lot of resources when doing graphical displays that make use of the same picture more than once, such as wallpapering multiple instances of a graphic across a form. You can use the *PaintPicture* method on PictureBoxes, Forms, Printers, and other objects that support it. The *PaintPicture* method has the following syntax:

object.**PaintPicture** picture, x1, y1, [width1], [height1], [x2], [y2], [width2], [height2], [opcode]

If you do not specify an object, then Visual Basic will apply the *PaintPicture* method to the form that currently has the focus. For the *picture* argument, simply assign the *Picture* property of a form or PictureBox control. The arguments *x1* and *y1* specify the top-left position of the graphic to be drawn. So, a simple *PaintPicture* method might look something like the following:

```
Form1.PaintPicture Picture1.Picture, 10, 10
```

To overcome the limitation of a PictureBox control's inability to resize a graphic, you can use the *PaintPicture* method. By specifying the arguments for width and height, the *PaintPicture* method will automatically resize the graphic by either compressing or enlarging it. Another handy trick you can do with the height and width arguments is flip a picture horizontally, vertically, or both by making the height or width arguments negative. A simple way to make a variable negative is to multiply it by −1.

The arguments *x2* and *y2* along with *width2* and *height2* specify a section of the source graphic to use. These arguments allow you to have a single large graphic and merely display parts of the whole at once, without having to load lots of little graphics in. This functionality is useful in many situations, but when you are dealing with any maps visually, either in games or for geographical purposes, the ability to view precise areas of the whole is invaluable.

To understand this concept more clearly, imagine if you had a picture that was 30 pixels wide and 50 pixels high. You can only ever display 10 pixels by 10 pixels at a time. By saving individual, even segments you only have 15 possible displays. By using the *PaintPicture* method properly you would have 1500 possible displays, and you have the additional bonus of not having had to manually split up the original picture into segments. Figure 15.6 shows the difference between saving sections manually as opposed to displaying sections of the whole.

**Figure 15.6**

*Saving individual graphics as opposed to* PaintPictures *section clipping.*

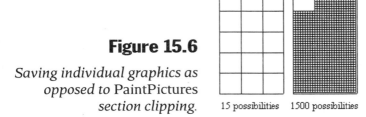

The final argument for *PaintPicture* is opcode, which is also optional. Opcodes deal with passing bitwise operations on bitmaps and are really a very advanced technique. You should only ever use the opcode argument with bitmaps, as it will cause errors with other file types. A detailed description of each possible constant that the opcode argument can take is beyond the scope of this lesson; however, Table 15.1 gives a brief description and shows you the constants you can use.

*Table 15.1 The possible constants for the* **PaintPicture** *method's opcode argument.*

| Constant | Definition |
|---|---|
| vbDstInvert | Inverts the destination bitmap. |
| vbMergeCopy | Combines the pattern and the source bitmap. |
| vbMergePaint | Combines the inverted source bitmap with the destination bitmap by using *Or*. |
| vbNotSrcCopy | Copies the inverted source bitmap to the destination. |
| vbNotSrcErase | Inverts the result of combining the destination and source bitmaps by using *Or*. |
| vbPatCopy | Copies the pattern to the destination bitmap. |
| vbPatInvert | Combines the destination bitmap with the pattern by using *Xor*. |
| vbPatPaint | Combines the inverted source bitmap with the pattern by using *Or*. Combines the result of this operation with the destination bitmap by using *Or*. |
| vbSrcAnd | Combines pixels of the destination and source bitmaps by using *And*. |
| vbSrcCopy | Copies the source bitmap to the destination bitmap. |
| vbSrcErase | Inverts the destination bitmap and combines the result with the source bitmap by using *And*. |

*Table 15.1 (continued)*

| Constant | Definition |
| --- | --- |
| *vbSrcInvert* | Combines pixels of the destination and source bitmaps by using *Xor*. |
| *vbSrcPaint* | Combines pixels of the destination and source bitmaps by using *Or*. |

On the companion Web site for this book is the *Opcode* example program with source code. (The Web site can be found at www.prima-tech.com/books/book/5250/945/.) The *Opcode* example program lets you experiment with the different opcodes at a rudimentary level, as shown in Figure 15.7.

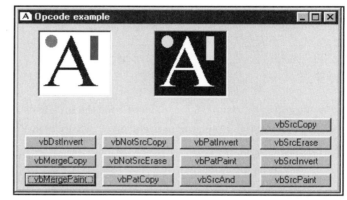

**Figure 15.7**

*The* Opcode *example program.*

 **Using the PictureClip Control**

> When you are animating graphics, rather than having to individually save each frame of the animation in a separate file, Visual Basic provides a control known as PictureClip, which you can use to load in a single bitmap file that holds all the frames in the animation. The PictureClip control can make it easier to create animations although if you choose to use this control you must add a reference to the file picclp32.ocx and also remember to include this file in your distribution packages.

# Creating the Ministry of *Silly Walks* Animation Example

In this example, you are going to create your own simple animation. In the process of creating this animation you will also learn about two new controls that you can use in your Visual Basic programs. One control is known as the Frame control and the other is known as the OptionButton control. Both of these controls, while simple to use, are highly useful and commonly seen in programs.

Please note that all source code for this book can be found at www.prima-tech.com/books/book/5250/945/.

Before you start this project you will need to have the bitmaps for the animation ready. You can copy the bitmaps that are in the *SillyWalks* folder on the companion Web site into your own project folder, or you can create your own bitmap animation graphics. The bitmaps should all be the same size or else your animation will appear jerky and strange. The graphics do not really matter here, as you should be concentrating on the Visual Basic techniques primarily.

1. Open a new project in Visual Basic. Select Project menu Properties, and in the Project Properties dialog box change the name of the project to **SillyWalk** before clicking your mouse on the OK button.

2. Change the form's *Caption* property to **Ministry of Silly Walks**.

3. Change the form's *Icon* property to something other than the default.

In the SillyWalks folder on the companion Web site, you will find the file *Misc02.ico* that you can use.

When you create a program you may need to use more space on the form for working than what you actually want to display to the user. You can specify the height and width of the form in the *Form_Load()* event so that at runtime you always have a constant and correctly sized form. Using Figure 15.8 as a guide to what the final program will look like, resize your form accordingly and then write down the values of the form's *Height* and *Width* properties.

**Figure 15.8**

*The Ministry of Silly Walks animation example in action.*

When you think of *Me* in terms of Microsoft Windows, you think of Microsoft's Millennium Edition operating system. However, Visual Basic has a different meaning of the term *Me* that you should not confuse with the operating system. Although you can specify the form's name explicitly, Visual Basic has the keyword *Me* that you can use to refer to the current form. Using the keyword *Me* can be shorter than your form name and is useful when you write routines that different forms might need to call. The keyword *Me* is good to be aware of so that when you are working with code written by other Visual Basic programmers you will be able to recognize this keyword. Be aware that using the *Me* keyword can detract from clarity of your code, so you should use the explicit form name whenever ambiguity would otherwise occur. Add the following lines to the *Form_Load()* event:

```
Me.Height = 4350
Me.Width = 4350
```

## Using a Frame Control

You use frames as a clear division of sections on a form so that a user may easily identify objects or options that relate closely to each other. When you position objects within a Frame control, you can also easily move that frame to a different position on the form without losing any positioning of the items contained within the frame. Add a Frame control to your form. The Frame control's icon is shown in Figure 15.9.

**Figure 15.9**

*The Frame control's icon.*

Change the Frame control's *Caption* property to **Speed**.

## Using an OptionButton Control

An option implies choice, and so OptionButton controls are usually together with other OptionButton controls. You should never use OptionButton controls in a solitary manner, not because of technical reasons, but because it is counter-intuitive for the user and goes against convention. By grouping OptionButtons within Frame controls, Visual Basic will automatically treat the OptionButton controls as a group and deselect all the other options whenever the user makes a selection. To find out if an OptionButton is currently selected by the user, you use the OptionButton's *Value* property. If the *Value* property is *True*, then the OptionButton is selected. You can also set the *Value* property from code to select an OptionButton.

Although you are using the OptionButton controls in a standard manner for the Ministry of Silly Walks program, you can also use OptionButtons graphically by assigning pictures to the *Picture* property and setting the *Style* property to **Graphical**. The OptionButton control's icon appears as shown in Figure 15.10.

### Figure 15.10

*The OptionButton control's icon.*

Add three OptionButton controls within the Frame control. Change the *Caption* property of the OptionButton controls to *&Slow*, *&Medium*, and *&Fast*, respectively.

## Creating Keyboard Shortcuts

Placing an ampersand sign before a character makes that character into a shortcut for users at runtime. Visual Basic will underline the character as an indication to users, who must use the character together with the Alt key to activate the shortcut. Users often appreciate the shortcut feature when they do not want to have to switch from keyboard to mouse to use a program. Also, if a user's mouse becomes faulty, having keyboard shortcuts in your program allows them a way to exit the program gracefully and save their work if necessary.

 **Using the Ampersand Sign (&)**

*As you have already learned, placing an ampersand sign before a character causes the character to be underlined by Visual Basic so that users can use the Alt key and that underlined character as a shortcut. While this functionality is very useful and easy to implement in Visual Basic, there are times when you actually want to display the ampersand sign itself! To display the ampersand sign, simply*

*type in a second ampersand sign directly after the first without leaving any spaces in between. Visual Basic will then realize that you want to actually display the ampersand sign and are not trying to underline a character. An example of using the ampersand sign to create a shortcut and also displaying an ampersand sign might look something as follows:*

```
Label1.Caption = "&Goods && Services"
```

*which will display as:*

```
Goods & Services
```

## Control Alignment

Hold the Shift key down and select all of the OptionButton controls. Select the Format menu Align submenu Lefts option. The OptionButtons all line up evenly. Without deselecting the OptionButton controls, select the Format menu Vertical Spacing submenu Make Equal option. The OptionButtons evenly space themselves. You can use the various alignment options under the Format menu for any control, not just the OptionButton control. Aligning your controls is aesthetically pleasing to the user and plays an important part in user-interface design.

Add a CommandButton to your form and change its *Caption* property to **&Animate**. Stretch your form so that it is a bit bigger and add five Image controls and a Timer control, as shown in Figure 15.11.

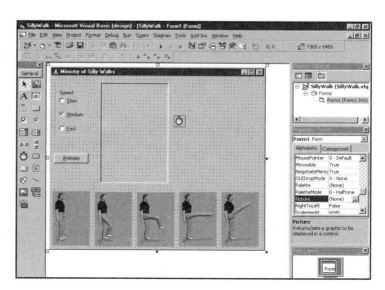

**Figure 15.11**

*Stretching the form to add more controls.*

In each of the first five Image controls, load in the five animation bitmaps that you copied at the outset of this project. Change the *Visible* property of these five Image controls to *False*. Set the *Stretch* property of these five Image controls to *True*, and then resize them so that you can easily see them all on your form. Add a sixth Image control and name it **imgMain**, placing it above the CommandButton. The *imgMain* Image control will be the main animation display for the program. We do not want *imgMain* to load in a bitmap, as this will waste resources unnecessarily. However, at the commencement of the program, *imgMain* will be empty. To remedy this situation add the following line to the end of the *Form_Load()* event:

```
imgMain.Picture = Image1.Picture
```

Set the Timer control's *Enabled* property to *False*. Add the following code for the CommandButton to allow the user to start and stop the animation:

```
Private Sub Command1_Click()
    If Timer1.Enabled = True Then
        Timer1.Enabled = False
        Command1.Caption = "&Animate"
    Else
        Timer1.Enabled = True
        Command1.Caption = "Sto&p"
    End If
End Sub
```

The Timer control's *Timer* event will handle the actual animation. You want the sequence of animation frames to ascend from 1 to 5 and then descend back to 1 again for smooth movement. To achieve this effect, use two static variables so that the *Timer* event retains knowledge of what direction the animation is going and also what animation frame it should display. Add the following code for the *Timer* event:

```
Private Sub Timer1_Timer()
Static foo As Integer
Static ASCEND As Boolean
    If foo < 1 Then foo = 1
    If foo = 1 Then ASCEND = True
    If foo = 5 Then ASCEND = False
    If ASCEND Then
        foo = foo + 1
    Else
        foo = foo - 1
    End If
```

```
     Select Case foo
     Case 1: imgMain.Picture = Image1
     Case 2: imgMain.Picture = Image2
     Case 3: imgMain.Picture = Image3
     Case 4: imgMain.Picture = Image4
     Case 5: imgMain.Picture = Image5
     End Select
End Sub
```

To change the speed of the animation, all you need to do is alter the Timer control's *Interval* property. Add the following code to allow the OptionButtons to control the animation speed:

```
Private Sub Option1_Click()
    Timer1.Interval = 500
End Sub

Private Sub Option2_Click()
    Timer1.Interval = 300
End Sub

Private Sub Option3_Click()
    Timer1.Interval = 100
End Sub
```

Save your project and run the program to see the Ministry of Silly Walks animation.

# What You Must Know

Visual Basic provides a way to assign icons to individual forms and also to the actual program itself. Picture-Box controls are an easy way to add pictures of a variety of format types and also allow multiple controls to be contained together. An Image control is a cut-down version of the PictureBox control that allows easy stretching of a graphic, faster displays, and fewer resource demands. In Lesson 16, "Adding Sound and Multimedia," you will learn how to use sounds and multimedia, such as *.avi* files, within your own Visual Basic projects. Before you continue with Lesson 16, however, make sure you understand the following key concepts:

◆ Each form in your project can be assigned a different icon. From the forms in your project you can select a form's icon for the actual program to use.

◆ Versatile and feature-filled, the PictureBox control allows you to easily add pictures from a variety of graphic formats. The PictureBox control can act as a container holding other controls offering Visual Basic programmers many possibilities for use in their own projects.

◆ An Image control is a cut-down version of the PictureBox control but with the advantage of using less resources, faster displays, and stretching of graphics.

◆ Add hot spots to your programs easily by simply placing empty Image controls on top of a larger Image control or PictureBox. The *Click* event of the smaller Image controls will contain the code for each hot spot.

◆ The *PaintPicture* method can achieve highly useful graphic effects such as flipping graphics vertically or horizontally, compressing or enlarging graphics, tiling a graphic multiple times, and copying sections of a graphic.

◆ You can reference the current form using the keyword *Me*.

◆ Frame controls are like containers that can hold other controls such as Label controls and OptionButton controls. Frame controls provide clarity of divisions and groups for the users.

◆ Using OptionButtons you can provide the user with a selection from which she can easily choose. OptionButton controls are most often placed within Frame controls for grouping purposes and can be textual or graphical.

◆ By placing an ampersand sign before a character you can easily create keyboard shortcuts. To indicate to the user the character to use for the shortcut, Visual Basic underlines the character. Use the Alt key with the shortcut character to activate the shortcut.

◆ Control alignment is important in user-interface design. The Format menu within the Visual Basic environment provides multiple tools to save time with alignment and centering of controls.

◆ By flipping through a sequence of still images, you can create a simple animation. A Timer control is central to flipping through the images, and the *Interval* property of the Timer control is directly proportional to the animation speed.

# Lesson 16

---

# Adding Sound and Multimedia

In Lesson 15, "Using Icons, Picture Boxes, and Image Controls," you learned how to create a silent animation using a sequence of still images. In this lesson, you will learn how to use Visual Basic to create simple sounds and to present animations with both sound and graphics. By the time you finish this lesson, you will understand the following key concepts:

◆ You can produce a simple sound in your Visual Basic programs by using the *Beep* statement with no arguments.

◆ The Multimedia control is an extremely powerful control that allows you to play *.wav* and *.avi* files as well as audio CDs.

◆ The Animation control lets you easily add system animations to your programs that run as a separate thread and allow program code to continue executing.

## Generating Sound Using the *Beep* Statement

The simplest way to produce a sound in your Visual Basic program is to use the *Beep* statement. The *Beep* statement takes no arguments, and the duration and frequency of the sound that the *Beep* statement produces depends upon the hardware and system software in use at the time. The following code shows how you might use the *Beep* statement to attract the user's attention:

```
Beep
MsgBox "Error saving your file!", vbCritical, "Save Error"
```

**Using the *mciExecute* API Function**

*In the advanced section of this book, you will cover APIs and how to use them in Visual Basic. One of the API functions that you may want to learn is the* mciExecute *function. The* mciExecute *function enables you to easily play .wav files and .avi files from within your Visual Basic programs. An example of the calls for the* mciExecute *function appears as shown:*

```
result = mciExecute("Play c:\mysound.wav")
result = mciExecute("Play c:\myanim.avi")
```

# Using the Multimedia Control

Visual Basic programmers can make use of the Multimedia control to perform a large number of tasks involving sound and multimedia. To add a Multimedia control to your project, you must add the component first. Within the Visual Basic environment, select Project menu Components to bring up the Components dialog box, as shown in Figure 16.1.

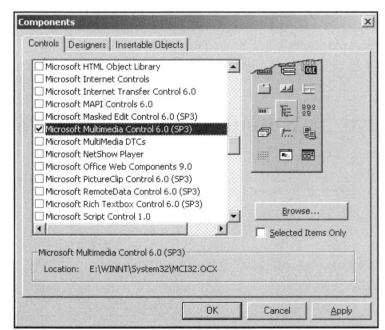

**Figure 16.1**

*Adding the component for the Multimedia control.*

Make sure that the component Microsoft Multimedia Control 6.0 has a check mark in its checkbox before clicking your mouse on the OK button.

In the control panel section of your Visual Basic environment, the Multimedia control's icon appears as shown in Figure 16.2.

### Figure 16.2

*The Multimedia control's icon.*

When you add a Multimedia control to your form regardless of the size you drag, the control will always take up at least a minimum preset size. You can make the control bigger than the minimum size but just not smaller. By setting the Multimedia control's *Orientation* property you can also select between a horizontal display and a vertical display. Figure 16.3 shows the Multimedia control in its default horizontal state with a minimum size. You can use the title bar, icon, and features of the standard form to give you an idea of comparative size.

### Figure 16.3

*The minimum size of the Multimedia control.*

Although you can add multiple Multimedia controls in a project, you can only use one Multimedia control per device. For example, you cannot have two Multimedia controls handling the same CD-ROM at the same time. You could, however, have two Multimedia controls handling different devices.

# Playing *.wav* Files

Using the Multimedia control, you can play multiple *.wav* sound files within your programs.

1. Open a new project in Visual Basic. Change the project name to **TestWAV** and the form name to **frmTestWAV**. Change the form's *Caption* property to **Testing .WAV Sounds**.

2. Add two Multimedia controls to the form and change the *Visible* property of both to **False** and then change the names of the two Multimedia controls to **mciSound1** and **mciSound2**. The position does not matter because both of the Multimedia controls will be invisible at runtime.

3. Add two CommandButtons to your form by changing the *Caption* property of one CommandButton to **Sound 1** and changing its name to **cmdSound1**. Change the *Caption* property of the second CommandButton to **Sound 2** and change its name to **cmdSound2**.

4. Before you can play a sound you must assign to the Multimedia control's *FileName* property the path and filename that it will use, as shown:

```
Private Sub Form_Load()
    'assign sound files to the controls
    mciSound1.FileName = App.Path & "\sound1.wav"
    mciSound2.FileName = App.Path & "\sound2.wav"
End Sub
```

5. Add the following code for the two CommandButtons to actually play the sounds:

```
Private Sub cmdSound1_Click()
    mciSound1.Command = "Sound"
End Sub


Private Sub cmdSound2_Click()
    mciSound2.Command = "Sound"
End Sub
```

6. To make sure that all the resources that the program has set aside for the Multimedia controls are properly returned to the system, you should close the Multimedia controls explicitly when the program ends by using the *Form_Unload()* event, as shown:

```
Private Sub Form_Unload(Cancel As Integer)
    'release the resources
    mciSound1.Command = "Close"
    mciSound2.Command = "Close"
End Sub
```

7. Save the program and run it to play the two *.wav* files.

Try playing other *.wav* files from the program.

# Playing an Audio CD

You can use the Multimedia control to easily play audio CDs from your programs.

1. Open a new project in Visual Basic and change the project name to **CDMadness** and the form name to **frmCDMad**.

2. Change the form's *Caption* property to **CD Madness**.

3. In the form's *Icon* property, assign an icon of a CD or any other icon that you prefer.

4. Add a Multimedia control to the form and then initialize it in the *Form_Load()* event, as shown:

```
Private Sub Form_Load()
    With mciCD
        .DeviceType = "CDAudio"
        .UpdateInterval = 1000
        .TimeFormat = mciFormatTmsf
        .Command = "Open"
    End With
End Sub
```

5. Add an Image control to hold a background pattern. Set the *Stretch* property to **True** and make the Image control very small in size so that you can see it on your form but not have it take up much space. Load a picture into the Image control that you want to use for a background. Paint the picture onto the form by using the *PaintPicture* method in the *Form_Paint()* event, as shown:

```
Private Sub Form_Paint()
    Me.PaintPicture Image1.Picture, 0, 0, _
    Me.Width, Me.Height
End Sub
```

6. Add a Shape control as a filled, black rectangle with a gray border.

7. Add a Label control on top of the Shape control and name it **lblTrack** and change the Label control's *BackColor* property to black and the *ForeColor* property to light green. The Label will indicate to the users what track they are listening to and how many tracks are on the CD.

8. Assign the Multimedia control's *Track* and *Tracks* properties to the Label control in the *mciCD_StatusUpdate()* event, as shown:

```
Private Sub mciCD_StatusUpdate()
    lblTrack.Caption = "Track " & mciCD.Track _
    & " of " & mciCD.Tracks
End Sub
```

9. Finally, you must release the resources taken by the Multimedia control back to the system, as shown:

```
Private Sub Form_Unload(Cancel As Integer)
    With mciCD
        .Command = "Stop"
        .Command = "Close"
    End With
End Sub
```

10. Save and run the *CD Madness* program, placing an audio CD into the CD-ROM drive.

Remember to stop the Windows default CD player from trying to play the CD automatically by closing the default CD player if it appears. The output of the *CD Madness* program should appear as shown in Figure 16.4.

**Figure 16.4**

*The* CD Madness *program in action.*

## Success HINT: Using DirectX

*If you are very serious about sound and music, then you really should look into DirectSound and DirectMusic, both of which are components of DirectX. Using DirectX from Visual Basic allows you to directly access hardware such as MIDI devices, sound cards, and more without having to write extremely low-level code.*

*Although this book cannot cover DirectX, you should understand all the concepts outlined in this book before you attempt to program DirectX in Visual Basic. DirectX is a complicated suite of tools that is recommended for intermediate or advanced Visual Basic programmers who want to push the limits of what they can do. Figure 16.5 shows an example of the serious type of things that you can do with sound using DirectX.*

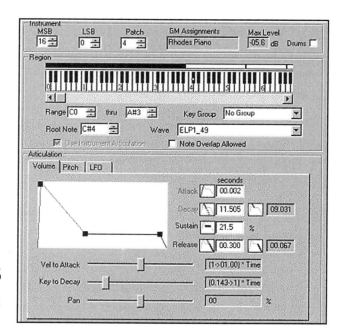

**Figure 16.5**

*The DLS Designer, a DirectMusic Producer module.*

*To work with DirectX, you must install the DirectX SDK (Software Developer's Kit). If you don't have this already installed on your computer you can download it for free from the following Microsoft site: www.microsoft.com/directx/.*

# Playing .avi Files

You no doubt already realize how useful the Multimedia control is. On top of what you have already done with the Multimedia control, you can also play .avi files, which are usually graphical animation files that can be accompanied by sound.

1. Open a new project in Visual Basic and change the project name to **TestAVI** and the form name to **frmTestAVI**.

2. Change the form's *Caption* property to **TestAVI**.

3. Add a Multimedia control to the form and change its name to **mciAVI**. Initializing the Multimedia control is similar to what you have previously done, as shown:

```
Private Sub Form_Load()
    With mciAVI
        .FileName = App.Path & "\age2.avi"
        .hWndDisplay = Me.hWnd
        .Command = "Open"
    End With
End Sub
```

4. As you have seen earlier, you must also make sure to free the resources used by the Multimedia control, as shown:

```
Private Sub Form_Unload(Cancel As Integer)
    mciAVI.Command = "Close"
End Sub
```

5. Save the *TestAVI* program and run it. You must press the Play button to start the animation. Figure 16.6 shows the *TestAVI* program playing an .avi file.

## Figure 16.6

*The* TestAVI *program in action.*

Remember that as the programmer, you are in control. To modify the *TestAVI* program to behave differently you only need to make some minor changes. For instance, if you want the animation to start playing automatically, you must add the following line at the end of the *Form_Load()* event:

```
.mciAVI.Command = "Play"
```

If you would like the animation to appear in its own window, simply remove the following line from the *Form_Load()* event:

```
.hWndDisplay = Me.hWnd
```

 **Advanced Multimedia Control Options**

*Although this lesson has shown you many of the tasks that can be accomplished by the Multimedia control, to really appreciate the power of this control you must spend some time working through its many features. There are too many properties, methods, events, and commands in the Multimedia control to cover in a lesson of this size. The main point being made here is that the Multimedia control is capable of far more than has been shown in this lesson, so if you like working with the Multimedia control, go out and look at what else it can do.*

# Using the Animation Control

The Animation control allows you a method of playing simple, uncompressed *.avi* files that do not contain sound. These types of animations are typically system animations, such as the searching flashlight or the files flying from one folder to another. The Animation control allows these animations to run as a separate thread, so the animation does not halt the Visual Basic program code from executing further until it ends, as is so often the case.

1. Start up a new Visual Basic project and name the project **SystemAnim** in the Project menu Properties dialog box and change the name of the form to **SysAnim** in the Properties section. Change the form's *Caption* property to **SystemAnim** and change the icon to something other than the default.

2. To use the Animation control, you must add the Microsoft Windows Common Controls-2 6.0 component from the Project menu Components dialog box. Add an Animation control to your form and name the Animation control **Anim1**.

3. Add four CommandButtons and change their properties, as shown in Table 16.1:

*Table 16.1 CommandButton Caption property values.*

| CommandButton Name | Property | Value |
| --- | --- | --- |
| cmdAction | Caption | &Play |
| cmdSearch | Caption | &Search |
| cmdFileMove | Caption | File &Move |
| cmdFindFile | Caption | &Find File |

Figure 16.7 shows the *SystemAnim* program at design time.

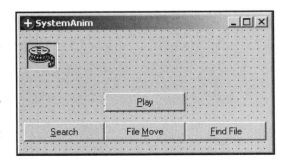

**Figure 16.7**

*The* SystemAnim *program at design time.*

Other than *cmdAction*, the CommandButtons are for selecting a system animation to load. The Animation control uses the *Open* method to open the system animations and takes the path to the file as its only argument. To load in the animation file you want to see, add the following code to the program's code window:

```
'======================================
' Load the possible system animations
'======================================
Private Sub cmdFileMove_Click()
    Anim1.Open App.Path & "\videos\filemove.avi"
End Sub


Private Sub cmdFindFile_Click()
    Anim1.Open App.Path & "\videos\findfile.avi"
End Sub


Private Sub cmdSearch_Click()
    Anim1.Open App.Path & "\videos\search.avi"
End Sub
```

When the *SystemAnim* program first starts, you must initialize the animation settings to avoid any errors or unexpected behavior from occurring. You must be able to discern whether the system animation is playing or stopped. By making use of the Animation control's *Tag* property, you can set a value to indicate that the animation is stopped (0) or playing (1). You can also load in a default system animation by calling one of the CommandButton's *Click* event. Place the initialization code in the *Form_Load()* event, as shown:

```
'======================================
' Program start - initialize animation
'======================================
Private Sub Form_Load()
    Anim1.Tag = 0
    cmdFileMove_Click
End Sub
```

So that the user does not try to load in a different system animation while another is currently playing, you must toggle between having the CommandButtons enabled and disabled. Create a simple routine that handles enabling and disabling the CommandButtons, as shown:

```
'=====================================
' Toggle between enabled and disabled
'=====================================
Private Sub ToggleButtons(ByVal mybool As Boolean)
    cmdSearch.Enabled = mybool
    cmdFileMove.Enabled = mybool
    cmdFindFile.Enabled = mybool
End Sub
```

Finally, all that is left for you to do is write the code for the *cmdAction* button. The *cmdAction* button must discern whether the system animation is playing or not and then, based on the result of this, toggle the other CommandButtons, change its own *Caption* property, and stop or start the system animation. The Animation control can start a system animation using the *Play* method. To stop a system animation the Animation control has a *Stop* method. Neither the *Play* nor *Stop* methods take any arguments. The code for the *cmdAction* button should appear something similar to the following:

```
Private Sub cmdAction_Click()
    If Anim1.Tag = 1 Then
        Anim1.Stop
        Anim1.Tag = 0
        cmdAction.Caption = "&Play"
        ToggleButtons True
    Else
        Anim1.Play
        Anim1.Tag = 1
        cmdAction.Caption = "Sto&p"
        ToggleButtons False
    End If
End Sub
```

Save and run the SystemAnim program, which should look something like Figure 16.8.

**Figure 16.8**

*The* SystemAnim *program in action.*

# What You Must Know

The *Beep* statement allows you to easily make a noise in your programs to get the user's attention. The Multimedia control lets you easily play *.wav* and *.avi* files in your programs and is capable of far more, such as playing audio CDs. To play system animations, which are silent, uncompressed *.avi* files, use the Animation control. In Lesson 17, "Working with the Mouse and Keyboard," you will learn how to control, change, and work with the mouse and keyboard from within your own Visual Basic projects. Before you continue with Lesson 17, however, make sure you understand the following key concepts:

◆ Visual Basic lets you produce a simple sound in your programs by using the *Beep* statement, which takes no arguments.

◆ Use the Multimedia control in your programs to easily play *.wav* and *.avi* files. You can also play audio CDs and more using the Multimedia control.

◆ System animations can be added to your programs by using the Animation control. The Animation control plays the animations in their own thread, allowing your program code to continue.

# Lesson 17

# Working with the
# Mouse and Keyboard

In earlier lessons, you learned how to use Visual Basic's graphics methods to affect the user interface. In this lesson, you will learn how to work with the mouse and keyboard from within your Visual Basic programs to improve the user interface in terms of both appearance and interaction. By the time you finish this lesson, you will understand the following key concepts:

◆ In Visual Basic, you can interchange the terms pointer and cursor as both refer to the icon representing the current mouse position.

◆ The appearance of the mouse is set by assigning one of the mouse pointer constants to the object's *MousePointer* property. Mouse pointer constants can be assigned at design time or at runtime.

◆ A form is not the only object that contains a *MousePointer* property, and different objects can use different mouse cursors.

◆ To use a custom mouse pointer, assign an icon or cursor file to the form's *MouseIcon* property and then set the *MousePointer* property to *vbCustom*.

◆ You can move the mouse cursor position using the Windows API call, *SetCursorPos*, and pass it the x- and y-coordinates as arguments.

◆ There are common mouse events associated with many objects that can make work involving mouse position and mouse buttons very straightforward in Visual Basic.

◆ The *KeyPress* event allows you to monitor ANSI character values that are received by individual objects, such as a TextBox control.

♦ Visual Basic provides a set of keycode constants for use in your programs rather than having to use raw ANSI character values.

♦ The *KeyUp* and *KeyDown* events let you check the physical state of all the keys on the keyboard and also provide a means by which you can see if the Shift, Ctrl, or Alt keys are being held down in combination with another key.

♦ The *KeyPreview* property in forms allows you to intercept keyboard events prior to the controls on the form for functionality such as global keyboard handling and hot key creation.

# Understanding Cursors and Pointers

When referring to the icon representing the mouse position in Visual Basic, the terms "cursor" and "pointer" can be interchanged as both refer to the same thing. Most programming languages and generic computer articles use the term cursor rather than pointer; however, for your own clarity be aware that in Visual Basic commands and articles you could see either term.

# Changing the Appearance of the Mouse Cursor

Good programs make use of multiple mouse cursors to give the user valuable feedback. An example of making use of multiple mouse cursors to provide the user with feedback would be changing the mouse cursor from an arrow to an hourglass when doing some task that may take quite a while. When the task is complete change the mouse cursor back to an arrow again. In this manner, the user can easily see that the program is busy doing something and will often wait until the mouse cursor reverts back to the default arrow before continuing.

Visual Basic provides easy methods for adding multiple mouse cursors in your own programs. Each form has a *MousePointer* property to which you can assign seventeen different mouse pointer constants, as shown in Figure 17.1.

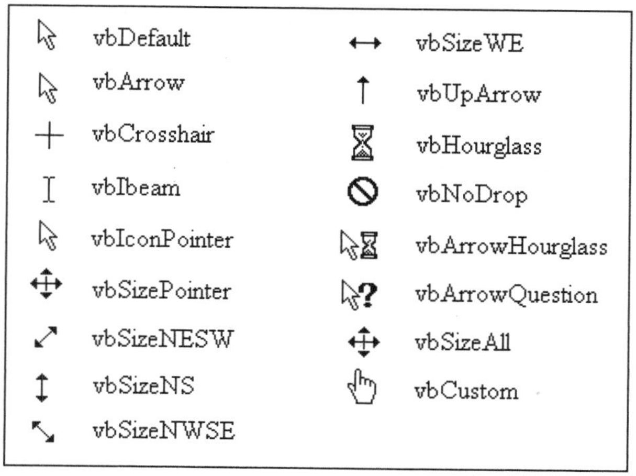

| | | | |
|---|---|---|---|
| ↖ | vbDefault | ↔ | vbSizeWE |
| ↖ | vbArrow | ↑ | vbUpArrow |
| + | vbCrosshair | ⧗ | vbHourglass |
| I | vbIbeam | ⊘ | vbNoDrop |
| ↖ | vbIconPointer | ↖⧗ | vbArrowHourglass |
| ✛ | vbSizePointer | ↖? | vbArrowQuestion |
| ↗ | vbSizeNESW | ✛ | vbSizeAll |
| ↕ | vbSizeNS | ☝ | vbCustom |
| ↘ | vbSizeNWSE | | |

**Figure 17.1**

*Visual Basic mouse pointer constants.*

Most of the constants are consistent; however, *vbDefault*, *vbIconPointer*, *vbSizePointer*, and *vbCustom* do not always appear the same. For instance, if you are working with a group and write some code that sets the form's *MousePointer* property to *vbCustom*, it may show a hand. Someone else writes some code that makes other changes and at one lengthy point changes the pointer to an hourglass. When your code executes again and sets the form's *MousePointer* property back to *vbCustom* again, it may show a black cat! Even though your code did not change, setting the *MousePointer* property to *vbCustom* can produce different mouse cursors. You will learn more about custom mouse cursors later in this lesson.

At runtime, you can change the mouse cursor from within your Visual Basic code by simply assigning one of the mouse pointer constants to the *MousePointer* property of the form, as follows:

```
Form1.MousePointer = vbHourglass
```

# Changing the Mouse Cursor for Different Objects

Although perhaps the most common, forms are not the only objects that you can assign mouse pointers to. Many objects contain the *MousePointer* property to which you can assign one of the Visual Basic mouse pointer constants. Some of the more commonly used objects that contain a *MousePointer* property are forms, Frames, CommandButtons, Images, PictureBoxes, Labels, ListBoxes, and TextBoxes, although there are many others.

1. Open a new Visual Basic project and name the project **Objects**.

2. Add a Frame control and set the *Caption* property to **Busy**. Change the Frame's *Mouse-Pointer* property to **11 – Hourglass**.

3. Add a CommandButton control and set the *Caption* property to **No Drops Here**. Change the CommandButton's *MousePointer* property to **12—No Drop**.

4. Save and run the program, pointing the mouse on the form, the Frame, and the Command-Button to see the mouse cursor change for the different objects, as shown in Figure 17.2.

**Figure 17.2**

*Using different pointers for different objects.*

# Customizing the Mouse Cursor

Although the common mouse cursors might often be all that your programs require, you may need to provide custom mouse cursors for special programs or functions. Visual Basic once again comes to the rescue by providing an easy way for you to use any icon or cursor file. With the object whose mouse cursor you want to change, set the *MouseIcon* property to the icon file that contains the image you want to use for your custom mouse cursor. At design time, you can simply use the Properties section for the object and click your mouse on the *MouseIcon* property to get the browse button, as shown in Figure 17.3.

**Figure 17.3**

*The* MouseIcon *property's browse button.*

Click your mouse on the browse button. Visual Basic will display the Load Icon dialog box from which you can navigate and select a file to use, as shown in Figure 17.4.

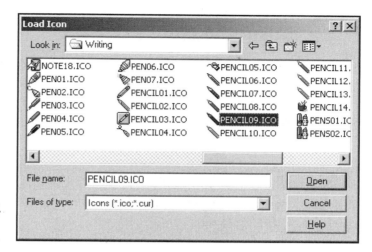

**Figure 17.4**

*The Load Icon dialog box.*

Next, simply set the object's *MousePointer* property to **vbCustom**, which appears as 99 — Custom in the drop-down, as shown in Figure 17.5.

**Figure 17.5**

*Setting the* MousePointer *property to **vbCustom** at design time.*

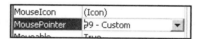

You can also set the mouse cursor from code by assigning an icon to the object's *MouseIcon* property from an Image control or ImageList control, as follows:

```
Form1.MouseIcon = Image1.Picture
Form1.MousePointer = vbCustom
```

You will learn more about ImageList controls later in Lesson 24, "Using ImageLists and TreeViews."

**NOTE:** *If you want to try customizing mouse cursors using icon and cursor files on your own hard drive, do a search for \*.ico and \*.cur. This will allow you to easily select the image you want to use. You might consider copying the icon or cursor files that you use into the project folder, so that you keep all the necessary pieces of the project in one place. Also, if you are looking for animated mouse cursors, do a search for \*.ani on your hard drive.*

**Hiding the Mouse Cursor**

*Sometimes, changing the appearance of the mouse cursor is not enough and your program really requires the ability to hide the mouse cursor completely. There are different ways to achieve this. One method would be to create a blank icon, assign the form's* MouseIcon *property to this icon, and then set the* MousePointer *property to* vbCustom.

*Another method would be to use an API call to hide the mouse cursor.* ShowCursor *is the API call to use, and you simply assign* False *to hide the mouse cursor or* True *to show it again. On the companion Web site (at* www.prima-tech.com/ books/book/5250/945/*) that comes with this book you can find the executable and source code for the program* HideCursor, *which gives you an example of hiding and showing the mouse cursor. You will learn about API calls in the advanced section of this book.*

# Changing the Position of the Mouse Cursor

From within your program code, you can change the position of the mouse cursor without the user having to physically move his mouse. Although moving the mouse cursor involves using a Windows API call, it is a simple one which you can easily follow instructions for.

Imagine that you have a program in which you must move the mouse cursor from within your code. You add a new module to the Visual Basic project and add the following line:

```
Public Declare Function SetCursorPos Lib "user32" _
(ByVal x As Long, ByVal y As Long) As Long
```

Then anywhere in your program where you must change the mouse cursor position, you type in *SetCursorPos* and then the values for the x and y coordinates. The following line moves the position of the mouse cursor to the coordinates (10, 40):

```
SetCursorPos 10, 40
```

You can use different values for x and y, of course.

# Understanding Common Mouse Events

Visual Basic provides an easy method to obtain common mouse events from many objects. A form, for example, contains the following five events that you can use for getting mouse information:

```
Click()
DblClick()
MouseDown(Button As Integer, Shift As Integer, X As Single, Y As Single)
MouseUp(Button As Integer, Shift As Integer, X As Single, Y As Single)
MouseMove(Button As Integer, Shift As Integer, X As Single, Y As Single)
```

The *Click* and *DblClick* events allow you to execute some code whenever the user clicks or double-clicks her mouse on the form. No arguments are passed by Visual Basic to these subroutines. Both of these events are often made use of by Visual Basic programmers because not only is it incredibly useful in many situations to know when the user has clicked or double-clicked her mouse somewhere on your form but also because Visual Basic makes it so easy for you to get this information.

The *MouseDown* and *MouseUp* events let you know when the user presses or releases any of the mouse buttons. Both of these events take arguments that Visual Basic supplies for your use. Button indicates which mouse button(s) the user is pressing. Table 17.1 shows you the different values for *Button* and the corresponding button description.

*Table 17.1 Button values for common mouse events.*

| Button Value | Description |
| --- | --- |
| 1 | Left button |
| 2 | Right button |
| 3 | Middle button |

The *Shift* argument lets you know if any special keys are being held down by the user. Table 17.2 shows you the different values for *Shift* and the corresponding key description.

*Table 17.2 Shift values for common mouse events.*

| Shift Value | Description |
| --- | --- |
| 0 | No special keys |
| 1 | Shift key |
| 2 | Ctrl key |

*Table 17.2 (continued)*

| Shift Value | Description |
|---|---|
| 3 | Shift and Ctrl keys |
| 4 | Alt key |
| 5 | Shift and Alt keys |
| 6 | Ctrl and Alt keys |
| 7 | Shift, Ctrl, and Alt keys |

x is the horizontal position of the mouse and y is the vertical position, with both being given in terms of the scalemode the form is using.

The *MouseDown* and *MouseUp* events are different from the *Click* and *DblClick* events because they give you a finer level of detail. For example, with the *Click* event you must wait until the user presses and then releases the mouse button before it triggers. However, as soon as the user presses the mouse button, the *MouseDown* event triggers and lets you know which button the user is pressing, which special keys are being held down, and what the current mouse position is.

The *MouseMove* event is very similar to the *MouseDown* and *MouseUp* events, utilizing the same arguments. The difference is that the *MouseMove* event will trigger whenever the user moves the mouse.

 **Using Animated Mouse Cursors**

*For some reason, the* MousePointer *property in Visual Basic does not support animated mouse cursors yet. However, as you will learn about in the advanced section of this book, you can use Windows API calls to work around this problem. This success hint may be a bit too advanced for you, so if you have any difficulty, come back to it later.*

*In a module, declare the following two APIs as shown:*

```
Public Declare Function LoadCursorFromFile Lib "user32" _
Alias "LoadCursorFromFileA" (ByVal lpFileName As String) _
As Long
Public Declare Function SetClassLong Lib "user32" _
Alias "SetClassLongA" (ByVal hwnd As Long, _
ByVal nIndex As Long, ByVal dwNewLong As Long) As Long
```

*In the code window for your form, add the following code:*

```
Option Explicit
Private lngOldMouse As Long


Private Sub Form_Load()
Dim lngNewMouse As Long
    lngNewMouse = LoadCursorFromFile("c:\piano.ani")
    'switch to the new mouse cursor
    lngOldMouse = SetClassLong(Form1.hwnd, -12, _
        lngNewMouse)
End Sub


Private Sub Form_Unload(Cancel As Integer)
    'switch back to the old mouse cursor
    lngOldMouse = SetClassLong(Form1.hwnd, -12, _
        lngOldMouse)
End Sub
```

*You can find cursor animations by searching for * .ani *on your own hard drive.*

# Using the *KeyPress* Event

Visual Basic provides you with the *KeyPress* event to determine when the user presses a key and contains a reference to an ASCII character value. The syntax for the *KeyPress* event is as shown:

```
Private Sub Form_KeyPress(KeyAscii As Integer)
```

You must convert this ASCII character value using the *Chr* function to get the actual character, as shown:

```
myChar = Chr(KeyAscii)
```

To modify the character, such as making it uppercase, and return it to an ASCII character value again, you must use the *Asc* function, as shown:

```
myChar = UCase(myChar)
KeyAscii = Asc(myChar)
```

Many objects contain a *KeyPress* event, including a form, TextBox, ListBox, CommandButton, PictureBox, RichTextBox, and many others. You can use the *KeyPress* event for all sorts of interesting and useful possibilities in your programs.

Imagine that you have a TextBox control on a form that you want the user to use only for entering numbers. Using the *KeyPress* event of the TextBox control, you can monitor each character for numerical validity. Having a TextBox control accept numerical values only is a very common requirement that often presents itself to programmers. The code for achieving a TextBox control that accepts only numerical input would look something as follows:

```
Private Sub Text1_KeyPress(KeyAscii As Integer)
    'Is it a numerical value?
    If Not ((KeyAscii >= 48) And (KeyAscii <= 57)) Then
        'Is it the backspace character?
        If Not (KeyAscii = 8) Then KeyAscii = 0
    End If
End Sub
```

Notice that an extra condition exists that checks if the user is trying to edit the TextBox control using the backspace key. The ASCII character value for the backspace key is 8. If you want to try a hands-on approach to finding the ASCII character values, open a new project, add a TextBox control to a form, and then add the following code:

```
Private Sub Text1_KeyPress(KeyAscii As Integer)
    MsgBox KeyAscii
End Sub
```

Run the program and press a key to see its ASCII character value.

Working with raw ASCII character values can sometimes cause difficulties or lead to errors that can be difficult to track down. Also, using raw ASCII values makes your code less readable and puts unnecessary strain on your memory when trying to work out what your code is trying to achieve. For this reason, Visual Basic contains a list of keycode constants that you can use within your code instead of putting in the raw ASCII character value. So, in the code example shown earlier, you could put the constant *vbKeyBack* instead of 8, *vbKey0* instead of 48, and *vbKey9* instead of 57. A complete list of the keycode constants Visual Basic provides can be found in Appendix B, "Keycode Constants."

# Using the *KeyUp* and *KeyDown* Events

Although the *KeyPress* event is very useful, it does not cater for all the possible keys on the keyboard and returns an ASCII character value but tells you nothing about the physical state of particular keys. The *KeyUp* and *KeyDown* events fill this gap and give you the functionality you require to be able to handle more complex keyboard events, such as checking if the user is holding the Shift key down in combination with another key. The *KeyDown* event triggers when the user presses a key down, and the *KeyUp* event triggers when the user releases a key that is being held down. The syntax for the *KeyDown* event is as follows:

```
Private Sub Form_KeyDown(KeyCode As Integer, _
Shift As Integer)
```

The *KeyUp* event has an identical syntax, only a different routine name. Of the two events, the *KeyDown* event is more often made use of by Visual Basic programmers, although both events can be very useful.

The argument *KeyCode* is one of the Visual Basic keycode constants, such as *vbKeyA*. The argument Shift is the same as you saw earlier for the *MouseDown* event, and Table 17.2 shows a breakdown of possible values.

 **Using Shift Key Masks**

*Although you already have the means to work out whether the Shift, Ctrl, or Alt keys are being held down, Visual Basic provides masks, which you can use to isolate the state of one of these keys easily. The masks are merely constants known as vbShiftMask, vbCtrlMask, and vbAltMask. So for example, if you only want to know if the Alt key is being held down by the user but do not care about the Shift key or Ctrl key, you could use something similar to the following to isolate the state of the Alt key:*

```
Private Sub Form_KeyDown(KeyCode As Integer, _
Shift As Integer)
Dim AltDown As Boolean
    AltDown = (Shift And vbAltMask)
    If AltDown = True Then
        MsgBox "The Alt key is down."
    Else
        MsgBox "The Alt key is up."
    End If
End Sub
```

# Using the *KeyPreview* Property

Forms in Visual Basic contain a property known as the *KeyPreview* property. The *KeyPreview* property by default is set to *False*, which means that the controls on the form, such as TextBox controls, etc., receive the keyboard events directly. By setting the *KeyPreview* property to *True*, a form intercepts keyboard events prior to any of the controls on that form. This early interception makes it possible to implement global key handling routines for all controls as well as an easy mechanism for creating hot keys in your programs.

As an example of global key handling, imagine if you had twenty-five TextBox controls on a form that each require numerical input. You saw earlier how to create TextBoxes that accept numerical input only. Instead of having twenty-five *KeyPress* event routines, you could set the form's *KeyPreview* property to *True* and have a single *KeyPress* event routine at the form level.

To create a hot key in your project, such as displaying a message when the user presses the F1 key, simply set the form's *KeyPreview* property to *True* and add an entry in the form's *KeyDown* event routine, as follows:

```
Private Sub Form_KeyDown(KeyCode As Integer, _
Shift As Integer)
    If KeyCode = vbKeyF1 Then MsgBox "F1 pressed!"
End Sub
```

# What You Must Know

Mouse cursors can have a different appearance depending on the state of the program and can provide the users with useful feedback that they can appreciate. You can easily create custom mouse cursors and assign different mouse cursors to different objects. Keyboard handling can be done at an individual level or at a global level, allowing you to control keyboard input in a powerful manner within your programs. In Lesson 18, "Using Common Dialogs," you will learn how to use the Microsoft CommonDialog control to add and use the common dialogs for opening files, printing, and more, within your own Visual Basic projects. Before you continue with Lesson 18, however, make sure you understand the following key concepts:

◆ You can use the terms pointer or cursor when referring to the icon representing the current mouse position.

◆ Mouse pointer constants can be used to easily set the appearance of the mouse cursor. At design time or at runtime, mouse pointer constants can be assigned to an object's *MousePointer* property.

◆ Forms are not the only objects that contain a *MousePointer* property and each object can make use of different mouse cursors.

◆ You can create custom mouse cursors by assigning an icon or cursor file to an object's *MouseIcon* property and then setting the *MousePointer* property to *vbCustom*.

◆ The position of the mouse cursor can be changed within your program using the Windows API call, *SetCursorPos*, and passing it x- and y-coordinates to use.

◆ Common mouse events make light work of handling mouse positions or the state of mouse buttons.

◆ Using the *KeyPress* event, you can check the validity of ANSI ASCII characters in your programs as they arrive.

◆ Rather than use the raw ANSI ASCII character values, you can use the keycode constants provided by Visual Basic to save possible errors from occurring and put less strain on your memory.

◆ The *KeyUp* and *KeyDown* events give you information concerning combinations of keys being used with the Shift, Ctrl, and Alt keys and their physical state.

◆ For global keyboard handling and hot key creation, use a form's *KeyPreview* property to intercept keyboard events prior to controls on that form.

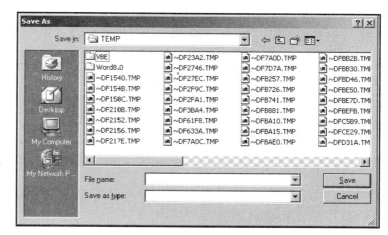

**Figure 18.4**

*The Save As common dialog appears only slightly different to the Open dialog.*

Unlike some of the other common dialog boxes, the Open and Save As dialogs do not require the *CancelError* property to be *True*, as you can simply check the *Filename* property to see if it is empty. And if this is the case, the Cancel button was used. You can set a title for the dialog box using the *DialogTitle* property, which simply takes a text string. You can also set the starting directory easily by setting the *InitDir* property. If you do not explicitly set the *InitDir* property then *InitDir* uses the last directory that the program was aware of.

Another useful feature to be aware of when using the Open and Save As dialogs is the *Filter* property. You can set the *Filter* property so that the only files the user will see are relevant files. For instance, if your program is expecting a batch file, you might want to filter for all files with *\*.bat* as an extension. You can have multiple filters and simply separate them with the *pipe* character. It is worth noting that each filter has two parts—the first is simply a display text while the second is the filter itself. These two parts of a filter are also separated by the *pipe* character.

The following example code shows you some of these techniques when using the Open common dialog:

```
Private Sub Form_Click()
    'Get the filename from the user
    With frmMain.dlgCmn
        .DialogTitle = "Load batch file"
        .InitDir = App.Path
        .FileName = ""
        .CancelError = False
        .Filter = _
        "Batch files (*.bat)|*.bat|All files (*.*)|*.*"
        .ShowOpen
```

```
        'check if cancel was pressed
        If .FileName = "" Then Exit Sub
        MsgBox "You selected the file: " & .FileName
    End With
End Sub
```

You do not need to use the Save As dialog box every time your program saves a file, as this would get very tedious for you. Once your program knows the name of a file, it can then save directly to that file rather than requesting a filename to save as.

# The Print Dialog

Producing a Print dialog is very easy using the common dialog control. Different options are available depending on the printer that the user selects, exactly the same as when a user prints from any other Windows application. You can simply call the *ShowPrinter* method for this dialog box or use the flags to create a more customized arrangement.

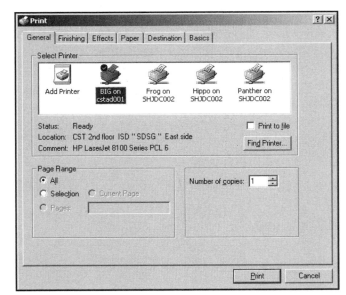

**Figure 18.5**

*The Print common dialog.*

Although the descriptions are omitted, the following flag constants show the possible flags that you can experiment with when working with the Print common dialog. If you require a description of these flags, then refer to Microsoft's online documentation.

| | | |
|---|---|---|
| *cdlPDAllPages* | *cdlPDCollate* | *cdlPDDisablePrintToFile* |
| *cdlPDHelpButton* | *cdlPDHidePrintToFile* | *cdlPDNoPageNums* |
| *cdlPDNoSelection* | *cdlPDNoWarning* | *cdlPDPageNums* |
| *cdlPDPrintSetup* | *cdlPDPrintToFile* | *cdlPDReturnDC* |
| *cdlPDReturnDefault* | *cdlPDReturnIC* | *cdlPDSelection* |
| *cdlPDUseDevModeCopies* | | |

The following code shows an example of calling the Print common dialog and setting some of its properties through code:

```
Private Sub cmdPrint_Click()
On Error GoTo err_handler
    dlgCmn.CancelError = True

    'set the number of copies and orientation
    dlgCmn.Copies = 10
    dlgCmn.Orientation = cdlLandscape

    'show the Print common dialog box
    dlgCmn.ShowPrinter
err_handler:
    MsgBox "A printing error occurred", vbExclamation
End Sub
```

# The Font Dialog

When you want the user to be able to select a font, you can use the Font common dialog, as shown in Figure 18.6.

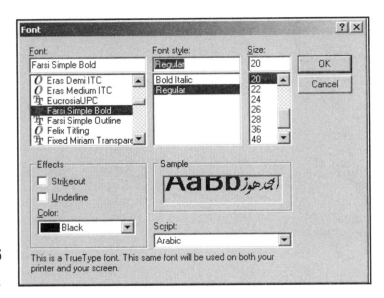

**Figure 18.6**

*The Font common dialog.*

Although the descriptions are omitted, the following flag constants show the possible flags that you can experiment with when working with the Font common dialog. If you require a description of these flags, then refer to Microsoft's online documentation.

| | | |
|---|---|---|
| *cdlCFANSIOnly* | *cdlCFApply* | *cdlCFBoth* |
| *cdlCFEffects* | *cdlCFFixedPitchOnly* | *cdlCFForceFontExist* |
| *cdlCFHelpButton* | *cdlCFLimitSize* | *cdlCFNoFaceSel* |
| *cdlCFNoSimulations* | *cdlCFNoSizeSel* | *cdlCFNoStyleSel* |
| *cdlCFNoVectorFonts* | *cdlCFPrinterFonts* | *cdlCFScalableOnly* |
| *cdlCFScreenFonts* | *cdlCFTTOnly* | *cdlCFWYSIWYG* |

The Font dialog requires that at least one of the flags, *cdlCFScreenFonts*, *cdlCFPrinterFonts*, or *cdlCFBoth*, be set in your program before it functions properly; otherwise, you will get an error message, as shown in Figure 18.7 and your program will crash.

**Figure 18.7**

*An error occurs if particular flags are not set prior to the ShowFont method.*

The following code shows an example of the correct way to call the Font common dialog:

```
Private Sub Form_Click()
    dlgCmn.Flags = cdlCFBoth Or cdlCFEffects
    dlgCmn.ShowFont
End Sub
```

# What You Must Know

Common dialogs can save you development time, help prevent avoidable errors creeping into your code, and provide users with a consistent interface to work with across programs. You can have common dialogs for file selections, printing, colors, and fonts. Using the common dialog flags gives you powerful customization and control capabilities. In Lesson 19, "Unleashing Fonts," you will learn about fonts, the different types of fonts, requesting fonts from the user, and how to generally manage fonts within your Visual Basic programs. Before you continue with Lesson 19, however, make sure you understand the following key concepts:

◆ Saving development time, preventing the unnecessary introduction of new errors, and providing users with a consistent interface across programs are the purposes for using common dialogs.

◆ The five types of common dialogs are Open, Save As, Print, Color, and Font.

◆ The Microsoft CommonDialog component must be included in your programs before you can add the CommonDialog control to your form.

◆ There are six different *Show* methods associated with the CommonDialog control—one for each common dialog plus one for Windows Help.

◆ To customize and control common dialog behavior and appearance you must use learn to set the common dialog flags.

◆ Although an error handling routine, catching the Cancel button is necessary to correctly handle common dialogs in your programs.

◆ You can use the CommonDialog error constants to provide more meaningful error messages to users of your programs as well as improve overall robustness.

# Lesson 19

# Unleashing Fonts

In Lesson 18, "Common Dialogs," you learned how to display the common dialog for selecting a font. In this lesson, you will learn what to do with the results of selecting a font, the different types of fonts, how to change and work with fonts in your programs, and generally the importance of fonts for the end user. By the time you finish this lesson, you will understand the following key concepts:

◆ Serif fonts have the small edges or lines that finish off letters and characters that you see and make reading sentences and paragraphs easier on the eye, while sans-serif fonts are usually more suitable for titles and headings.

◆ You can preset a control's font at design time by using the browse button and selecting a font from the Font dialog box.

◆ To change a font through code you must reference the object first, followed by Font and then the individual font characteristics, such as Name, Size, Bold, etc.

◆ The *FontTransparent* property determines whether the background will show through the gaps between text characters or if a solid background will be displayed behind each character.

◆ Unicode fonts can be utilized in your Visual Basic programs for powerful language capabilities by using the Microsoft Forms 2.0 Library controls or other Unicode compliant controls.

◆ Multiple fonts can easily be displayed in your programs by using different Label or TextBox controls or making use of the multifont capabilities of RichTextBox and PictureBox controls.

◆ Scaling fonts so that you can see a font displayed in different sizes is a common practice and easily done using Visual Basic.

# Introducing Fonts

You have probably used fonts in many standard programs such as text editors and drawing packages, and although you may think you know all about fonts, you would be surprised at the number of people who create programs with an awful selection of gaudy fonts or no fonts at all besides the default. Fonts are the shape and style of text, with each font conforming to a specified pattern. For example, some handwriting fonts may make all of the letters in that font lean to the right even though italic style has not been specified. Others are always big and bold because they are intended by their maker for headlines or such. Do not use lots of different fonts and styles in your programs but rather choose one or two fonts that complement each other and stay consistent. Screen fonts are usually bitmap fonts with set sizes, while printer fonts and true-type fonts can be resized indefinitely.

# Contrasting Serif and Sans-Serif Fonts

One of the first things about fonts that you must learn is the difference between serif and sans-serif fonts. A serif font has small edges or lines that are attached to the end of letters. These edges are known as serifs and their purpose is to make it easier for the eye to flow from one letter to the next. A sans-serif font is a font that does not have a serif and is typically used for headings, titles, and short labels.

Figure 19.1 shows both the correct and the incorrect use of serif and sans-serif fonts. The left window correctly uses a sans-serif font for the heading and a serif font for the body of the text, but the right window incorrectly uses the serif font for the heading and a sans-serif font for the body of the text.

**Figure 19.1**

*Using serif and sans-serif fonts correctly at left and incorrectly at right.*

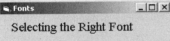
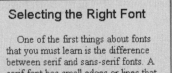

The use of serif and sans-serif fonts does not have to be strictly adhered to by you, and there are times when you choose to make an exception for stylistic reasons. Many programs will, for instance, use only one font throughout, changing properties such as size and style for differentiation. It is important that you choose fonts suitable for your target audience, although in the end the choice comes down to you. However, without restricting your creative ideas, a good font selection can enhance your program significantly.

# Presetting Fonts Within Controls

At design time, you can select what font a particular control or object should use very easily by selecting the *Font* property in the Properties section in the Visual Basic environment and then clicking your mouse on the small browse button, as shown in Figure 19.2.

### Figure 19.2

*The browse button for the* Font *property.*

Visual Basic will display the common dialog for selecting a font. Within the font dialog you can select the font, the font size, the font style of regular, italic, or bold, and even special font effects such as underline or strikeout.

# Changing Fonts Using Code

To change the font of an object, such as a Label control, at runtime, you merely have to reference the font properties of the object, as shown:

```
Label1.Font.Name = "Garamond"
```

To change aspects other than just the name of the font, simply reference those font properties as you did with the *Name* property. When assigning multiple font properties you should use a *With* statement.

```
With Label1.Font
    .Name = "Garamond"
    .Size = 18
    .Bold = True
    .Italic = False
    .Strikethrough = True
    .Underline = False
End With
```

The standard font properties you will be aware of from general computer use are *Name*, *Size*, *Bold*, *Italic*, *Underline*, and *Strikethrough*. However, there are two font properties available at runtime that may require some further explanation as they are not obvious at first.

The *Weight* property of a font refers to how thick or bold to make the characters. There are basically only two possible values for this property: 400 or 700. Selecting a value other than 400 or 700 will result in Visual Basic replacing your value with the closest of the two values. The default value for weight is 400, which is usually for regular or italic settings. When you use bold or bold italic settings, however, you should set the weight to 700. So, the two typical weight settings would appear similar to the following in your code:

```
Label1.Font.Weight = 400
Label1.Font.Weight = 700
```

The *Charset* property of a font refers to the character set to use. There are four possible settings for the *Charset* property, as shown in Table 19.1, but the character set can only be used if the font supports the setting.

**Table 19.1 Possible settings for the Charset *property.***

| *Charset* Value | Description |
| --- | --- |
| 0 | Standard Windows character set |
| 2 | Symbol character set |
| 128 | Double Byte Character Set (DBCS) for Japanese Windows versions |
| 255 | Extended character set (DOS applications) |

An example of setting a Label control to use the symbol character set might look similar to the following:

```
Label1.Font.Charset = 2
```

# Understanding the *FontTransparent* Property

Forms, PictureBoxes, and Printer objects all have a *FontTransparent* property. When the *FontTransparent* property is set to True it allows the background to show through the spaces around characters. When the *FontTransparent* property is set to *False* a solid background color is seen behind the characters.

To see the difference between having the *FontTransparent* property set to *True* or *False*, open a new project in Visual Basic. In the form's *Picture* property load in a picture file from your hard drive. Add the following code to the code window:

```
Private Sub Form_Click()
    Me.FontTransparent = False
    Me.ForeColor = vbBlack
    Print "Hello"
```

```
    Print "FontTransparent is False."
End Sub
```

Run the program and click your mouse on the form a few times. Observe the way the characters have a solid background color behind them. Quit the program and return to the Visual Basic environment. Change the two occurrences of *False* in your code to *True*, as follows:

```
Me.FontTransparent = True
Print "FontTransparent is True."
```

Run the program again and click your mouse on the form a few times. Figure 19.3 shows the difference between having the *FontTransparent* property set to *True* or *False*.

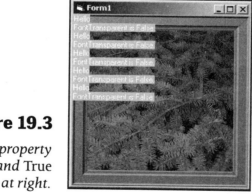 

**Figure 19.3**

FontTransparent *property set to* False *at left and* True *at right.*

The *FontTransparent* property only affects graphics and text that have not yet been drawn, and you can change the *FontTransparent* property at either design time or runtime.

# Handling Unicode Characters and Fonts

Unicode characters are two byte characters which basically take up twice as much space as their ASCII counterparts yet allow an incredibly greater range of possible characters. This makes Unicode fonts ideal for Japanese, Chinese, and other languages that your programs may need to support. By default, Visual Basic does not handle Unicode characters, although there are certain Microsoft controls that you can use which do.

**NOTE:** *Although the following project involving Unicode can be created on systems running Windows 95 or 98, neither of these two operating systems actually support Unicode, and so obtaining Unicode characters to test the program will be difficult without some third-party software.*

You are going to create a program that will compare standard Label controls and TextBox controls with similar controls from the Microsoft Forms 2.0 Object Library. By entering some Unicode characters into both of the TextBox controls, you will learn not only how to work with Unicode characters in your programs but also what would happen when you use controls that do not support Unicode. The result of the Unicode program is shown in Figure 19.4, to give you an idea of what you are trying to accomplish.

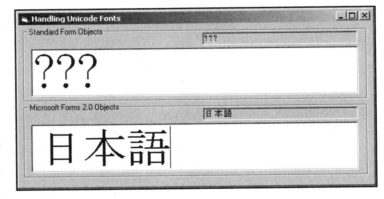

**Figure 19.4**

*The Unicode program in action.*

1. Open a new project in Visual Basic and name the project **Unicode**.

2. Change the form's *Caption* property to **Handling Unicode Fonts**.

3. Add two Frame controls to the form and change the *Caption* property of one to **Standard Form Objects** and the other to **Microsoft Forms 2.0 Objects**. Drag the second Frame control so that it is below the first.

4. Inside the Frame control for the standard object, add a Label control and name it **lblF1**, and then add a TextBox control and name it **txtF1**.

   For both objects, lblF1 and txtF1, change the font to a Unicode font, such as MS Mincho. Make the font size 11 for lblF1 and 48 for txtF1.

5. Next you must add the component Microsoft Forms 2.0 Object Library to your project. From the Project menu select Components. Visual Basic opens the Components dialog box, from which you must select Microsoft Forms 2.0 Object Library by placing a check mark in the component's checkbox. Click your mouse on the OK button.

6. The Microsoft Forms 2.0 Object Library adds 14 new controls to your control panel, including new Label and TextBox controls. Add a new Label control inside the second Frame control and name it **lblF2**. Add a new TextBox control inside the second Frame control and name it **txtF2**.

   For both objects, *lblF2* and *txtF2*, change the font to the same Unicode font that you are using for *txtF1*. Make the font size 11 for *lblF2* and 48 for *txtF2*.

7. You now want to write some code so that whatever text you enter into either of the TextBox controls is duplicated by your program into the companion Label control. Enter the following code in the code window:

```
Option Explicit

Private Sub txtF1_Change()
    lblF1.Caption = txtF1.Text
End Sub

Private Sub txtF2_Change()
    lblF2.Caption = txtF2.Text
End Sub
```

8. Save the project and then run the program. Open the Microsoft Character Map program, which has a different look and options depending on the operating system you are running. Using the Character Map program, as shown in Figure 19.5, enter in some Unicode characters and then copy them and paste them into both *txtF1* and *txtF2*.

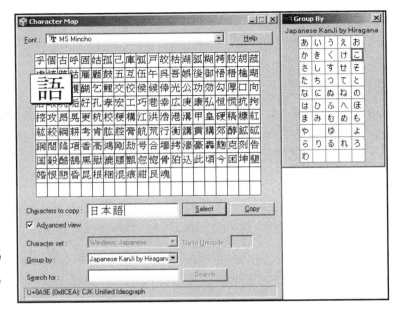

**Figure 19.5**

*Using the Character Map program.*

You will notice that the standard form objects are unable to display the Unicode characters properly and display a question mark symbol to indicate this. The new form objects, however, are able to handle the display of Unicode characters.

# Displaying Multiple Fonts

To display multiple fonts in your programs, you can either make use of different Label controls and set the font to be different for each one or you could make use of a RichTextBox control. You can easily lock a RichTextBox control for display-only purposes by using the *Locked* property or leave it unlocked to provide the user with an input area that allows multiple fonts.

1. Open a new project in Visual Basic and name it **RTBMulti**.

2. Add a RichTextBox control to the form and name it **rtbText**. (In Lesson 8, "Using Text Boxes," you learned how to add a RichTextBox control to your projects.) Add the following code to the code window:

```
Option Explicit

Private Sub Form_Load()
```

```
With rtbText
      .SelFontName = "Garamond"
      .SelFontSize = 48
      .SelBold = True
      .SelColor = vbBlack
      .SelText = "Garamond 48 Bold" & vbCrLf

      .SelFontName = "Arial"
      .SelFontSize = 36
      .SelBold = False
      .SelItalic = True
      .SelColor = vbBlue
      .SelText = "Arial 36 Italic" & vbCrLf

      .SelFontName = "Times New Roman"
      .SelFontSize = 24
      .SelItalic = False
      .SelUnderline = True
      .SelColor = vbRed
      .SelText = "Times New Roman 24 Underline"
   End With
End Sub
```

3. Save the project and run the program.

Your output should look similar to Figure 19.6.

**Figure 19.6**

*Multiple fonts and font styles using a RichTextBox control.*

You can also use a PictureBox control to display multiple fonts. To print text in a PictureBox, you simply use the PictureBox control's *Print* method and follow it with the text you want to display. Any text that has already been drawn in the PictureBox is not affected by you when you change the font properties.

# Displaying Multiple Font Sizes

Although displaying multiple font sizes is very easy in Visual Basic, it is also one of the most commonly seen depictions of fonts and many programs offer this capability to the users.

1. Open a new project in Visual Basic and name it **FontSizes**.

2. Change the form's name to **frmMain** and the *Caption* property to **Font Sizes**.

3. Add a CommandButton control to your form and name it **cmdFont**.

4. Change the *Caption* property of the CommandButton control to **&Font**.

5. Add a CommonDialog control to your form and name it **dlgCmn**. Resize the form so that it is only slightly larger than the CommandButton that you have added.

   Add the following code to the code window:

```
Option Explicit

Private Sub cmdFont_Click()
On Error GoTo err_CANCEL
Dim i As Single
    'let user select a font
    With dlgCmn
        .CancelError = True
        .Flags = cdlCFBoth
        .ShowFont
        frmDisplay.Show
        frmDisplay.Font.Name = .FontName
    End With

    'disable the button until display form closes
```

```
        cmdFont.Enabled = False
        Exit Sub
    err_CANCEL:
    End Sub
```

6. Add a second form to your project and name it **frmDisplay**. Make it a reasonable size and change the *BackColor* property to White.

   Add the following code to the code window:

```
Option Explicit

Private Sub Form_Paint()
Dim i As Single
    'display the font in various sizes
    i = 4
    Do
        Me.Font.Size = I
        Print Me.FontName & "  (" & Me.FontSize & ")"
        i = i * 1.2
    Loop Until i > 64
End Sub

Private Sub Form_Unload(Cancel As Integer)
    frmMain.cmdFont.Enabled = True
End Sub
```

7. Save the project and run the program. Each time you select the Font button, the program presents you with the Font common dialog and then disables itself until you close the font display window. The font display shows you the name of the font and the size, as shown in Figure 19.7.

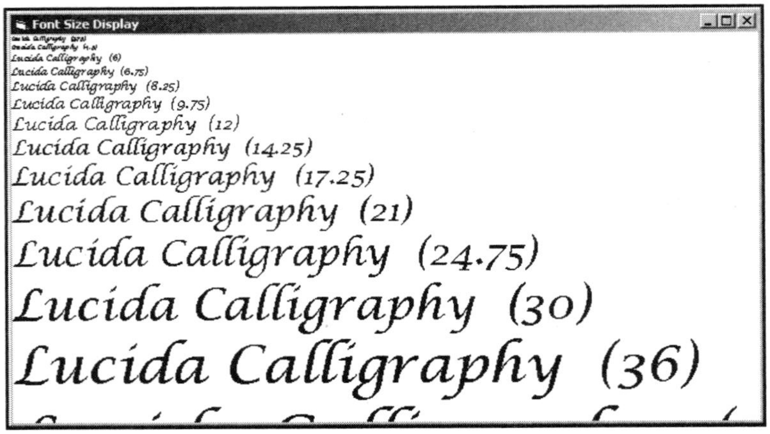

**Figure 19.7**

*The font sizes displayed in a window.*

# What You Must Know

You can preset individual fonts for each control at design time or change fonts at runtime using code. By using Unicode compliant controls it is possible to include support for Unicode fonts in your Visual Basic applications, giving you the capability to handle foreign language alphabets. Within your programs, you can display multiple fonts in a variety of ways and scale fonts to different sizes. In Lesson 20, "Using Menus," you will learn how to incorporate menus into your own Visual Basic programs, as well as how to customize menus at both design time and runtime. Before you continue with Lesson 20, however, make sure you understand the following key concepts:

◆ Sans-serif fonts are usually used for titles, headings, and labels while serif fonts loan themselves more to sentences and paragraphs where more reading is required.

◆ Each control that has a *Font* property can be preset at design time by using the browse button and selecting a font from the Font dialog.

◆ Fonts are changed through code by accessing an object's Font attributes, such as Name, Size, Bold, etc.

◆ Setting the *FontTransparent* property determines whether a solid background will be displayed behind each character or if the background will show through the gaps between text characters.

◆ By using the Microsoft Forms 2.0 Object Library controls or other Unicode-compliant controls, Unicode fonts can be utilized in your Visual Basic programs for powerful language capabilities.

◆ You can display multiple fonts in your programs by using different Label or TextBox controls or making use of the multifont capabilities of RichTextBox and PictureBox controls.

◆ A common requirement is to be able to size fonts and display a font that has been scaled incrementally.

# Lesson 20

---

# Using Menus

E arlier in this book, you learned how to use such features as CommandButton and ComboBox controls to give the user a selection to choose options from. In this lesson, you will learn another method of giving the user a selection to choose from called menus, as well as how to add menus to your programs and also how to easily manipulate those menus. By the time you finish this lesson, you will understand the following key concepts:

◆ To add a menu to your Visual Basic program you must first select the Menu Editor from the Tools menu.

◆ You use the Menu Editor to create menus in your Visual Basic programs and also to modify existing menus.

◆ To change the order of menu items you simply click your mouse on the up and down arrow buttons in the Menu Editor after selecting the menu item to move.

◆ You can insert, enable, disable, and delete menu items easily by using the appropriate buttons on the Menu Editor.

◆ Menu items that are toggled on and off should have an indication of status through use of a check mark.

◆ The only event handled by the menu object is the *Click()* event, in which you place any code that you want to run when the user selects that particular menu item.

◆ Menu items can have both shortcut keys and access keys assigned to them making it convenient for users to quickly utilize common menu item functions.

◆ Up to four levels of submenus are permissible in your Visual Basic programs and are created in the Menu Editor by increasing the indent of menu items.

◆ Pop-up menus can be shown either in the current location of the mouse or at a location that you specify, and only one pop-up menu can be displayed at a time.

# Introducing Menus

Many programs make use of menus because they are an efficient way to offer a lot of functionality without having to compromise on valuable display space. Imagine five menus each with ten items and the amount of space that they take up. Now imagine if you had to use a CommandButton control for each and every one of those same items! The amount of space that the buttons would require would be quite significant and definitely have a choking impact on the user interface.

As a direct result of so many programs using menus, most users know how to use menus and feel instantly comfortable and at ease when navigating with them. Utilizing features that make your program's user interface appealing to users is a significant point when designing any program.

# Opening the Menu Editor

To add a menu to your Visual Basic programs you must first click your mouse on the Tools menu Menu Editor option, as shown in Figure 20.1.

**Figure 20.1**

*Displaying the Menu Editor.*

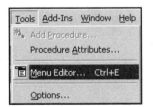

Visual Basic will display the Menu Editor, as shown in Figure 20.2.

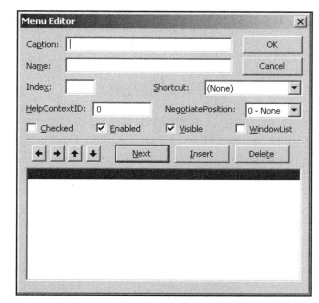

**Figure 20.2**

*The Menu Editor with default settings.*

The Menu Editor is the key to creating menus in your Visual Basic programs. You also use the Menu Editor to edit existing menus and modify the appearance or behavior of menus within your programs. The Menu Editor contains a number of text boxes, checkboxes, buttons, and other various options that you must learn properly to be able to produce professional menus in your programs.

# Selecting Menu Names and Captions

The two most significant fields in the Menu Editor are the Caption and Name text boxes.

The Caption field is the actual string or text that the user will see in the final program and can be for menu titles or menu items. The Caption field does not necessarily have to be unique, although usually it is clearer and more practical to name it uniquely.

The Name field is the tag or label by which you reference a menu or menu item within your program code. The Name field must be unique. By convention, menus in Visual Basic always begin with the prefix *mnu* followed by the name of the menu title then the menu item. For example, the item Save, which is under the File menu, would have the name *mnuFileSave,* and you or anyone else reading your code would be able to immediately tell what menu or menu item the code is referring to.

# Creating Menu Titles and Menu Items

To create new menu and menu items in your program:

1. Open a new project in Visual Basic and name the project **Menus**.

2. Change the form's *Caption* property to **Menus**. Open the Menu Editor by selecting the Tools menu Menu Editor option. In the Caption field enter **Color** and in the Name field enter **mnuColor**. *Color* is now a menu title.

   You will see the menu caption appear in the Menu Editor's list box. The Menu Editor's list box lists all menu titles, menu items, submenu titles, and submenu items.

3. You must now add some menu items to place beneath your Color menu. Click your mouse on the Menu Editor's Next button. Visual Basic moves the list box's highlight bar to the next line beneath *Color* and clears the entries in the Caption and Name fields for you.

4. In the Caption field, enter **Blue** and in the Name field enter **mnuColorBlue**. You will notice in the Menu Editor's list box that the menu caption *Blue* is directly below the menu caption *Color*. At this stage you actually have two menu titles! With the menu caption *Blue* highlighted, click your mouse once on the right arrow button, as shown in Figure 20.3.

### Figure 20.3

*Creating a menu item by using the right arrow button.*

Visual Basic will change the menu caption *Blue* from a menu title into a menu item. You can see the difference between a menu title and a menu item in the Menu Editor's list box by the four dots that precede all menu items.

 **Reversing Menu Item Promotion**

*If you accidentally click your mouse on the right arrow button and turn a menu title into a menu item, you can easily reverse the process by clicking your mouse on the left arrow button.*

5. In the same manner, create four more menu items using Table 20.1 as a guideline.

*Table 20.1 Additional menu items.*

| Caption | Name |
| --- | --- |
| Red | *mnuColorRed* |
| Green | *mnuColorGreen* |
| Yellow | *mnuColorYellow* |
| Magenta | *mnuColorMagenta* |

6. Save the project and run the program. Click your mouse on the Color menu and see if all the menu items appear, as shown in Figure 20.4.

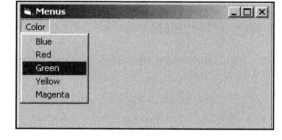

**Figure 20.4**

*The Color menu in the* Menus *example program.*

# Changing the Order of Menu Items

Often in Visual Basic programming, as with life, people do not always get something perfect the first time they do it. Changing the order of menu items seems to be a common occurrence, due to changes in a program, additional features, aesthetic requirements, or any number of other reasons. Thankfully, changing the order of menu items is a very easy thing to do in Visual Basic.

1. Open up the *Menus* project if it is not already open.

2. Select the Tools menu Menu Editor option. Notice that the order of the menu items beneath the Color menu are not in alphabetical order.

3. Click your mouse on the Green menu item in the Menu Editor's list box. Visual Basic highlights the Green menu item to show that it is selected. To change the position of this menu item, simply click your mouse on the up arrow once, and Visual Basic will move the Green

menu item up one position so that it is now between the *Blue* and *Red* menu items, as shown in Figure 20.5.

**Figure 20.5**

*Using the up arrow button to move the Green menu item.*

4. Using the up arrow button and the down arrow button, change the order of the menu items so that they are all in alphabetical order.

# Creating Multiple Menus

In the real world, most programs have more than one menu. In Visual Basic, creating multiple menus is incredibly easy, and you have actually already created multiple menus when you were first creating menu items but had not yet learned about the right arrow button.

1. Open the Menus project if it is not already open and select the Tools menu Menu Editor option.

2. Click your mouse on the space beneath the menu item Yellow. Add a new menu with the Caption **Shape** and the Name **mnuShape**. Table 20.2 shows the list of menu items to add to the Shape menu, and Figure 20.6 shows the Menu Editor after completing the addition of the second menu.

*Table 20.2 Menu items to add to the Shape menu.*

| Caption | Name |
| --- | --- |
| Circle | *mnuShapeCircle* |
| Oval | *mnuShapeOval* |
| Rectangle | *mnuShapeRectangle* |
| Square | *mnuShapeSquare* |

**Figure 20.6**

*The Menu Editor after adding a second menu.*

3. Save the *Menus* project and run the program. Try clicking your mouse on both of your menus separately and selecting menu items.

# Inserting Separator Bars in Your Menus

Often you will notice that programs have clearly made logical groups of some menu items by clustering them together and then placing a separator bar between them and any other menu items that are in the same menu. The reason for this behavior is to provide the users with an optimal user interface by increasing clarity of related options and decreasing the time taken to locate a menu item, thereby making users feel immediately more comfortable with the program.

To insert separator bars in your own menus, simply add a menu item in the position where the separator bar is to go and in the Caption field enter a hyphen (-). Only menu items, not menu titles, can be separator bars. Menu bars cannot be disabled, checked, have shortcut keys assigned, or submenus attached to them.

1. Open the *Menus* project if it is not already open and select the Tools menu Menu Editor option.

2. Insert a separator bar at the end of the Shape menu, and then add two more menu items with the Captions **Rounded Rectangle** and **Rounded Square**. Assign the Names as **mnuShape RndRect** and **mnuShapeRndSquare**, respectively.

3. Save the *Menus* project and run the program. Clicking your mouse on the Shape menu should now bring up a menu that contains a separator bar, as shown in Figure 20.7.

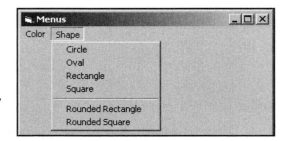

**Figure 20.7**

*A separator bar in a menu.*

 **Viewing Menus at Design Time**

*Although, you may find it straightforward to simply compile your Visual Basic program and view the result of this minor menu change or that minor menu tweak, it can become rather tedious as the program gets bigger and takes longer to compile. At design time you can simply click on the menu titles on each form to see the menus below. Do not click on the menu items or Visual Basic will assume that you are trying to write code for the menu item, which you will learn more about later in this lesson.*

# Inserting, Disabling, and Deleting Menu Items

These three often-used routines are easily handled in Visual Basic. To try all three features, you will insert a menu item into the middle of an already existing menu, then disable the menu item so that it is grayed out and the user is unable to select it, and then, finally, delete the menu item. The menu item that you will add you should name *Doomed* and should insert it in the Color menu above the Magenta menu item.

To insert a menu item into an existing menu, click your mouse on the menu item above which you want to insert, in your case the Magenta menu item. Within the Menu Editor, click your mouse on the Insert button. Visual Basic inserts a new menu item in the place where the Magenta menu item was. Enter *Doomed* for the new menu item's Caption and *mnuColorDoomed* for its Name. Save and run your program, checking to see if the new item has been inserted properly.

To disable a menu item, you must click your mouse on the menu item and then uncheck the Enabled checkbox. Alternatively, you can edit the menu item in code. Add the following line to the *Form_Load()* event:

```
mnuColorDoomed.Enabled = False
```

Save the *Menus* project and run the program, checking to see if the new item has been disabled.

To delete a menu item, click your mouse on the menu item that you want to delete within the Menu Editor, and then click your mouse on the Delete button. Visual Basic will delete the menu item from the menu. Try deleting the *Doomed* menu item in this manner. Figure 20.8 shows the different stages of the *Doomed* menu item that you have just seen.

**Figure 20.8**

*Inserting, disabling, and finally deleting the* Doomed *menu item.*

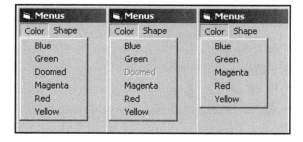

# Assigning Code to Menu Items

You should now have a good grasp of setting up menus; however, you must learn how to make your menu items do something when a user clicks his mouse on them. To make your menu items do something when a user clicks his mouse on them, you must make use of the *Click()* event that belongs to each menu item. Menu items only have one event to associate with, so event handling for menu items is very straightforward.

1. Open the *Menus* project if it is not already open.

2. Add a Shape control to the form and name it **shpAny**.

3. Change the *FillStyle* property of *shpAny* to **0—Solid** in the Properties section.

4. Click your mouse on the *Circle* command on the Shape menu. Visual Basic opens the code window and automatically writes the event wrapper code for you. Add a command to change the Shape control, **shpAny**, into a circle so that the *Click()* event looks similar to the following:

```
Private Sub mnuShapeCircle_Click()
    shpAny.Shape = vbShapeCircle
End Sub
```

5. Now click your mouse on the Color menu Blue option. Visual Basic once again writes the *Click( )* event wrapper code for you. Add a command to change the Shape control's *FillColor* property to Blue so that the event code looks similar to the following:

```
Private Sub mnuColorBlue_Click()
    shpAny.FillColor = vbBlue
End Sub
```

6. Assign code to all of the remaining Shape menu and Color menu items appropriately. The *Menus* program is on the companion Web site that comes with this book if you want to either reference the full code or copy and paste it into your own program. To locate this Web site, go to www.prima-tech.com/books/book/5250/945/.

7. Save the *Menus* project and run the program, checking to see if the menu options all work as you expect. The shape should change as you select different menu items from the Shape menu, and the color of the shape should change as you select different menu items from the Color menu.

# Using the Keyboard with Menus

You can also create keyboard shortcuts and access keys for your menu titles and menu items through the Menu Editor. You have already seen how to assign an access key in CommandButton controls and other objects simply by placing an ampersand (&) in front of the letter you want to use with the Alt key. Menus are no different to other Visual Basic objects in this respect, and in the Menu Editor you simply place an ampersand in the *Caption* property to create an access key.

In the *Menus* program, open the Menu Editor and create an access key for the Color menu title by placing an ampersand before the letter C in the *Caption* property, so that the *Caption* is now *&Color*. Add an access key for the *Green* menu item by changing the *Caption* property to *&Green*.

Shortcut keys are usually more direct than access keys, and you use shortcut keys only for very common functions that a user is most likely to select often. To assign a shortcut key to a menu item you must use the Menu Editor. Select the menu item first, and then use the Shortcut combo box to select the shortcut key to use. When you assign a shortcut key to a menu item, Visual Basic will automatically indicate this beside the menu item.

In the Menu Editor, assign the keys F1 to F5 to the menu items under the Color menu. Notice that you can assign both an access key and a shortcut key to the same menu item simultaneously, as in the case of the Green menu item. Save the *Menus* project and run the program, trying out the new keyboard shortcuts, as shown in Figure 20.9.

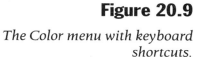

**Figure 20.9**

*The Color menu with keyboard shortcuts.*

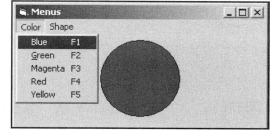

# Using Check Marks in Menus

If you ever have menu items that the user can toggle on or off, it adds greatly to the user interface of your program to indicate the current state to the user using a check mark. You can also use check marks to indicate the current selection out of a group of menu items. Visual Basic allows you to easily add check marks to menu items by setting the menu item's *Checked* property to *True* or *False* in your code or by using the Menu Editor and clicking your mouse on the Checked checkbox.

To indicate the current color of the shape in your *Menus* project, add a line to each of the menu items under the Color menu to check that item, similar to the following:

```
mnuColorBlue.Checked = True
```

You can see a problem with this logic, however, because the code is not unchecking the menu item that was previously checked. To remedy the situation, add the following subroutine to your code:

```
Private Sub UncheckAllColors()
    mnuColorBlue.Checked = False
    mnuColorGreen.Checked = False
    mnuColorMagenta.Checked = False
    mnuColorRed.Checked = False
    mnuColorYellow.Checked = False
End Sub
```

In each *Click()* event for the *Color* menu items, add a call to your new subroutine immediately before the line that checks the menu item, so that it looks similar to the following:

```
Private Sub mnuColorBlue_Click()
    shpAny.FillColor = vbBlue
    UncheckAllColors
    mnuColorBlue.Checked = True
End Sub
```

Save the *Menus* project and run the program. As you change the color of the shape you should notice a check mark appear next to the current color's menu item.

# Creating Submenus

To create submenus and submenu items in your programs, simply increase the indent amount of any menu item. You use an ellipsis (…) after any menu item that leads to a dialog box, such as the *Save As…* menu item in many programs, but not necessarily after a submenu title because Visual Basic will supply a small arrow to indicate that there is a further submenu. You can have up to four levels of submenus branching off any menu, which should be ample for any program. Use submenus sparingly to avoid causing user frustration, as there are many users who have difficulty navigating multiple levels of submenus.

# Dynamically Changing Menus at Runtime

You have already seen how to dynamically change menus at runtime using the menu item's *Checked* property. You can do a lot more with menu items by similarly modifying their other properties. For instance, you can dynamically gray out menu items that are not applicable at a particular time by setting the *Enabled* property to *False*. Perhaps as an alternative to toggling a check mark on or off you could change the *Caption* property dynamically instead. Although this is not often done, you may have a client that insists on such functionality rather than relying on the check mark.

Making menus invisible and visible is a simple way to change menus at runtime. For instance, you may have two different modes that your program operates in, with each mode having the same menu titles but different menu options. You can simply create all of the menus at design time and set the menus that you want to be initially hidden to invisible by unchecking the Visible check box in the Menu Editor or setting the menu title's *Visible* property to *False* in the *Form_Load()* event, similar to the following code:

```
Private Sub Form_Load()
    mnuShape.Visible = False
End Sub
```

# Using Pop-Up Menus

Although static menus are very useful, there are circumstances where a program benefits from providing a menu either right where the user's current mouse position is or in a location other than across the top of the form. Such menus are known as pop-up menus but are sometimes referred to as floating menus, shortcut menus, or context menus. In Visual Basic you can also create pop-up menus, although you can only have one pop-up menu at a time.

To create a pop-up menu you must use the *PopupMenu* method and pass it the name of the menu that you want to display. The usual method in Windows is to produce a pop-up menu when the user clicks the right button of her mouse in a specific region. You can use the *PopupMenu* method in a variety of places in your code, but the most common places would be in the *MouseUp* events of forms or Image controls.

Add the following code to the *Menus* program in the code window and add an Image control so that it is directly over the Shape control:

```
Private Sub Image1_MouseUp(Button As Integer, Shift As Integer, X As Single,_
Y As Single)
    If Button = vbRightButton Then
        PopupMenu mnuShape
    End If
End Sub
```

Right-clicking on the shape will now produce the Shape menu, from which you can select another shape. You can also pass the *PopupMenu* method a number of flags to further customize the pop-up location and behavior, as shown in Table 20.3.

*Table 20.3 PopupMenu method flags for customization.*

| Constant | Type | Description |
|---|---|---|
| *vbPopupMenuLeftAlign* | Location | Uses x as the coordinate for the left of the menu. |
| *vbPopupMenuCenterAlign* | Location | Centers the menu at x. |
| *vbPopupMenuRightAlign* | Location | Uses x as the coordinate for the right of the menu. |
| *vbPopupMenuLeftButton* | Behavior | Selects menu items with the left mouse button. |
| *vbPopupMenuRightButton* | Behavior | Selects menu items with either left or right mouse buttons. |

To make one of the menu items bold in the pop-up menu, simply give the name of the menu item as the final argument to the *PopupMenu* method. For a more complex pop-up menu, replace the line

```
PopupMenu mnuShape
```

with

```
PopupMenu mnuShape, vbPopupMenuRightAlign, Me.Width, _
20, mnuShapeSquare
```

Save the *Menus* project and run the program. Right-clicking your mouse on the shape should bring up a pop-up menu similar to the one shown in Figure 20.10.

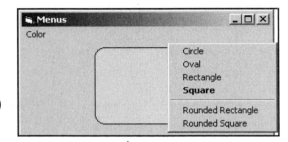

**Figure 20.10**

*Producing a pop-up menu.*

 **Advanced Menu Techniques**

Although, you have learned almost all of the features of menus in Visual Basic, there are two further advanced techniques that you may want to look into yourself. One technique is the use of control arrays with menus, whereby a single point of reference together with an index number can be used to loop through all the menu items in a menu. You will learn more about control arrays in Lesson 27, "Using Arrays and Collections."

The other technique involving menus is only useful if you are creating Multiple Document Interface (MDI) programs and wish to do menu negotiations for positioning when placing menus on MDI child forms. The Menu Editor contains a combo box for the NegotiatePosition property, but you have to also set your MDI child form's NegotiateMenus property to True. This is an advanced technique that you can read more on if you require.

# What You Must Know

The Menu Editor is the tool to use in Visual Basic for both creating new menus and modifying existing menus. You can create multiple menu titles, menu items, submenu titles, and submenu items all by altering the indentation of an item in the Menu Editor's list box. By manipulating a menu's properties at runtime you can enable or disable menu items, place a check mark beside menu items, or hide menus via the *Visible* property. In Lesson 21, "Using StatusBars, ProgressBars, and Toolbars," you will look further into user interface design and providing visual feedback in your own programs. Before you continue with Lesson 21, however, make sure you understand the following key concepts:

◆ To work with menus in your Visual Basic programs, the first thing you must do is select the Tools menu Menu Editor option.

◆ The Menu Editor is used to create new menus or modify existing menus in your Visual Basic programs.

◆ You can change the order of existing menu items by selecting the item you want to move and using the up and down arrows within the Menu Editor.

◆ The Menu Editor provides buttons to insert, enable or disable, and delete menu items easily.

◆ You can use a check mark to indicate the status of a particular menu item, which is especially useful for menu items that can be toggled or that are part of a selection of related menu items.

◆ Menu items only handle one event, the *Click()* event, in which you can place any code that must be executed when that menu item is selected by the user.

◆ Accessing menu items through the keyboard is made possible through the use of access keys and shortcut keys.

◆ In Visual Basic, submenus can be implemented up to four levels deep and are created in the Menu Editor by increasing the indent of menu items.

◆ Through use of the *PopupMenu* method you can easily have pop-up menus in your programs that you can customize to an extent for both location and behavior.

# Lesson 21

---

# Using StatusBars, ProgressBars, and Toolbars

In Lesson 20, "Using Menus," you learned about providing the user with menus and using a check mark to give the user some indication of a menu item's current state. In this lesson, you will take that concept further by learning about the use of other controls, such as the StatusBar control and ProgressBar control, whose sole purpose is to provide some form of status indication or feedback to the user and the Toolbar control, which you use to give the user a quick method of getting to common features. By the time you finish this lesson, you will understand the following key concepts:

◆ To use the StatusBar, ProgressBar, or Toolbar controls you must add the component Microsoft Windows Common Controls to which all three controls belong.

◆ Each StatusBar control can contain up to 16 Panel objects, each of which has independent settings for alignment, size, bevel state, picture, style, and text.

◆ Setting a Panel object's *Style* property allows you to easily add the functionality of displaying the status of certain keys, time, and date in your StatusBar control.

◆ A StatusBar can be configured at design time using the Property Pages dialog or the standard Properties section. At runtime, the StatusBar control can be handled by code.

◆ By setting the StatusBar's *SimpleText* and *Style* properties you can easily use the StatusBar control to convey a message to the user concerning the program's current state or intention.

◆ You can use a ProgressBar control to indicate to the user the status of a lengthy process, such as a loop, where the minimum and maximum values are known.

◆ The height of a ProgressBar control affects the accuracy of the graphical display when smooth scrolling is not in use.

◆ ProgressBar controls can be aligned to the top, bottom, left, and right edges of a form and can have a vertical or horizontal orientation.

◆ Toolbar controls contain Button objects on which you can display text and images or certain other controls under special circumstances.

◆ A toolbar can be configured at design time using the Property Pages dialog or the standard Properties section. At runtime, the Toolbar control can be handled by code.

◆ Use a toolbar's *ButtonClick()* event in combination with a *Select* structure to respond to the individual toolbar buttons that the user clicks her mouse on.

◆ The styles available to a Toolbar Button object can offer a broader variety and allow greater customization of a toolbar.

◆ Toolbar controls can be aligned to the top, bottom, left, or right edges of a form or to none of a form's edges and will automatically adjust to a vertical or horizontal orientation depending on alignment.

# Adding the Common Controls Component

The StatusBar, ProgressBar, and Toolbar controls are all part of the Windows Common Controls Component. You must add the component *Microsoft Windows Common Controls 6.0* using the Project menu Components option, as you have already learned earlier in this book.

# Using the StatusBar Control

The StatusBar control is a very good method of supplying your programs with a standard and unobtrusive interface for providing small pieces of useful data to the user. You have probably seen status bars in many other Windows programs, such as Internet Explorer or Microsoft Word. Figure 21.1 shows a status bar from a common Windows Explorer session, which not only does practically every user of Windows see but is also a good example of status bar usage.

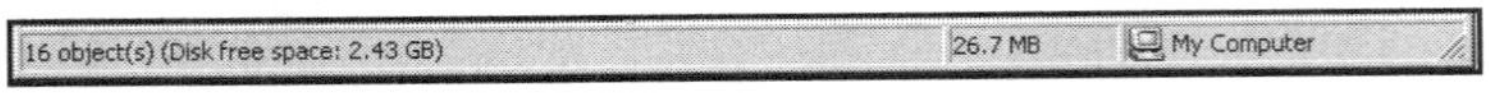

**Figure 21.1**

*A status bar.*

16 object(s) (Disk free space: 2.43 GB)          26.7 MB     My Computer

To add a StatusBar object to your form you must click your mouse on the StatusBar control icon in the control panel, as shown in Figure 21.2, and then drag the size of the StatusBar on your form.

**Figure 21.2**

*The StatusBar control icon.*

The StatusBar control can contain up to 16 Panel objects, each of which can be a different width and can contain different information. The Panel objects are really the heart of the StatusBar control and are highly customizable yet easy to configure. You can configure a Panel object at both design time and runtime. To configure a Panel object at design time, you must right-click your mouse on the StatusBar control and select Properties from the pop-up menu that appears. Visual Basic will display the Property Pages dialog, which contains a Panels tab for configuring all the Panels in a StatusBar control at design time, as shown in Figure 21.3.

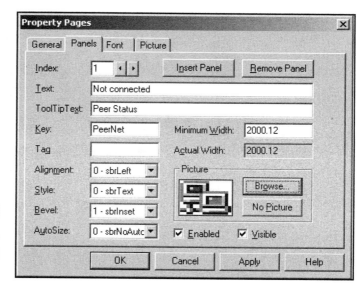

**Figure 21.3**

*The Property Pages dialog for setting the StatusBar control at design time.*

Using the Panels tab of the Property Pages dialog, you can set each panel with individual settings.

To set the *Picture* property simply click your mouse on the Browse button to select an image to use or the No Picture button if you want the panel to contain only text.

The *Alignment* property can be set to *sbrLeft*, *sbrRight*, or *sbrCenter* and refers to the alignment of the text within an individual panel. Notice that if *sbrRight* is set, the picture positions itself to the far right of the panel and on the right of the actual text. Figure 21.4 shows the result of setting the *Alignment* property.

### Figure 21.4

*The result of setting the* Alignment *property.*

The *Bevel* property can be set to *sbrNoBevel*, *sbrInset*, or *sbrRaised* and refers to the border of an individual panel. The default setting is *sbrInset*, which gives the appearance of being sunken. Clever use of the *Bevel* property can enhance the user interface of a program so long as you are consistent in your usage. Figure 21.5 shows the result of setting the *Bevel* property.

### Figure 21.5

*The result of setting the* Bevel *property.*

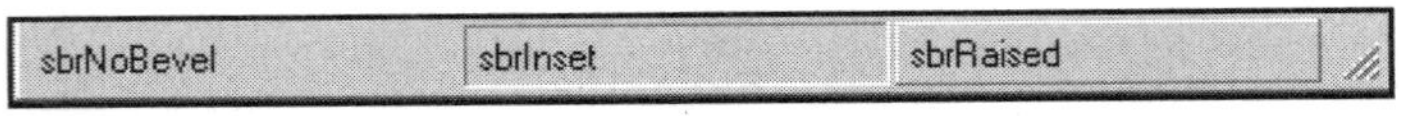

The *AutoSize* property can be set to *sbrNoAutoSize*, *sbrSpring*, or *sbrContents* and refers to the behavior of the individual panel with regard to its width. The default setting is *sbrNoAutoSize*, which does not change the width. The *sbrSpring* constant will make use of empty space by springing in or out depending on the need, while the *sbrContents* constant will make the width just large enough to hold the panel's contents. Figure 21.6 shows a status bar with three panels all set to *sbrNoAutoSize*, and Figure 21.7 shows the same status bar after setting the last two panels to *sbrSpring* and *sbrContents*, respectively.

### Figure 21.6

*A status bar with three panels all set to* sbrNoAutoSize.

### Figure 21.7

*The same status bar after setting the* AutoSize *properties.*

# Setting the Style of Panels

If you want to show the state of certain keys, the time, or the date in the StatusBar control, Visual Basic makes it very easy for you by letting you set the *Style* property of each Panel object to do this and also handles all the code for you. For the state of certain keys, the resulting text is gray if the key is not on and black otherwise. One special style, *sbrKana*, is only of use for Japanese systems and indicates if the Kana lock is on. Table 21.1 shows the available constants that the Panel object's *Style* property can be set to.

*Table 21.1 The Style constants for the Panel object.*

| Style Constant | Description |
|---|---|
| sbrText | (Default) Displays the *Text* property. |
| sbrCaps | Displays the status of the Caps Lock key. |
| sbrNum | Displays the status of the Num Lock key. |
| sbrIns | Displays the status of the Insert key. |
| sbrScrl | Displays the status of the Scroll Lock key. |
| sbrTime | Displays the system time. |
| sbrDate | Displays the system date. |
| sbrKana | Displays the status of the (Japanese) Kana lock. |

Figure 21.8 depicts the various styles available for the Panel object.

## Figure 21.8

*The various Style settings in action.*

 **Adding Panels at Runtime**

*To add a Panel object at runtime you must declare a variable of type Panel and then use the Set command to assign it to the StatusBar control. So, if you had a StatusBar control in your program which you call sbrMain, you would add a Panel as follows:*

```
Dim pnlX As Panel
Set pnlX = sbrMain.Panels.Add
```

# Setting Toolbar Button Styles

One of the real secrets to using toolbars well is to make use of Toolbar Button styles. You can assign each individual button a different style by using one of the various style constants, as shown in Table 21.2.

*Table 21.2 Toolbar Button object style constants.*

| Style Constant | Definition |
| --- | --- |
| *tbrDefault* | (Default) A standard pushbutton that pops back out when the mouse button is released. |
| *tbrCheck* | A button will toggle between being checked and unchecked on each successive mouse click. |
| *tbrButtonGroup* | A button, along with other buttons in the group, can only remain pressed until one of the other buttons in the group is pressed. |
| *tbrSeparator* | A button becomes an 8 pixel separator between adjacent buttons. |
| *tbrPlaceholder* | A button can be sized and becomes a placeholder for another type of control to be added to the toolbar. |
| *tbrDropDown* | A button becomes a drop-down for MenuButton objects. |

Figure 21.19 shows all of these styles, although the features to note are that the Stop, Change, and Go buttons are all part of a *tbrButtonGroup*, that there is a ComboBox control sitting on a *tbrPlaceholder* button, and that the drop-down menu is created within the Toolbar Property Pages dialog.

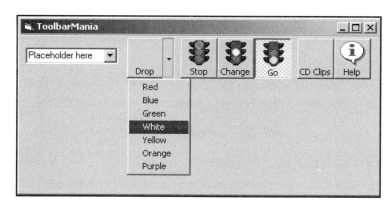

**Figure 21.19**

*All of the Toolbar Button object styles in action.*

# Changing Toolbars at Runtime

You can change toolbars at runtime by editing the toolbars' properties. You can change whether the Button text is shown on the bottom or on the right by setting the *TextAlignment* property. By using a pop-up menu with your toolbar you can easily offer alignment options or even customization options to users. You can set a toolbar to align to the top, bottom, left, or right edges of a form or not to align to any of the form's edges by setting the *Alignment* property, as shown:

```
tbrA.Align = vbAlignLeft
```

Besides offering your users customization features, other realistic reasons to change the toolbar at runtime might be to gray out buttons whose features cannot currently be used, to change the icon for buttons for different modes or perhaps to modify the toolbar due to an error.

A more thorough example of toolbar alignment and the Visual Basic code to handle it from a pop-up menu is given at www.prima-tech.com/books/book/5250/945/ and shown in Figure 21.20.

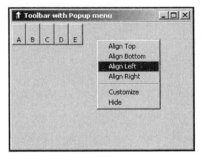 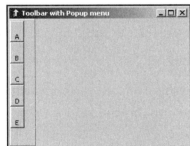

**Figure 21.20**

*Changing alignment at runtime—before and after.*

The Customize option requires two key changes. First, you must set the *AllowCustomization* property to *True*, and secondly, you must call the Toolbar's *Customize* method, as shown:

```
tbrA.AllowCustomize = True
tbrA.Customize
```

The *Customize* method will display a dialog to the user for customizing the toolbar at runtime.

# What You Must Know

You can supply your programs with a standard and unobtrusive interface for providing small pieces of useful data to the user by using a StatusBar control. When your programs do any lengthy operations, use a ProgressBar control to inform the users so that they have some indication of what stage the operation is up to. Use a Toolbar control to offer users a comfortable and visually attractive method to perform common tasks without using up too much space. In Lesson 22, "Using Sliders and Scrollbars," you will learn how to either display or receive measurements and values using graphical means and how to display only a portion of a larger object using scrollbars. Before you continue with Lesson 22, however, make sure you understand the following key concepts:

◆ The StatusBar, ProgressBar, and Toolbar controls all belong to the component Microsoft Windows Common Controls, which you must add to use any of the three controls.

◆ You can have up to 16 Panel objects in each StatusBar control, with each Panel having independent settings for alignment, size, bevel state, picture, style, and text.

◆ You can display the status of certain keys, time, or date in your StatusBar control by setting a Panel object's *Style* property.

◆ A StatusBar can be configured at runtime through code and at design time using the Property Pages dialog or the standard Properties section.

◆ You can set the StatusBar's *SimpleText* and *Style* properties to convey a message to the user concerning the program's current state or intention.

◆ A ProgressBar control is used to indicate to the user the status of a lengthy process for which the minimum and maximum values are known.

◆ The accuracy of a ProgressBar control's graphical display is directly related to its *Height* property when smooth scrolling is not in use.

◆ You can align ProgressBar controls to the top, bottom, left, and right edges of a form, where they can have a vertical or horizontal orientation.

◆ You can display text and images on Button objects which are contained in Toolbar controls.

◆ A toolbar can be configured at runtime through code or at design time using the Property Pages dialog or the standard Properties section.

◆ You can use the *ButtonClick( )* event of a Toolbar control in combination with a *Select* structure to respond to mouse clicks on Button objects.

◆ The *Button* object's *Style* property offers a broad variety of customization options for use within a toolbar.

◆ You can align a Toolbar control to the top, bottom, left, or right edges of a form or to none of a form's edges and the toolbar will automatically adjust to a vertical or horizontal orientation depending on alignment.

# Lesson 22

# Using Sliders and Scrollbars

In Lesson 21, "Using StatusBars, ProgressBars, and Toolbars," you learned how to use some of the controls from the Microsoft Windows Common Controls component. In this lesson, you will learn how to use another control from this component—the Slider control—to display or receive measurements and values using graphical means. You will also learn how to display only a portion of a larger object using scrollbars. By the time you finish this lesson, you will understand the following key concepts:

◆ There are two standard scrollbar controls in Visual Basic, known as HScrollBar and VScroll-Bar, with the only difference between the two being orientation.

◆ Scrollbars contain a *Value* property, which indicates the current value and position of a scroll-bar's thumb.

◆ You can set a minimum and maximum value for a scrollbar, thereby setting a valid range from which the user may select.

◆ The movement of a scrollbar's thumb is determined by the *SmallChange* and *LargeChange* properties, which can be set at both design time and runtime.

◆ The two key events that Visual Basic programmers use in conjunction with scrollbars are the *Change()* event and the *Scroll()* event.

◆ FlatScrollBar controls have all of the properties of the HScrollBar and VScrollBar controls plus additional properties and features.

◆ A FlatScrollBar has an *Orientation* property to select horizontal or vertical orientation without the need for two controls.

◆ You can disable either end of a FlatScrollBar control by using the *Arrows* property for an improved user interface when the thumb of the scrollbar is at the limit of the range.

◆ A FlatScrollBar can have one of three possible appearances and can be changed at runtime using the *Appearance* property.

◆ Slider controls are similar to scrollbars except that they have an *Orientation* property that allows them to display in either a vertical or horizontal position.

◆ You can easily customize the frequency of ticks and the style of ticks for a Slider control by setting the *TickFrequency* and *TickStyle* properties.

◆ Slider controls allow a user to select an entire range of values as well as having the ordinary option of selecting a single value from within a given range.

# Understanding Scrollbars

Visual Basic makes a lot of controls very easy to use by having them automatically contain scrollbars that appear when necessary, such as when the user enters more text into a TextBox control than the control can visually display at any one moment. However, not all controls have such functionality built in, and to cater for these types of controls Visual Basic contains two standard scrollbar controls known as HScrollBar and VScrollBar. Figure 22.1 shows the HScrollBar and VScrollBar control icons.

### Figure 22.1

*The HScrollBar and VScrollBar control icons.*

Scrollbars are made up of different components, some of which you can individually control. The two most significant parts of a scrollbar are the thumb and arrows, as shown in Figure 22.2 and which you will see reference to throughout this lesson.

### Figure 22.2

*Scrollbar components.*

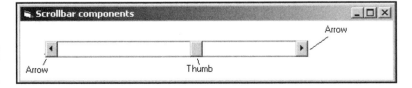

HScrollBar and VScrollBar are identical in the properties that each contains and the method of assigning values to those properties. The difference between the two controls is simply that HScrollBar has a horizontal orientation and VScrollBar has a vertical one.

The *Value* property of a scrollbar indicates the position of the thumb on the scrollbar. As the user moves the thumb of a scrollbar, Visual Basic updates the *Value* property.

With both scrollbars you must set a minimum and maximum value to indicate clearly the range that the scrollbar covers. You use the *Min* and *Max* properties to set the minimum and maximum values. For instance, if a picture was 400 pixels in height and you could only display 100 pixels at any given moment, you would set the *Max* property of the VScrollBar control to 300 pixels and the *Min* property to 1 pixel. As the user changes the *Value* property of the scrollbar either by clicking her mouse on the arrows or scrolling the thumb, your program need only display the portion of the picture between the current *Value* property and 99 pixels more than that. To change the minimum and maximum values at runtime, you would use code similar to the following:

```
vsbBig.Max = 299
vsbBig.Min = 1
```

The HScrollBar and VScrollBar controls have a *SmallChange* property and a *LargeChange* property. *SmallChange* refers not to the amount of petty cash you have in your purse or wallet but to the amount that the *Value* property of the scrollbar should increment or decrement when the user clicks his mouse on the arrows at either end of the scrollbar. The *LargeChange* property refers to the amount of change to the *Value* property when the user clicks his mouse on the gap between the scrollbar's thumb and arrow. The *LargeChange* property also determines the size of the thumb in a scrollbar, as you will notice when creating scrollbars in your own programs. Both the *SmallChange* property and the *LargeChange* property can be set at design time through the Properties section or at runtime through code.

Scrollbars have two key events that Visual Basic programmers most often work with. One such event is the *Change()* event, which triggers when either the user or code changes the *Value* property of a scrollbar. The other event is the *Scroll()* event, which triggers whenever the thumb moves. Although at first the two events look the same, the important difference between them is that the *Change()* event occurs only once at the end of a change to the *Value* property whereas the *Scroll()* event occurs multiple times throughout the duration of the change. For example, if a user was scrolling the thumb from 0 to 400 using her mouse, the *Change()* event would only fire when the user let go of the mouse button.

To avoid confusion, the general naming convention adopted by the Visual Basic community is to use a *vsb* prefix for *VScrollBar* objects and *hsb* as the prefix for *HScrollBar* objects. When you are looking at code written by other Visual Basic programmers or reading documentation from various sources, you will often see this naming convention in use.

Although the primary usage of scrollbars is for a means to determine what portion of a larger whole to display, there are many other uses for scrollbars too. You could use scrollbars to allow the user to select a range of questions from a database, or if you did not want to use the common dialog for selecting a color you could use scrollbars to create an RGB color picker, as shown in Figure 22.3. Basically, anywhere that uses a range of values that the user can select from is a potential place to use a scrollbar, although if you are imaginative you can come up with many other uses as well.

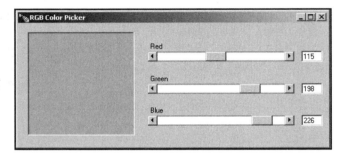

**Figure 22.3**

*The RGB Color Picker showing an example of scrollbar usage possibilities.*

## Success HINT: Using the RGB Color Picker

*Although this lesson cannot accommodate the entire source code for the RGB Color Picker example program, you can access the executable at www.prima-tech.com/books/book/5250/945/ to see an example of scrollbar usage in a Visual Basic program. The entire source code for the program is on this Web site as well, giving you a good example of how to use scrollbars in your programs, handle key press events, and perform some error handling too. Error handling will be shown in greater detail in the advanced section of this book in Lesson 28, "Handling Program Errors."*

# Creating the *ScrollPic* Example Program

The *ScrollPic* example program shows you how you would use the scrollbar controls to view a portion of a picture that is larger than can actually be displayed in the viewable area at any given moment. The *ScrollPic* example program is a short program but gives you a practical example of using scrollbars in your Visual Basic programs. Figure 22.4 shows the *ScrollPic* example program in action.

**Figure 22.4**

*The* ScrollPic *example program in action.*

1. Open a new project in Visual Basic and name it **ScrollPic**.

2. Add a small Image control, name it **imgSmall**, and set its *Visible* property to *False* and its *Stretch* property to *True*.

3. Load the image file *bahai.jpg* into the *Picture* property of the Image control.

4. Add a Timer control to your form and set its *Interval* property to *5*.

5. Add a large PictureBox control to your form and name it **picBig**. Below the Image control, add two Label controls and name them **lblX** and **lblY**. Near the bottom and right of your PictureBox control, add the appropriate scrollbar. Name the vertical scrollbar *vsbBig* and name the horizontal scrollbar **hsbBig**.

6. Add the following code to the *ScrollPic* project's code window:

```
Option Explicit

'=================================================
' Initialize settings for program scrollbars
'=================================================
Private Sub Form_Load()
    'assign minimum and maximum values
```

```
        vsbBig.Max = 5978
        vsbBig.Min = 0
        hsbBig.Max = 9853
        hsbBig.Min = 0

        'assign large and small change values
        vsbBig.LargeChange = 500
        vsbBig.SmallChange = 50
        hsbBig.LargeChange = 500
        hsbBig.SmallChange = 50
End Sub



'=================================================
' Update the display
'=================================================
Private Sub Timer1_Timer()
    Timer1.Enabled = False
    BigPicUpdate
End Sub


Private Sub BigPicUpdate()
    picBig.PaintPicture imgSmall.Picture, 0, 0, _
    picBig.ScaleWidth, picBig.ScaleHeight, hsbBig.Value, _
    vsbBig.Value, picBig.ScaleWidth, picBig.ScaleHeight
    lblX = "x: " & hsbBig.Value
    lblY = "y: " & vsbBig.Value
End Sub



'=================================================
' Handle Change and Scroll events for scrollbars
'=================================================
Private Sub hsbBig_Change()
    BigPicUpdate
End Sub
```

```
Private Sub hsbBig_Scroll()
    BigPicUpdate
End Sub

Private Sub vsbBig_Change()
    BigPicUpdate
End Sub

Private Sub vsbBig_Scroll()
    BigPicUpdate
End Sub
```

7. Save the *ScrollPic* project and run the program. Try moving the scrollbars and observing the effect on the program. For interest, you might like to comment out the *Scroll()* event code and compile and run your program again to see the difference the *Scroll()* event has on the program.

The first thing that the *ScrollPic* program does is set the limits of the scrollbars and set the amounts to increment when changes occur. The call to update the big picture is not in the *Form_Load()* event but rather in the *Timer*'s event to allow the form to actually load before trying to redraw the contents of the big picture. Making the Timer's *Enabled* property *False* means that this event will only fire once, five milliseconds after the program starts. The *ScrollPic* program will fire an event when either of the scrollbars is changed by the user. With two scrollbars, a vertical and a horizontal one, and two possible change increments, this leaves four events to cater to all possible scrollbar changes. Each one of these events simply makes a call to the subroutine *BigPicUpdate()*, which handles the redrawing of the big picture.

# Working with FlatScrollBars

The FlatScrollBar control is very similar to the HScrollBar and VScrollBar controls. The FlatScrollBar control has every property of the HScrollBar and VScrollBar controls plus additional properties and features. You might think of the FlatScrollBar control as an upgrade to the other two scrollbar controls, and in effect that is exactly what the FlatScrollBar control is.

To use the FlatScrollBar control you must first add the Microsoft Windows Common Controls-2 component. Figure 22.5 shows the FlatScrollBar control icon as it appears in the control panel.

### Figure 22.5

*The FlatScrollBar control icon.*

Unlike the HScrollBar and VScrollBar controls, which are two separate controls with a fixed orientation, the FlatScrollBar control has an *Orientation* property, which allows it to be set to either a vertical or horizontal view.

The FlatScrollBar is also capable of disabling either end of the scrollbar by using the *Arrows* property. You should disable the arrow at the end of a scrollbar when the user reaches either the maximum or minimum value set. Visually disabling the end of the scrollbar is constructive feedback for the user, which enhances the user interface that your programs present. The *Arrows* property can be set to any of three values, as shown in Table 22.1.

*Table 22.1 Possible constants for use with the Arrows property.*

| Arrows Constant | Description |
| --- | --- |
| cc2Both | Both arrows are enabled on the scrollbar. |
| cc2LeftUp | When the scrollbar is horizontal the left arrow is enabled, and when the scrollbar is vertical the top arrow is enabled. |
| cc2RightDown | When the scrollbar is horizontal the right arrow is enabled, and when the scrollbar is vertical the bottom arrow is enabled. |

There are three different appearance modes that you can assign to a FlatScrollBar control which do not affect the functionality of the scrollbar but do give you further customization options. The three appearance modes are shown in Table 22.2.

*Table 22.2 Possible constants for use with the Appearance property.*

| Appearance Constant | Description |
| --- | --- |
| fsb3D | The scrollbar takes on a standard 3-D or beveled look. |
| fsbFlat | The scrollbar takes on a flat 2-D look, and the arrows and thumb change color when the user clicks her mouse on them. |
| fsbTrack3D | The scrollbar takes on a flat look, but when the mouse pointer passes over a mouse-sensitive area such as the arrows or the thumb, the mouse-sensitive area becomes beveled and 3-D like in appearance. |

You can actually change the appearance of any FlatScrollBar controls at runtime by simply assigning a different constant to the FlatScrollBar control's *Appearance* property. Figure 22.6 shows the three types of appearances that a FlatScrollBar control can have, as well as disabling the left scroll arrows and placing a standard HScrollBar control in for comparison.

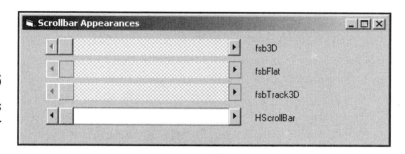

**Figure 22.6**

*A comparison of various scrollbars and their appearances.*

## Success HINT: Creating Custom Scrollbars

*Although Visual Basic provides a variety of scrollbars to use in your programs, if you are trying to achieve a custom look with your scrollbars, then you can easily create your own custom scrollbar by using a PictureBox control and some imagination. The algorithms behind the scrollbar are not very complex, and you could easily mimic the* Change() *and* Scroll() *events of a scrollbar by using the* Change() *and* MouseMove() *events of the PictureBox control.*

*For the scrollbar arrows you might think about using separate Image controls because this would greatly simplify handling* Click() *events. You could even customize the thumb of the scrollbar dynamically, as shown in Figure 22.7.*

**Figure 22.7**

*Customizing the thumb of the scrollbar.*

# Understanding Sliders

Sliders are similar to scrollbars in the fact that they can be horizontal or vertical in orientation and really just graphically represent a value within a given range. Slider controls also have in common with scrollbars a *Min* and *Max* property, a *SmallChange* and *LargeChange* property, and a *Value* property. With so many similarities, you may well be wondering to yourself what need there is for a Slider control. Where a scrollbar is primarily for situations when only a portion of a larger whole can visually be shown at any one moment, a Slider control is primarily for allowing the user to select either a value from within a given range or a range of values.

A common example of Slider control usage is shown in Figure 22.8, displaying Slider controls in both a horizontal and vertical orientation, as well as using tick marks in both left and right sides and also across the bottom.

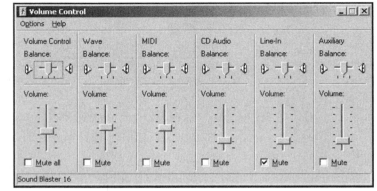

**Figure 22.8**

*The Volume Control dialog box is a good example of Slider control usage.*

To use the Slider control you must first add the Microsoft Windows Common Controls component. Figure 22.9 shows the Slider control icon as it appears in the control panel.

**Figure 22.9**

*The Slider control icon.*

When adding a Slider object to your form, you can only dictate the length of the Slider object, but the width is fixed. The default is to use a horizontal orientation, but you can change a Slider control's *Orientation* property to vertical in the Properties section. To change a Slider control's orientation at runtime, you use something similar to the following:

```
Slider1.Orientation = ccOrientationVertical
Slider1.Orientation = ccOrientationHorizontal
```

The frequency of ticks that a Slider control uses, as well as the position of the ticks, can be set by you at both design time or runtime. A Slider control's *TickStyle* property takes one of four possible constants to specify the position of the ticks, as shown in Table 22.3.

*Table 22.3* TickStyle *property constants for the Slider control.*

| *TickStyle* Constant | Description |
|---|---|
| *sldBottomRight* | The tick marks are located on the bottom when the Slider has a horizontal orientation and on the right when a vertical orientation. |
| *sldTopLeft* | The tick marks are located on the top when the Slider has a horizontal orientation and on the left when a vertical orientation. |
| *sldBoth* | The tick marks are located on both the top and bottom when the Slider has a horizontal orientation and on both the left and right when a vertical orientation. |
| *sldNoTicks* | The Slider does not use tick marks. |

Figure 22.10 shows all of the *TickStyle* property options in both horizontal and vertical orientations.

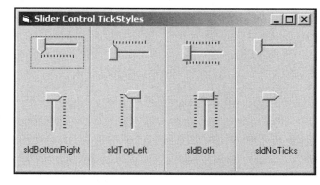

## Figure 22.10

*The various* TickStyle *property options.*

Setting the *TickFrequency* property of a Slider control allows you to customize the frequency of ticks that visually appear on a Slider control. The higher the value set, the lower the frequency of ticks that Visual Basic will display for the Slider control.

Probably the most significant feature of the Slider control is its ability to allow the user to select an entire range of values. You could duplicate this feat using two scrollbars, but having a single control is more elegant in both program terms and user-interface terms. To make a Slider control accept a range, you must set the *SelectRange* property to *True*. By setting the *SelStart* property to a value and the *SelLength* property to a value higher than or equal to *SelStart*, you create the range. There are different methods that you could use to set these values depending on the way you want your program to behave. One method is to set the *SelStart* property when the *MouseDown()* event triggers and then set the *SelLength* property when the *MouseUp()* property triggers. Or you may want the user to hold down special keys such as Shift, Ctrl, or Alt when creating a range. The implementation is really up to you. At www.prima-tech.com/books/book/5250/945/ is the code for *SliderRange*, which gives you a simple example of setting a range with a Slider control, as shown in Figure 22.11.

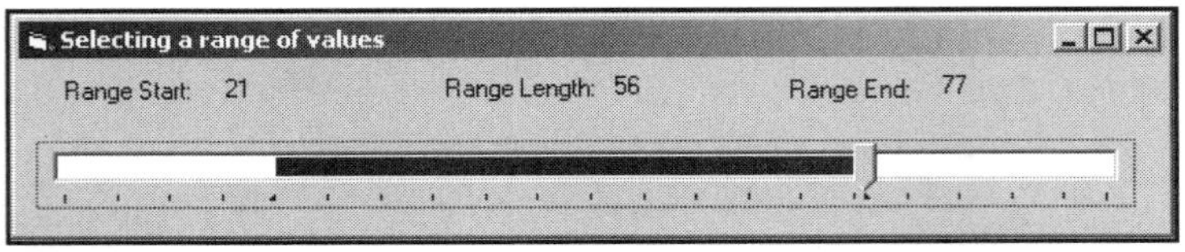

**Figure 22.11**

*Displaying a range of values using a Slider control.*

## What You Must Know

The two standard scrollbars in Visual Basic are the HScrollBar and the VScrollBar controls. Instead of the standard scrollbars, you can use a FlatScrollBar control, which has additional properties and features such as disabling the scrollbar's arrows and using different styles. A Slider control is similar to scrollbars but allows you to select an entire range of values in addition to selecting a single value from a given range. In Lesson 23, "Using Frames and Tabs," you will learn how to use Frames, TabStrips, and SSTab controls as containers for logically related objects, such as radio buttons and checkboxes. Before you continue with Lesson 23, however, make sure you understand the following key concepts:

◆ HScrollBar and VScrollBar are the two standard scrollbar controls in Visual Basic, with the only difference between the two being orientation.

◆ A scrollbar's *Value* property indicates the current position and value of a scrollbar's thumb.

◆ You can set the *Min* and *Max* properties for a scrollbar to create a valid range from which the user may select.

◆ The *SmallChange* and *LargeChange* properties determine the movement of a scrollbar's thumb and can be set at both design time and runtime.

◆ The *Change()* event and the *Scroll()* event are the two key events that Visual Basic programmers use in conjunction with scrollbars.

◆ You can replace HScrollBar and VScrollBar controls with FlatScrollBar controls because they have all of the same properties as well as additional properties and features.

◆ To select horizontal or vertical orientation without the need for two controls, use a FlatScrollBar and change its *Orientation* property .

◆ The FlatScrollBar control allows you to disable either end of a scrollbar by changing the *Arrows* property, resulting in an improved user interface when the thumb of the scrollbar is at the limit of the range.

◆ You can change the *Appearance* property of a FlatScrollBar control to have one of three possible appearances, *fsbFlat*, *fsb3D*, and *fsbTrack3D*.

◆ Similar to scrollbars, Slider controls have an *Orientation* property that allows them to display in either a horizontal or vertical position.

◆ By setting the *TickFrequency* and *TickStyle* properties, you can easily customize the frequency of ticks and the style of ticks for a Slider control.

◆ In addition to having the option of selecting a single value from within a given range, Slider controls also allow a user to select an entire range of values by setting the *SelectRange* property to *True*.

# Using Frames and Tabs

In this section, you have learned how to use various controls to enhance the user interface. In this lesson, you will learn how to further enhance the user interface by containing the controls you have already seen, as well as other controls such as OptionButton and CheckBox controls, in manageable areas using frames and tabs. By the time you finish this lesson, you will understand the following key concepts:

◆ You can easily add CheckBox and OptionButton controls to your Visual Basic projects to enhance your program's user interface for selections.

◆ To use multiple groups of OptionButton controls, you must use some form of container for controls, such as Frame or PictureBox controls, that keep the groups of controls functionally separate from each other.

◆ A Frame control can not only hold multiple controls but also provides an improvement in the user interface by clearly delineating groups of controls from each other.

◆ Moving a Frame control will result in all the controls contained within the Frame also moving yet maintaining their position relative to each other, saving you time, effort, and code.

◆ When you disable or hide a Frame control through use of the *Enabled* and *Visible* properties, you effectively disable or hide all the controls that the Frame contains too.

◆ To add controls to a Frame control at design time, you must either drag the new control directly on the Frame control or cut and paste already existing controls, but you cannot drag and drop an already existing control into a Frame control.

◆ The Forms 2.0 Frame control has many additional features and properties than the standard Frame control, such as border styles, pictures, zoom, tiling, stretch, scrollbars, and more, which could provide functionality that you require in your programs.

◆ Part of the Windows Common Controls 6.0 component, the TabStrip control is the common control for adding tabs to your programs in Visual Basic.

◆ Use the Property Pages dialog box to edit and customize a TabStrip control at design time using the General tab for style, width style, and placement and the Tabs tab for adding new tabs, tab captions, tab keys, and ToolTips.

◆ The TabStrip's *Click()* event and *SelectedItem* property are used at runtime to handle tab switching, by making Frame controls visible and invisible as appropriate.

◆ Using the SSTab control from the Microsoft Tabbed Dialog Control 6.0 component is far easier for beginners and less frustrating even for more experienced programmers mostly because it is a real container object that lets you work with the individual tabs at design time.

# Understanding OptionButton and CheckBox Controls

You will have seen both radio buttons and checkboxes in many Windows programs. In fact, you learned about them a little in Lesson 15, "Using Icons, Picture Boxes, and Image Controls" although now you will cover them more thoroughly. In Visual Basic, radio buttons are known as option buttons and you use them whenever you need the user to select one item from a group of items. At any given moment, only one option button may be selected with all the other option buttons becoming unselected. Checkboxes can also be in groups, but each individual checkbox is really independent and is either checked or unchecked regardless of the other checkboxes. Figure 23.1 shows the control panel icons for the OptionButton and CheckBox controls.

### Figure 23.1

*The control panel icons for the OptionButton and CheckBox controls.*

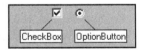

1. Open a new project in Visual Basic and name it **CheckOpt**.

2. Change the *Caption* property of the form to **CheckBox and OptionButton controls**.

3. Add two CheckBox controls and three OptionButton controls, using Table 23.1 and Figure 23.2 as a guide.

*Table 23.1 Controls to add and properties to set.*

| Control Type | Name | Caption |
|---|---|---|
| CheckBox | *chkVerbose* | Use verbose logging |
| CheckBox | *chkOverwrite* | Overwrite log after 7 days |
| OptionButton | *optRed* | Red |
| OptionButton | *optWhite* | White |
| OptionButton | *optBlue* | Blue |

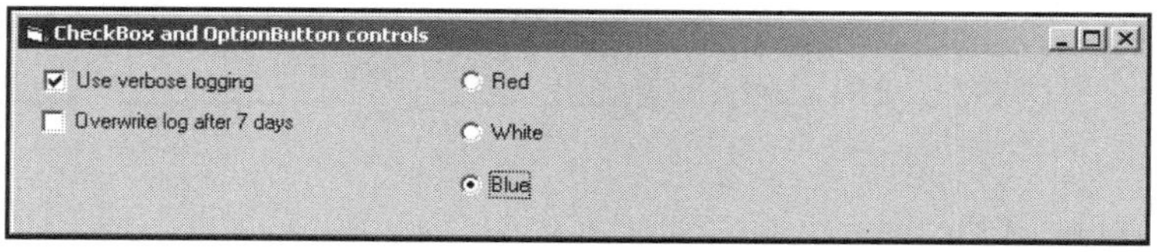

**Figure 23.2**

*The* CheckOpt *program in its early stage.*

4. Save the *CheckOpt* project and run the program. Try checking and unchecking the two CheckBox objects. Notice that you can select either of them, both of them, or neither of them. Now try using the OptionButton objects to select a color. Notice that the previous selection returns to an unchosen state with each new selection so that only one OptionButton is selected at any given moment.

In code, you can find out the status of a CheckBox or an OptionButton object through its *Value* property. An OptionButton has a *Value* property of *True* when selected and *False* otherwise. A CheckBox has a *Value* property of *vbChecked*, *vbUnchecked*, or *vbGrayed*. It is easy then to check the status of one of these objects and then do something, as you can see by the following code snippets:

```
If chkVerbose.Value = vbChecked Then ...
If optRed.Value = True Then ...
```

Now suppose that you must also have the user select a number in addition to the color that she is already selecting. Open your *CheckOpt* project if it is not already open, and add three more OptionButton controls, using Table 23.2 and Figure 23.3 as a guide.

*Table 23.2 Additional controls to add and properties to set.*

| Control Type | Name | Caption |
|---|---|---|
| OptionButton | *optOne* | One |
| OptionButton | *optTwo* | Two |
| OptionButton | *optThree* | Three |

**Figure 23.3**

*The* CheckOpt *program with a second group of OptionButtons.*

Ideally, you want the user to select a color from the group of colors as well as a number from the group of numbers. However, as soon as the user selects a number from the group of numbers, all of the other OptionButton objects become unselected. This scenario is unacceptable, and you must have some method of containing groups of controls so that they are functionally separate from other groups of controls, which brings you to the next topic—Frame controls.

# Understanding the Use and Purpose of Frames

Frame controls are very simple to use in Visual Basic, and often a programmer will apply Frame controls simply to enhance the user interface. Frames make the distinction between groups of items very clear to the user and by using the *Caption* property, allow an overall description of the objects contained by the Frame to also be given to the user.

You can use any form, Frame, or PictureBox control as a container to hold other controls, including other Frame or PictureBox controls. You can use Frame controls to keep items functionally separate from each other, which solves the problem of having multiple groups of OptionButton controls, as shown in Figure 23.4.

**Figure 23.4**

*Using multiple groups of controls with Frames.*

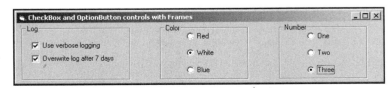

Frame controls are also capable of saving a lot of code, not to mention vastly simplifying that code by acting as a guide to all the other controls that it contains. For instance, imagine that you have a Frame control with thirty different controls in it and you must dynamically enable and disable all of the controls. By setting the Frame's *Enabled* property to *False*, all of the child controls that the Frame contains will automatically become disabled too. In Figure 23.5 the *Color* Frame's *Enabled* property has been set to *False* using the following line of code:

```
fraColor.Enabled = False
```

**Figure 23.5**

*Disabling multiple controls by disabling their Frame container.*

**Success HINT: Improving the User Interface**

*Although disabling a Frame renders the controls within it temporarily unusable, the controls still appear active (not grayed out) and this can be confusing for many users. This may appear counterproductive from a programming point of view; however, you might like to entertain the possibility of writing a simple subroutine to disable or enable all of the controls that are within a Frame. Although doing so removes the Frame control's advantage of code saving, it pays off in user satisfaction. Figure 23.6 shows the improvement in clarity of the user interface after adding the following code:*

```
Private Sub Form_Load()
    EnableColorFrame False
End Sub


Private Sub EnableColorFrame(ByVal ecf As Boolean)
    fraColor.Enabled = ecf
    optRed.Enabled = ecf
    optWhite.Enabled = ecf
    optBlue.Enabled = ecf
End Sub
```

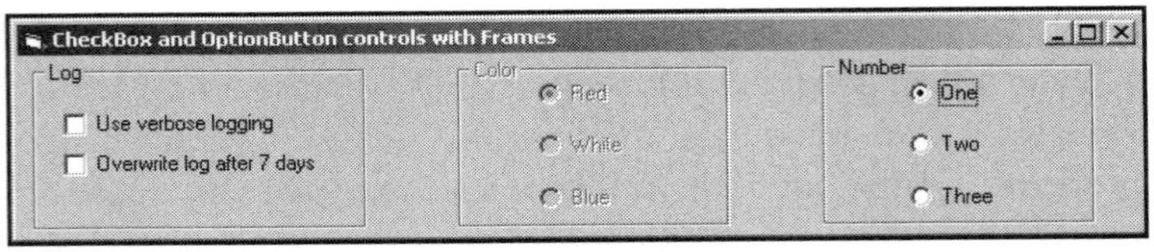

**Figure 23.6**

*Disabling the Color Frame with attention to user interface.*

You do not have to take the option of disabling a Frame and all the controls it contains. Another alternative which leaves no room for user confusion is to set the Frame's Visible property to False, which hides the Frame and all its controls, as shown in Figure 23.7, with a single line of code:

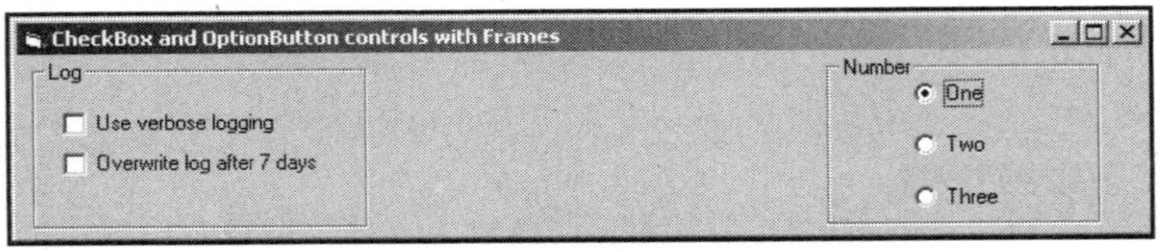

**Figure 23.7**

*Setting a Frame to be invisible hides all the controls it contains as well.*

```
fraColor.Visible = False
```

Another very useful instance where Frame controls can save not only code but also design time is when you must move multiple controls. Imagine having about twenty controls all neatly laid out on a form and then discovering later that you must move them all five pixels to the right. Rather than having to select these controls and move them, by placing them all in a Frame you only need to move the Frame and all the child controls will move as well, maintaining their position in relation to each other. You can move Frame controls at runtime too and make use of this feature.

All of this functionality makes Frame controls potentially very useful in Visual Basic programs.

# Using Frames

To use Frame controls in your own Visual Basic programs, simply click your mouse on the Frame control icon on the control panel, as shown in Figure 23.8, and then drag the size of Frame that you desire on your form, in the same manner as other Visual Basic controls.

## Figure 23.8

*The Frame control icon.*

To add new controls to a Frame, you must drag the size of the new control directly inside the Frame control's borders. For an existing control that you want to add to a Frame, you must click your mouse on the existing control, cut it using the Edit menu Cut option or equivalent, then select the Frame to which the control is to be added and paste the control using the Edit menu Paste or equivalent option.

**NOTE:** *You cannot simply drag an existing control over a Frame object to add the control to the Frame. Doing this gives the appearance of the existing control being inside the Frame, but in effect the existing control is merely on top of the Frame. You can prove this for yourself by trying to add an existing control to a Frame in this manner and then moving the Frame to see if the existing control moves with it.*

**Success HINT:** **Selecting Multiple Controls in a Frame**

*When you have multiple controls inside a Frame, it becomes awkward to select a group of them for alignment or moving. Hold down the control key (Ctrl) and then select multiple controls within the Frame by clicking your mouse on them or dragging a box around the controls you want with your mouse.*

# Using the Forms 2.0 Frame Control

There is another Frame control with additional features that comes with the Microsoft Forms 2.0 Object Library component. Figure 23.9 displays the Forms 2.0 Frame control icon as it appears in the control panel.

## Figure 23.9

*The Forms 2.0 Frame control icon.*

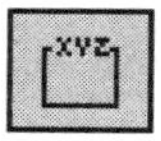

You can specify the color of the Frame's border with the *BorderColor* property; however, the border color is only used when the *BorderStyle* property is set to *fmBorderStyleSingle*. Setting the border to *fmBorderStyleSingle* changes the *SpecialEffect* property to be set to *fmSpecialEffectFlat*. Table 23.3 shows the different possible constants you can assign the *SpecialEffect* property and Figure 23.10 displays the effect of these constants.

*Table 23.3 The* SpecialEffect *property constants.*

| Constant | Description |
|---|---|
| *fmSpecialEffectBump* | Single line bump effect with caption twice |
| *fmSpecialEffectEtched* | (Default) Etched two tone lines |
| *fmSpecialEffectFlat* | Flat border with single line |
| *fmSpecialEffectRaised* | Frame appears raised |
| *fmSpecialEffectSunken* | Frame appears sunken |

**Figure 23.10**

*Displaying the various* SpecialEffect *property constants.*

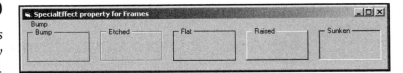

You cannot add controls to a Forms 2.0 Frame in the same manner as you can with a standard Frame. Dragging and dropping or cutting and pasting will not work. To add a control to a Forms 2.0 Frame you must right-click your mouse on the Frame. Visual Basic will display a pop-up menu, as shown in Figure 23.11, from which you must select the Edit option. When you select the Edit option, Visual Basic hides the pop-up menu and displays the Toolbox dialog, from which you can select controls to add to your Forms 2.0 Frame.

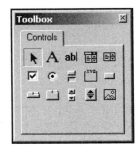

**Figure 23.11**

*The Forms 2.0 Frame's Toolbox dialog.*

You can add a picture to the Frame control using the *Picture* property that can be stretched, zoomed, tiled, or more. There are even five alignment settings for the picture using the *PictureAlignment* property. You can also easily add scrollbars to your Frame control, again with great control over customizing this feature. Figure 23.12 shows a Frame control using PictureTiling and Scrollbars, with controls inside and outside the Frame as a comparison.

**Figure 23.12**

*Using the PictureTiling and Scrollbar features in a Frame.*

The Frame control also has a *Zoom* property. The *Zoom* property allows you to magnify the viewing area within the Frame. The following code shows you how easy it is to implement a three-stage zoom effect whenever the user clicks her mouse within the Frame:

```
Private Sub fraView_Click()
    With fraView
        .zoom = .zoom + 100
        If .zoom = 400 Then .zoom = 100
    End With
End Sub
```

You could be far more elaborate with the *Zoom* property and its usage, using different mouse pointers or having a pop-up menu with zoom options. You can set the *Zoom* property anywhere from 10 to 400, with 100 being the normal size. Figure 23.13 displays a good range of *Zoom* property values and the results they bring about.

**Figure 23.13**

*A range of* Zoom *property values.*

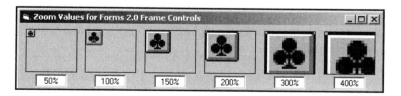

In summary, the Forms 2.0 Frame control has many additional features than the standard Frame control that you may want to make use of in your own programs.

# Adding TabStrips

Tabs are made use of in many Windows programs for their ability to save valuable screen space or real-estate, yet still leave an easy means of getting to a lot of information or many options, which is important to many users. In Visual Basic, the TabStrip control is the common control for adding tabs to your programs, and it is part of the Windows Common Controls 6.0 component, which you have made use of many times already so far in this book. The control icon for the TabStrip control is shown in Figure 23.14.

### Figure 23.14

*The control icon for the
TabStrip control.*

When you add a TabStrip control to your form, the first thing you will probably notice is that you cannot actually add controls directly onto it or flip between multiple tabs. To configure a TabStrip control you must right-click your mouse on the control and select the Properties option from the pop-up menu. Visual Basic will display the Property Pages dialog, as shown in Figure 23.15.

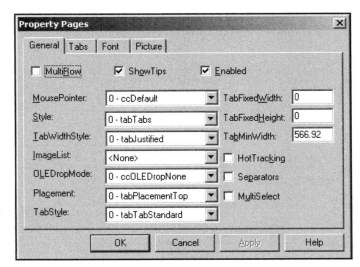

### Figure 23.15

*The TabStrip control's
Property Pages dialog.*

TabStrips are complex controls with many options and settings. Although this may put some programmers off using them, try to see that the complexity of options is really to give you an abundance of customization capability so that you can achieve the effect you desire in your programs. As you learn about some of the features and options of the TabStrip control, play around with what you learn within Visual Basic so that you become more familiar and comfortable with the control.

# Assigning General Settings

Within the Property Pages dialog box, in the General tab you can set the checkbox for the *MultiRow* property. Figure 23.16 shows the difference between having the *MultiRow* option and not having it.

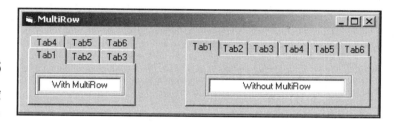

**Figure 23.16**

*The difference between using* MultiRow *and not using it.*

You can set the *Style* property to *tabTabs*, *tabButtons*, or *tabFlatButtons*. When you use *tabButtons* or *tabFlatButtons* style you can also select the MultiSelect checkbox, which allows the user to make multiple selections by holding down the Ctrl key and clicking his mouse on different buttons. You can also check the Separators checkbox to have Visual Basic place a small line between your buttons. Figure 23.17 shows the different styles for the TabStrip control.

**Figure 23.17**

*The different styles for the TabStrip control.*

When the *Style* property is set to *tabFlatButtons* you can also set the *HotTracking* property to *True* by checking the HotTracking checkbox. HotTracking causes the TabStrip to track the mouse and automatically depress tabs when the mouse hovers over them.

The *TabWidthStyle* property can have three possible values: *tabJustified*, *tabNonJustified*, and *tabFixed*. When the tabs are justified they evenly use up the space that you allocate to the TabStrip control. When the tabs are not justified they can be different sizes from each other and are just big enough to contain the text. When the tabs are fixed they are all the same size, which you set using the *TabFixedWidth* and *TabFixedHeight* properties.

Setting the *TabStyle* property to *tabTabOpposite* causes every row of tabs between the currently selected tab and the main tab page or area to shift to the opposite side of the TabStrip control, as shown in Figure 23.18.

**Figure 23.18**

*Various* TabStyle *and* TabWidthStyle *settings.*

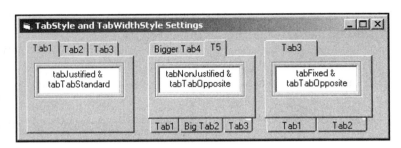

Although setting the *TabStyle* property to *tabTabOpposite* can change the position of tabs in relation to the Tab-Strip control itself, you do not have control over when this occurs as it is dependent on the current tab that the user is selecting. However, the *Placement* property does allow you to control the placement of tabs in relation to the TabStrip control. There are four possible settings, one for each side of the TabStrip control, as shown in Figure 23.19.

**Figure 23.19**

*Various settings for the* Placement *property.*

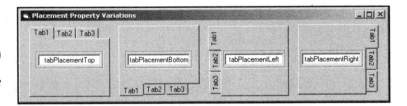

# Adding Tabs at Design Time

To add tabs to your TabStrip at design time, you must use the Property Pages dialog's Tabs tab, as shown in Figure 23.20.

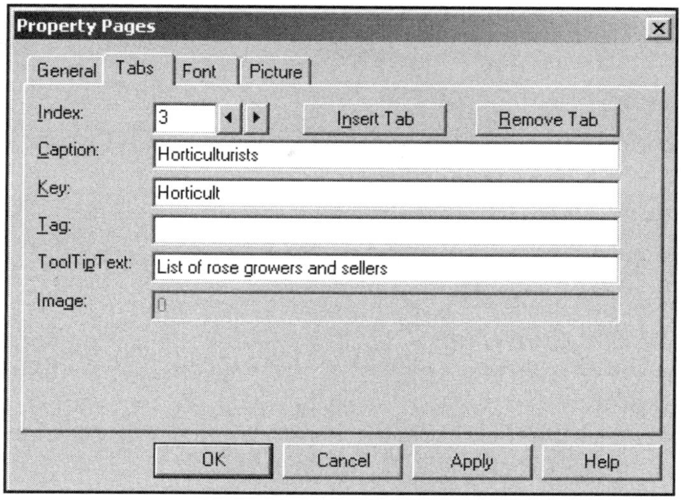

**Figure 23.20**

*Using the Property Pages dialog's Tabs tab to add tab entries.*

To add a new tab, click your mouse on the Insert Tab button. In the *Caption* property, type in the text that you want to display on the tab as the user will see it. In the *Key* property, type in the text that you want to use to reference this tab from your Visual Basic code. To remove the current tab, simply click your mouse on the Remove Tab button. You can use the Index field's arrow buttons to move through the current list of tabs. To add a ToolTip to a tab, enter the text that you want to display in the *ToolTipText* property field.

# Using the TabStrip

As a TabStrip cannot act as a container at design time, you must react to the user clicking her mouse on different tabs by displaying the appropriate objects. One of the best methods of doing this is by using a Frame control to hold the contents of each tab. At design time you can place the TabStrip control and one Frame control in position. All of the other Frame controls should be located elsewhere at design time and simply made to move into position at runtime. By flipping the Frames between visible and invisible, you can easily display different options to the user when he clicks his mouse on different tabs.

You must use the TabStrip's *Click()* event in combination with the *SelectedItem* property to work out when to switch tabs and which tab to switch to. The following code shows one method of flipping tabs at runtime:

```
Private Sub TabStrip1_Click()
    Select Case TabStrip1.SelectedItem.Key
    Case "General":
        fraGeneral.Visible = True
```

```
        fraRoses.Visible = False
        fraHort.Visible = False
    Case "Roses":
        fraGeneral.Visible = False
        fraRoses.Visible = True
        fraHort.Visible = False
    Case "Horticult":
        fraGeneral.Visible = False
        fraRoses.Visible = False
        fraHort.Visible = True
    End Select
End Sub
```

Although not a real database, the *Rose Database* example program at www.prima-tech.com/books/book/5250/945/ gives you an example of how to flip Frame controls when the user selects a different tab, as shown in Figure 23.21.

**Figure 23.21**

*Selecting the second tab in the TabStrip control—before and after.*

## Using the Forms 2.0 TabStrip Control

*As you probably know by now, the Microsoft Forms 2.0 Library component contains variations of many of the standard controls, and the TabStrip is one of those controls. The control icon for the Forms 2.0 TabStrip control is shown in Figure 23.22.*

**Figure 23.22**

*The control icon for the Forms 2.0 TabStrip control.*

*Some features or properties are in one control but not the other, such as the Hot-Tracking property. Other properties have different names for the same thing, such as the Placement property in the standard TabStrip control and the TabOrientation property in the Forms 2.0 TabStrip control. If you have a strong interest in tabs and are looking for a particular feature or type of functionality for your own programs, be aware that the Forms 2.0 TabStrip control exists, as do many third-party tab controls.*

# Using the Tabbed Dialog Control (SSTabs)

Although the TabStrip control is quite powerful it can be rather tedious at design time or overly difficult for new programmers. Visual Basic offers another tab control, the SSTab control, which is a real container and therefore allows you to add objects directly onto each tab. The SSTab control also allows you to simply click your mouse on each tab at design time, and it will display that tab without you having to compile and run the program each time. Features such as these can make using the SSTab control quite time-saving and often far less frustrating in comparison to the TabStrip control.

To add the SSTab control to your projects you must add the Microsoft Tabbed Dialog Control 6.0 component. As with the TabStrip control, you must right-click your mouse on the SSTab control and select the Properties option from the pop-up menu that Visual Basic displays. Visual Basic will then display the Property Pages dialog for the SSTab control. The Property Pages dialog for the SSTab control does not contain as many options as the TabStrip control; however, it is easy to use. Many options and properties are so similar that they will be easily recognizable to you after learning about the TabStrip control. One special point to note is that there is no Tabs tab with the SSTab's Property Pages dialog box. Instead you simply supply the text for the tab's label in the Caption field for each tab and move through the range of tabs by using the left and right arrow buttons or the tab index in the Current Tab section.

Generally, the SSTab control is easier to use for beginners and less frustrating at first. Later, when you want to be able to do more with tabs from your code, you may opt to use the TabStrip control instead.

# What You Must Know

You can easily add CheckBox and OptionButton controls to your programs for an intuitive selection of user options in your programs. Groups of OptionButtons must belong in a container, such as a Frame control, which can provide both functionality and clarity for groups of controls. TabStrip controls are powerful but not as easy to use as SSTab controls, which allow you to work with the individual tabs at design time. In Lesson 24, "Using ImageLists and TreeViews," you will learn how to use ImageList and TreeView controls to create Explorer-like windows that can view items using icons or hierarchically in a tree-like manner. Before you continue with Lesson 24, however, make sure you understand the following key concepts:

◆ To enhance your program's user interface for selections, you can easily add CheckBox and OptionButton controls to your Visual Basic projects.

◆ You must use some form of container for controls, such as Frame or PictureBox controls, that keep the groups of controls functionally separate from each other, to use multiple groups of OptionButton controls.

◆ Not only can a Frame control hold multiple controls but it also clearly separates groups of controls from each other, providing an improvement in the user interface.

◆ You can move all the controls contained within a Frame simply by moving a Frame control and they will maintain their position relative to each other, saving you time, effort, and code.

◆ You can effectively disable or hide all the controls that a Frame contains, by disabling or hiding a Frame control using the *Enabled* or *Visible* properties.

◆ To add controls to a Frame control at design time, you cannot drag and drop an already existing control into a Frame control—you must either drag the new control directly on the Frame control or cut and paste already existing controls.

◆ Border styles, pictures, zoom, tiling, stretch, and scrollbars are some of the many additional features and properties of the Forms 2.0 Frame control, which, in comparison to the standard Frame control, could provide functionality that you require in your programs.

◆ The common control for adding tabs to your programs in Visual Basic, the TabStrip control is part of the Windows Common Controls 6.0 component.

◆ To edit and customize a TabStrip control at design time, use the Property Pages dialog box, using the General tab for style, width style, and placement and the Tabs tab for adding new tabs, tab captions, tab keys, and ToolTips.

◆ You use the TabStrip's *Click()* event and *SelectedItem* property at runtime to handle tab switching. Tab switching is achieved through your code by making Frame controls visible and invisible as appropriate.

◆ Far easier for beginners and less frustrating even for more experienced programmers, the SSTab control from the Microsoft Tabbed Dialog Control 6.0 component is a real container object that lets you work with the individual tabs at design time.

# Lesson 24

---

# Using ImageLists and TreeViews

In Lesson 23, "Using Frames and Tabs," you learned how to use the TabStrip control and other tab controls to act as a container type structure for an improved user interface but did not make use of image lists with those controls, even though they support this feature. You covered earlier many other controls that could also make use of image lists. In this lesson, you will learn how to further enhance the user interface by covering the ImageList control and then use it extensively with the TreeView control to achieve some very professional looking and powerful effects in your programs. By the time you finish this lesson, you will understand the following key concepts:

◆ The ImageList control is simply a repository for images that many controls can make use of allowing you to load all the graphics beforehand and then simply write code that refers to a particular item in the repository and not have to load them from various places in your code.

◆ Part of the Microsoft Windows Common Control 6.0 component, the ImageList control has a Property Pages dialog that makes working with the ImageList control at design time easy for Visual Basic programmers.

◆ Use the Insert Image button within the Images tab to add new images to the ImageList control.

◆ You can assign keys to the images using the *Key* property, which allows you to reference a particular image within an ImageList control by a permanent name rather than an index number, which is subject to change.

◆ You can manipulate an ImageList control at runtime by adding images, removing images, reading the image size, and performing a variety of different methods for displaying the image.

◆ You can create composite images made up from two images within an ImageList control by using the *Overlay* method in conjunction with the *UseMaskColor* and *MaskColor* properties.

◆ The TreeView control is part of the Microsoft Windows CommonControl 6.0 component and can make use of ImageList controls for node icon usage.

◆ Many settings for a TreeView can be configured at design time in the Property Pages dialog for the TreeView control.

◆ Nodes are added to TreeView controls at runtime using the *Add* method, at which point you can set images, text, and node position within the tree.

◆ Each node can have individual color and boldness settings as well as an image associated with its *ExpandedImage* property to customize its appearance.

◆ TreeViews can make use of checkboxes, provide properties and methods for node selection and visibility, and prevent node editing by the user.

# Understanding the Use and Purpose of the ImageList Control

The ImageList control is simply a repository for images that you can use with many controls in Visual Basic. The main controls that can make use of images in an ImageList control are the Image, PictureBox, ImageCombo, CommandButton, Toolbar, TabStrip, ListView, and TreeView controls, although some other controls can also take advantage of images stored in an ImageList control. One of the nice benefits of using a single repository for all your images is that you can load all the graphics beforehand and then simply write code that refers to a particular item in the repository, referencing all your images from a single point and not having to load them from lots of places in your code. Whenever you want to change an image you do not have to concern yourself with going to all the places that use that image in code, as nothing in code has to change.

# Adding Images to an ImageList Control

The ImageList control is part of the Microsoft Windows Common Control 6.0 component, and its control icon appears in the control panel, as shown in Figure 24.1.

**Figure 24.1**
*The ImageList control icon.*

The ImageList control is similar to the Timer control that you covered earlier in this book because it is only visible at design time and also has a fixed size when you add it to your form. Right-clicking your mouse on an ImageList control will cause a pop-up menu to display. Selecting the Properties option from this pop-up menu will cause Visual Basic to display the Property Pages dialog for the ImageList control, as shown in Figure 24.2.

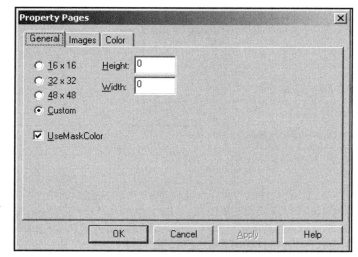

**Figure 24.2**

*The General tab of the ImageList's Property Pages dialog.*

In the General tab of the ImageList's Property Pages dialog, you can select a particular image size, although doing so means that all images within the ImageList control must be the same size. Having an ImageList with a fixed size can be useful when precision is important. Leaving the default setting of *Custom* allows you to add images of varying sizes to the ImageList control, which is often the best setting to use. The General tab also contains a checkbox for the *UseMaskColor* property, which is set to *True* by default. The *UseMaskColor* property together with the *MaskColor* property are for using transparent colors in your images, and you will see an example of how to use these properties later in this lesson when you learn about creating composite images.

In the General tab of the ImageList's Property Pages dialog, you can add images to your ImageList control by simply clicking your mouse on the Insert Image button and selecting a graphic file to load from the standard file open dialog that Visual Basic presents. The types of graphic files that the ImageList control can handle are bitmap (*.bmp*), JPEG (*.jpg*), GIF (*.gif*), icon (*.ico*), and cursor (*.cur*). Figure 24.3 shows the Images tab of the ImageList control's Property Pages dialog after inserting a variety of images.

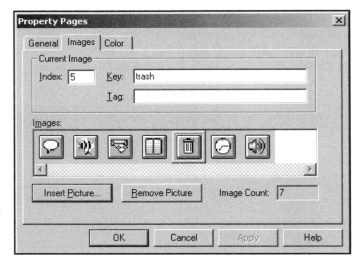

**Figure 24.3**

*The Images tab of the ImageList's Property Pages dialog.*

To remove images at design time, you simply click your mouse on the image you want to remove and then click your mouse on the Remove Picture button. To look at or work with the properties of another image in the Image-List control, either enter the index number of the image in the Index property field or simply click your mouse on the image. Visual Basic provides a scrollbar in case you have more images than you can see at once.

You can assign keys to each of the images to be able to easily reference a particular graphic from within your code without having to remember the index number. Using the *Key* property to reference individual images within an ImageList control is also very useful because it prevents the need to go back and change any of these references when you delete some images from the ImageList control and thereby alter the index value of subsequent images. When those references are scattered throughout your code, assigning keys to images becomes a big time and effort saver.

# Using the ImageList Control from Code

Making the most of an ImageList control from code can sometimes appear challenging to new programmers as there are a variety of options to choose from. However, you only have to use a single method that works for you and just be aware of alternative methods in case you either come across them in someone else's code or require them for a new purpose.

You can add images to an ImageList control by using the *Add* method, the syntax for which is as follows:

Add [Index], [Key], [Picture]

The arguments are optional, and you will often leave the *Index* field for Visual Basic to determine and concern yourself with the *Key* and *Picture* arguments, such as in the following code example:

```
ImageList1.ListImages.Add , "disk", "c:\images\disk.jpg"
```

To remove an image from the ImageList control, you would use the *Remove* method, as follows:

```
ImageList1.ListImages.Remove "disk"
```

To remove all the images, you would use the *Clear* method, as follows:

```
ImageList1.ListImages.Clear
```

To see the number of images inside an ImageList control, you would use the *Count* property, as follows:

```
lblTotal.Caption = ImageList1.ListImages.Count
```

Although you can delve down through an ImageList control's image properties to get the width or height of an image, Visual Basic provides you with the *ImageWidth* and *ImageHeight* properties at a higher level to make these more easily accessible. The following two lines of code return the height of an image:

```
ImageList1.ListImages.Item(1).Picture.Height
ImageList1.ImageHeight
```

There are numerous ways to display the actual image when using an ImageList control. When you use a PictureBox control or some other object that supports the *PaintPicture* method you can write something similar to the following:

```
pic1.PaintPicture ImageList1.ListImages(1).Picture, 0, 0
```

You can use the ImageList control's *Draw* method to paint the picture directly onto an object such as a form, as follows:

```
ImageList1.ListImages("disk").Draw Form1.hDC
```

Yet another method is to directly assign the *Picture* property to some other object that contains a *Picture* property, such as an Image control, as follows:

```
Image1.Picture = ImageList1.ListImages.Item("disk").Picture
```

```
If tvw1.Nodes("aqua").Checked = True Then ...
If tvw1.Nodes("aqua").Checked Then ...
```

# Understanding Node Selection and Visibility

To determine if a particular node is selected, you only need query the TreeView's *SelectedItem* property or that node's *Selected* property. The following code shows both methods, and both lines achieve the same result:

```
If tvw1.SelectedItem.Key = "aqua" Then MsgBox "Aqua!"
If tvw1.Nodes("aqua").Selected = True Then MsgBox "Aqua!"
```

To determine if a particular node is visible at present within the TreeView's displayable area, you can query the node's *Visible* property. If a node is hidden beneath a non-expanded (collapsed) node, then Visual Basic considers that node as invisible. You can ensure that a node becomes visible by calling its *EnsureVisible* method. The following code checks if a particular node is visible and if not ensures that it becomes visible:

```
If tvw1.Nodes("aqua").Visible = False Then
    'Make Node visible
    tvw1.Nodes("aqua").EnsureVisible
End If
```

You can also determine the number of nodes that are currently visible by using the TreeView's *GetVisibleCount* method.

# Preventing Node Editing

Although easily fixed when you know how, preventing users from editing the text of the individual nodes can be both frustrating to find and damaging to sales when programs are released without handling this aspect properly. By default, a TreeView control does not prevent the user from editing the individual nodes. By changing the *LabelEdit* property to *tvwManual* you can keep your TreeView's nodes from having their text accidentally edited.

# What You Must Know

ImageList controls are useful for holding a selection of images in a single repository, which can be easily accessed by other controls within the program. TreeViews have a positive effect on most user interfaces because almost every Windows user is comfortable with the concept of using a TreeView control. The heart of the Tree-View control is its collection of nodes for which numerous properties and options exist. In Lesson 25, "Using Files to Store and Retrieve Information," you will learn how to use files in your Visual Basic programming for saving data to hard drives or loading data for use within your programs, as well as cover a variety of useful methods and controls to enhance working with files. Before you continue with Lesson 25, however, make sure you understand the following key concepts:

◆ A repository for images that many controls can make use of, the ImageList control allows you to load all the graphics in beforehand and then simply write code that refers to a particular item in the repository and not have to load them in from various places in your code.

◆ The ImageList control is part of the Microsoft Windows Common Control 6.0 component and has a Property Pages dialog box that makes working with the ImageList control at design time very easy.

◆ To add new images to the ImageList control, use the Insert Image button within the Images tab.

◆ Each image within an ImageList control lets you assign keys to them using the *Key* property, which allows you to reference images by a permanent name rather than an index number, which is subject to change.

◆ At runtime, you can work with an ImageList control by adding, removing, and displaying images, as well as reading image sizes.

◆ By using the *Overlay* method in conjunction with the *UseMaskColor* and *MaskColor* properties, you can create composite images made up from two images within an ImageList control.

◆ The TreeView control is part of the Microsoft Windows Common Control 6.0 component and can make use of ImageList controls for node icon usage.

◆ At design time you can configure many settings for a TreeView control in the Property Pages dialog box.

◆ Using the *Add* method at runtime, you can add nodes to TreeView controls and also set images, text, and node position within the tree.

◆ You can change the appearance of each node by setting the *ForeColor*, *BackColor*, and *Bold* properties as well as having an image associated with its *ExpandedImage* property to customize its appearance.

◆ TreeViews can make use of checkboxes, provide properties and methods for node selection and visibility, and prevent node editing by the user.

## Using FileCopy, Name...As, and Kill

*As an alternative to copying, moving, renaming, and deleting files using the FileSystemObject and the Microsoft Scripting Runtime Library, Visual Basic has some low-level alternatives that you may want to use. Although programmers will make use of the FileSystemObject's clean methods most of the time, there are always those few occasions when you must make your final code a bit smaller for distribution reasons or you just do not want to use the Microsoft Scripting Runtime Library.*

*You can delete a file easily using the Kill statement, which takes a single argument— a string representing the pathname. The pathname can also include wildcards but only for the filename part of the string. You represent a single character wildcard with the ? character and a multiple character wildcard with the * character. Visual Basic will give an error if no file exists matching the criteria. The Kill statement can also include drives and directories, as shown in some of the following examples:*

```
Kill "greenfish.txt"
Kill "c:\*fish.txt"
Kill "e:\temp\gr*sh.t?t"
```

*To copy a file you can use the FileCopy statement, which takes a source filename for its first argument and a destination filename for its second argument. Visual Basic will give an error if the file that you are trying to copy is in use. An example of the FileCopy statement is shown in the following line:*

```
filecopy "c:\redfish.txt", "e:\temp\bluefish.txt"
```

*Moving and renaming files also have an alternative to the FileSystemObject, known as the Name statement, although this is often seen as the Name ... As statement. The Name statement takes one argument before the As keyword and another argument directly after. The first argument refers to the old pathname and the second argument to the new pathname. You cannot use wildcards in either of the arguments, and Visual Basic will give an error if you use an open file with the Name statement. Some examples of moving and renaming files are as follows:*

```
Name "c:\purplefish.txt" As "c:\bluefish.txt" 'Renaming
Name "c:\purplefish.txt" As "e:\purplefish.txt" 'Moving
```

# Working with File Attributes

Files can have different attributes that affect whether you can copy, move, or delete them, whether they are hidden or not, whether they are system files or not, and also if they require archiving. From within your Visual Basic programs you can alter the attributes that a file has by using the *GetAttr* function and *SetAttr* statement.

To get a file's attributes, you must use the *GetAttr* function, which has the following syntax:

GetAttr(*PathName As String*)

The *PathName* argument should include both the path and the name of the file whose attributes are being sought. The *GetAttr* function will use the directory in which the application is run if no path is specified. The *GetAttr* function returns a value that equates to the sum of all the attributes currently held by the file and you can store this value in a variable of type *Variant* or *Long*. An example of getting a file's attribute might appear as follows:

```
Dim lngFA As Long
    lngFA = GetAttr("c:\finance.txt")
```

Due to the fact that all the attributes have been put together into one variable, you must have a method to determine individual attribute settings. Table 25.1 shows the values of the individual attributes and gives a description.

*Table 25.1 File attribute constants and their values and descriptions.*

| Constant | Value | Description |
| --- | --- | --- |
| *vbNormal* | 0 | File is normal |
| *vbReadOnly* | 1 | File is only for reading |
| *vbHidden* | 2 | File is hidden |
| *vbSystem* | 4 | File is a system file |
| *vbDirectory* | 16 | File is a directory |
| *vbArchive* | 32 | File has been altered since the last backup |

In the example shown above, if the file *c:\finance.txt* had the attributes *vbNormal*, *vbReadOnly*, and *vbArchive*, then the value in *lngFA* would be 33 (0 + 1 + 32). To easily determine if an individual attribute is set, you must use bitwise comparisons on the result of the *GetAttr* function, as shown in the following example:

```
If lngFA And vbArchive Then MsgBox "Archive is set."
If lngFA And vbHidden Then MsgBox "Hidden is set."
```

To set a file's attributes is very easy using the *SetAttr* statement, which has the following syntax:

SetAttr *PathName As String, Attributes As vbFileAttribute*

The *PathName* argument is similar to the *GetAttr* function's *PathName* argument. Simply supply a string that contains the path and filename of the file whose attributes you want to set. The *Attributes* argument is simply a list of any of the file attribute constants from Table 25.1. The following is an example of setting a file's attributes:

```
SetAttr "c:\finance.txt", vbArchive + vbReadOnly
```

# Using DriveListBox, DirListBox, and FileListBox

To easily add functionality to your programs that allows the user to select directories and files from media such as the local hard drive or a mapped network share, Visual Basic provides you with the FileListBox and the DirListBox controls. Together with a DriveListBox control, these three controls provide a powerful element to your programs with a minimum of code on your part. The control icons for the three controls appear as shown in Figure 25.2.

### Figure 25.2

*The control icons for the DriveListBox, DirListBox, and FileListBox controls.*

The DriveListBox control is the simplest of the three controls because it does not depend on the values of the other two controls. The DriveListBox control is a drop-down combo box, as shown in Figure 25.3, which you can size as necessary on your form.

### Figure 25.3

*The drop-down combo box of the DriveListBox control.*

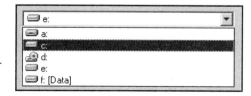

You can find out the current drive from the DriveListBox's *Drive* property, which is a String value that you can easily copy. The DriveListBox has a *Change()* event that you can make use of by placing in it any code that your program must do whenever the user selects a different drive, such as updating a DirListBox object.

You can add a DirListBox control to your form and size it to your needs. Because the number of folders in the current directory may be more than can be shown in the viewable area, the DirListBox automatically provides a scrollbar when necessary, as shown in Figure 25.4.

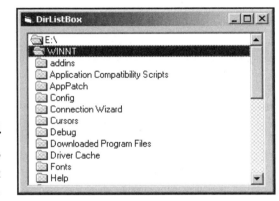

**Figure 25.4**

*The DirListBox automatically provides a scrollbar when necessary.*

The path that a DirListBox object displays can be found in the *Path* property, and Visual Basic will automatically update this property whenever the user makes changes within the DirListBox object. You can easily set the *Path* property, as you can see from the following example:

```
dlbSource.Path = "e:\winnt"
```

As your users navigate through drives and directories you can use a FileListBox control to show them the available files in each of the locations. Like the DirListBox control, the FileListBox control does automatically provide a vertical scrollbar if necessary but does not provide a horizontal scrollbar, even if a filename is longer than the viewable area can support, as shown in Figure 25.5.

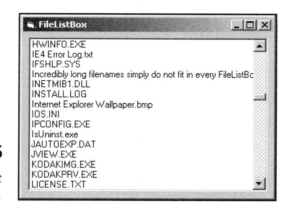

**Figure 25.5**

*The FileListBox does not provide a horizontal scrollbar.*

The FileListBox control's *Path* property holds the value of the current path of the files that it is displaying, and you can easily set this to the *Path* property of the DirListBox to synchronize the two controls. By default, not all files are shown in the FileListBox control, but its boolean properties *Archive*, *Hidden*, *ReadOnly*, and *System* allow you to determine if the FileListBox object will display files of these types.

To get the filename of the current file selected by the user in a FileListBox object, you must use the *FileName* property, as shown in the following line of code:

```
MsgBox "The current file is... " & flbSource.FileName
```

# Working with Folders and Drives

Although the *FileSystemObject* is primarily for use with files, you can also use it to great effect with folders and drives too. For instance, you can check if a folder exists or list all the available drives on the local computer.

When working with folders, some of the most useful methods of a *FileSystemObject* are the *FolderExists*, *Copy-Folder*, *MoveFolder*, and *DeleteFolder*. The following code gives you an example of how these methods are used:

```
Private Sub Form_Load()
Dim fs As New FileSystemObject
    If fs.FolderExists("c:\temp") = True Then
        fs.CopyFolder "c:\temp", "c:\temp2"
        fs.DeleteFolder "c:\temp", True
        fs.MoveFolder "c:\temp2", "c:\temp3"
    End If
End Sub
```

You can also declare a variable of type *Folder* and assign a folder to it using various methods such as *GetFolder* or *CreateFolder*, as shown:

```
Private Sub Form_Load()
Dim fs As New FileSystemObject
Dim fldNew As Folder
    fldNew = fs.CreateFolder("c:\green")
    fldNew = fs.GetFolder("c:\temp")
End Sub
```

A *Folder* object also has many useful properties and methods, such as *Size*, *DateLastModified*, *SubFolders*, and *Files* plus many others that you can easily make use of when working with folders in your own programs.

The *FileSystemObject* also has support for drives. You can use the *DriveExists* method to determine if a particular drive letter is mapped on the local computer or not. The *DriveExists* method takes a drive letter as its only argument and returns *True* if the drive letter is mapped or *False* otherwise, as shown by the following code:

```
Private Sub Form_Load()
Dim fs As New FileSystemObject
Dim MAPPED As Boolean
    MAPPED = fs.DriveExists("C")
    MsgBox MAPPED
End Sub
```

You can do a lot more with drives than simply check if they exist. The *FileSystemObject*'s *Drives* property lets you find out drive sizes, free space, share names, volume names, and many other facts about each of the drives connected to the local computer. Add a ListBox control to a form in a new project and add the following code, which shows how to iterate the unknown number of drives connected and report some information about the total size of each of them:

```
Private Sub Form_Load()
Dim fs As New FileSystemObject
Dim MAPPED As Boolean
Dim myDrives
Dim aDrive As Drive
Dim s As String
    MAPPED = fs.DriveExists("C")

    If MAPPED = True Then
```

```
      Set myDrives = fs.Drives
      For Each aDrive In myDrives
            s = aDrive.DriveLetter
            s = s & " has size "
            If aDrive.IsReady Then
                s = s & aDrive.TotalSize & " bytes"
            Else
                s = s & "unknown"
            End If
            List1.AddItem s
      Next
   End If
End Sub
```

# Building the *FileMaster* Example Program

Putting together lots of Visual Basic features covered in this lesson, as well as drawing on features from previous lessons, the *FileMaster* example program at www.prima-tech.com/books/book/5250/945/ is a good example of manipulating files within Visual Basic. Although the entire source code is too large to print in its entirety for this lesson, key areas are worth mentioning so that you understand what the code is accomplishing. You can feel free to edit the source code to add further functionality if you so desire. Figure 25.6 shows the *FileMaster* example program in action with the source file on the left and the destination path on the right.

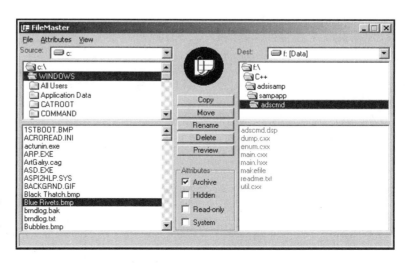

**Figure 25.6**

*The* FileMaster *example program in action.*

The View menu options determine what types of files are shown in the FileListBox, *flbSource*, and you can not only check and uncheck the menu item but also assign it to the appropriate attribute property of the FileListBox object, as shown:

```
Private Sub mnuViewHidden_Click()
    mnuViewHidden.Checked = Not mnuViewHidden.Checked
    flbSource.Hidden = mnuViewHidden.Checked
End Sub
```

The Preview button in *FileMaster* allows users to preview graphic files in a tiny thumbnail size Image control. The following code snippet shows not only how to determine what the current file is but also how to find the file extension and prevent the user from trying to display a file that the Image control does not support:

```
' Enable the preview button if right format
    Select Case Right(flbSource.FileName, 4)
    Case ".bmp": cmdPreview.Enabled = True
    Case ".ico": cmdPreview.Enabled = True
    Case ".jpg": cmdPreview.Enabled = True
    Case ".gif": cmdPreview.Enabled = True
    Case Else: cmdPreview.Enabled = False
        imgPreview.Visible = False
    End Select
```

The following code shows how to load and display a graphic file:

```
Private Sub cmdPreview_Click()
    imgPreview.Picture = LoadPicture(PathAndFile(Source))
    imgPreview.Visible = True
End Sub
```

To prevent the program from writing over an existing file, you must give the user some sort of feedback and let her decide what she wants to do. If the file does not already exist or the user indicates that it is OK to proceed, then the value of *result* is *vbOK*, as shown:

```
If fs.FileExists(PathAndFile(Dest)) Then
    result = MsgBox("Overwrite the existing file?", _
    vbQuestion + vbOKCancel, "File Already Exists")
Else
    result = vbOK
End If
```

When the user changes drives, you should update the directories and files that your program is displaying by simply assigning the new value to his or her *Path* property, as shown:

```
Private Sub drvSource_Change()
    dlbSource.Path = drvSource.Drive
    flbSource.Path = drvSource.Drive
End Sub
```

For the renaming of a file, the *FileMaster* program uses a separate form to display to the user, although an Input-Box is another alternative. To place the value of the FileListBox object's *FileName* property in the form *frmFM* to the TextBox object's *Text* property in the form *frmRename,* you must use the name of the form explicitly in the reference, as shown:

```
Private Sub cmdRename_Click()
    frmRename.Show
    frmRename.txtRename.Text = flbSource.FileName
End Sub
```

When setting attributes in response to the user selecting attribute changes for a file, you must check that it is not the program simply setting the attributes for a new file that the user has selected. A boolean value, *LOADING_ATTRIBS,* prevents file settings from being incorrectly set, as shown:

```
Private Sub SetMyFileAttribs()
Dim lngFA As Long
    If LOADING_ATTRIBS = False Then
        lngFA = 0
        If chkArchive.Value = vbChecked Then lngFA = ...
        If chkHidden.Value = vbChecked Then lngFA = ...
        If chkRead.Value = vbChecked Then lngFA = ...
        If chkSystem.Value = vbChecked Then lngFA = ...
        SetAttr PathAndFile(Source), lngFA
    End If
End Sub
```

# What You Must Know

The Microsoft Scripting Runtime Library's *FileSystemObject* makes working with files in Visual Basic extremely easy. *TextStream* variables have the *FileSystemObject*'s *CreateTextFile* or *OpenTextFile* methods assigned to them, allowing easy reading or writing of data to files. You can also make use of copy, move, rename, and delete

For greater control, you can set the *PrintQuality* property to any positive number for the dpi value. For example, the following lines of code set the print quality to 600dpi and 1200dpi respectively:

```
Printer.PrintQuality = 600
Printer.PrintQuality = 1200
```

## Orientation

To specify whether the page should print in landscape or portrait mode, you must set the *Printer* object's *Orientation* property to either *vbPRORLandscape* or *vbPRORPortrait*, as shown:

```
Printer.Orientation = vbPRORLandscape
Printer.Orientation = vbPRORPortrait
```

Portrait mode is more commonly seen in use and has the narrow ends of the paper at the top and bottom. Landscape mode looks very wide and has the narrow ends on the sides. Figure 26.3 shows clearly the difference between the two modes.

**Figure 26.3**

*Portrait and landscape modes.*

## Paper Size

Setting the paper size to print is one option that many users expect from a program, and Visual Basic supports many different paper sizes. To set the paper size, you must set the *Printer* object's *PaperSize* property to one of the paper size constants. Some of the more commonly used paper size constants are shown in Table 26.2.

*Table 26.2* PaperSize *constants.*

| *PaperSize* Constant | Description |
| --- | --- |
| *vbPRPSLetter* | Letter, $8\frac{1}{2}$" × 11" |
| *vbPRPSLetterSmall* | Letter Small, $8\frac{1}{2}$" × 11" |
| *vbPRPSLedger* | Ledger, 17" × 11" |
| *vbPRPSLegal* | Legal, $8\frac{1}{2}$" × 14" |
| *vbPRPSA3* | A3, 297 × 420 mm |
| *vbPRPSA4* | A4, 210 × 297 mm |
| *vbPRPSA4Small* | A4 Small, 210 × 297 mm |
| *vbPRPSA5* | A5, 148 × 210 mm |
| *vbPRPSFanfoldUS* | U.S. Standard Fanfold, $14\frac{7}{8}$" × 11" |
| *vbPRPSUser* | User defined |

# Paper Tray/Paper Bin

By setting the *Printer* object's *PaperBin* property, you can specify which tray or bin the printer should use paper from. Table 26.3 shows the available constants to use with the *Printer* object's *PaperBin* property.

*Table 26.3* PaperBin *constants.*

| *PaperBin* Constant | Description |
| --- | --- |
| *vbPRBNAuto* | (Default) Uses the default bin |
| *vbPRBNLower* | Uses the lower bin |
| *vbPRBNMiddle* | Uses the middle bin |
| *vbPRBNUpper* | Uses the upper bin |
| *vbPRBNManual* | Waits for manual paper insertion |
| *vbPRBNEnvelope* | Uses the envelope feeder |
| *vbPRBNEnvManual* | Waits for manual envelope insertion |
| *vbPRBNTractor* | Uses the tractor feeder |
| *vbPRBNSmallFmt* | Uses the small paper feeder |
| *vbPRBNLargeFmt* | Uses the large paper bin |
| *vbPRBNLargeCapacity* | Uses the large capacity feeder |
| *vbPRBNCassette* | Uses the attached cassette cartridge |

# Duplex

Printing something in a duplex style is when you are printing double-sided, or on both sides of the paper, similar to pages in a book. Not all printers come with a duplexer, although many laser printers have duplexers as optional extras that you may purchase, and most companies do because it saves paper and cuts costs. Therefore, it is important to support duplex printing within your programs if you are hoping to write programs intended for more than a stand-alone home user's computer. To set the duplex style in Visual Basic, change the *Printer* object's *Duplex* property to one of the constants in Table 26.4.

*Table 26.4* Duplex *constants.*

| *Duplex* Constant | Description |
| --- | --- |
| *vbPRDPSimplex* | Print single-sided |
| *vbPRDPHorizontal* | Print double-sided horizontally |
| *vbPRDPVertical* | Print double-sided vertically |

# Color Mode

Setting the *Printer* object's *ColorMode* property to *vbPRCMColor* allows you to print in color mode. If you set the *ColorMode* property to *vbPRCMMonochrome* you will print in monochrome (black and white).

# Number of Copies

To set the number of copies that you want to print, change the *Printer* object's *Copies* property. The following example sets the number of copies to print to five:

```
Printer.Copies = 5
```

# Using the *Printer* Object

You know how to set the *Printer* object's main properties, which brings you to actually using the *Printer* object. One of the first things you must learn about using the *Printer* object is that you cannot see it, and unlike forms at design time, you are unable to drag text and graphics around using your mouse. To add text to the *Printer* object, you simply use the *Print* statement, as follows:

```
Printer.Print "This is some text."
```

There are different ways that you can declare arrays. Depending on your programming needs and personal preferences you can decide which method to use.

# Declaring Arrays Using the *Dim* Statement

Using the *Dim* statement or keyword to declare a variable is probably a good place to start because you are already familiar with it and its usage. To declare a variable of type *integer*, you would write something like the following:

```
Dim intSky As Integer
```

As you are already aware by now, the variable *intSky* can hold exactly one integer value, and when you reference *intSky* a single value Visual Basic would return a single integer value. To declare an array of integers using the *Dim* statement, you simply specify the number of elements you want in the array, surround this with brackets, and place it directly after the variable name. For example, to make *intSky* an array of 5 integer values, you could alter the code as follows:

```
Dim intSky(5) As Integer
```

The variable *intSky* can now hold 6 separate integer values! You can assign values to the different elements using an explicit reference, with the lower bound for the elements starting from 0, as follows:

```
intSky(0) = 40
intSky(1) = 37
intSky(2) = 21
intSky(3) = 78
intSky(4) = 40
intSky(5) = 95
```

Each item can contain a different integer although this is not necessary, as you can see above with elements 0 and 4 both containing the value 40.

# Declaring Multi-Dimensional Arrays

You can also declare arrays of multiple dimensions. You may be wondering why you would use a multi-dimensional array. You would use a multi-dimensional array for the same reasons that you would use an array instead of a lot of variable declarations. Imagine that you were writing a role-playing game and you had to keep track of the upper and lower bounds for different character attributes, as well as the current value, and that you had to do this for up to eight different characters. By using a standard, single-dimension array you would need 8 declarations for hit points, 8 declarations for strength, and 8 declarations for magic. Alternatively, you could declare each attribute variable as a multi-dimensional array, with the first dimension representing the 8 characters (0-7) and the second dimension representing the current value (0), lower bound (1), and upper bound (2), as follows:

```
Dim HitPoints(7, 2) As Integer
Dim Strength(7, 2) As Integer
Dim Magic(7, 2) As Integer
```

To set the current value of character 3's strength, you would write something like:

```
Strength(2, 0) = 76
```

To set the upper bound of character 7's hit points, you would write something like:

```
HitPoints(6, 2) = 120
```

You can see how easy it would be to write functions for working with all the characters and their attributes. You could also use more dimensions in your arrays. Continuing on with the character attribute scenario, rather than assigning a different array variable for each attribute, simply use one array variable with the first dimension representing HitPoints (0), Strength (1), and Magic (2), as follows:

```
Dim ChrAttrib(2, 7, 2) As Integer
```

You could change the order of the array's dimensions to suit ease of access. For instance, it might seem more logical to make the first dimension represent the player, the second dimension the attribute, and the third dimension the current value, lower and upper bounds, as shown in the following examples:

```
Dim ChrAttrib(7, 2, 2) As Integer

'Set player 3's current strength to 40
ChrAttrib(2, 1, 0) = 40

'Get player 5's upper bound for hit points
result = ChrAttrib(4, 0, 2)
```

# Declaring Arrays Using the *Array* Function

Another method of assigning arrays is to use the *Array* function and assign it to a variable of type *Variant*, as follows:

```
Dim arrFish As Variant
arrFish = Array(10, 5)
```

You can assign values or text to the individual items in the array. Unlike the arrays you have seen so far in the lesson, the *Array* function does not take dimensions for arguments but the actual values. It is a single array consisting of the same number of elements as the number of arguments that you supply, as shown by the following code:

```
Private Sub Form_Load()
Dim arrFish As Variant
Dim s As String
    arrFish = Array(10, 5, "Salmon")
    s = "arrFish(0) = " & arrFish(0) & vbCrLf
    s = s & "arrFish(1) = " & arrFish(1) & vbCrLf
    s = s & "arrFish(2) = " & arrFish(2)
    MsgBox s, vbInformation, _
    "Using: arrFish = Array(10, 5, 'Salmon')"
End Sub
```

The result of running this code is shown in Figure 27.1.

**Figure 27.1**

*The result of assigning values using the Array function.*

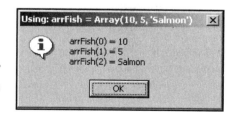

# Removing Items from Collections

Removing items from collections is extremely straightforward, as collections contain a *Remove* method whose only argument is the index or key of the item to remove. For example, to remove the item *Stephen* from the *Names* program, you could use the following line:

```
colNames.Remove "keyStephen"
```

To remove all the items from a collection, you could either loop through all the items and remove them or you could simply set the collection to *Nothing*, as follows:

```
Set colNames = Nothing
```

The trick with setting your collection to *Nothing* is to re-create it again when you must next use it, by declaring a new instance of the collection class, as follows:

```
Set colNames = New Collection
```

# Referencing and Counting Collection Items

To reference any item in a collection to retrieve its current value, simply use the collection's *Item* method, which takes either the index or key of the item you want as its only argument. The following line of code shows you how to retrieve the second item from the collection:

```
name = colNames.Item(2)
```

You cannot assign a different value to an existing item in a collection using the *Item* method, but instead you should remove the item and insert it again with the new value. However, many new Visual Basic programmers get caught out by this, so it is worth being aware of how to change the value of an item. For instance, if you had to change the item *Stephen* to *Steven,* you cannot assign it directly but must remove and add the item, as shown:

```
Set colNames("keyStephen") = "Steven" 'Incorrect method!

'Correct method.
'Inserting the new item first can assist with placement
colNames.Add "Steven", "keySteven", "keyStephen"
colNames.Remove "keyStephen"
```

When trying to determine the total number of items within a collection, you only have to use the collection's *Count* method with no arguments. You can use this value if you want to display the total number of items in a collection to the user or if you want to iterate through a subset of the items without going past the last item. The following line of code shows how you might use the *Count* method:

```
lblTotal.Text = "Total: " & colNames.Count
```

 **Using the *Dictionary* Object**

*Although collections are commonly seen in Visual Basic and are often used by programmers, there is a similar object for handling dynamic arrays known as the* Dictionary *object. The* Dictionary *object is quite simple and straightforward to use, having similar methods as the* Collection *object but without some of the limitations. Some of the handy extra features that a* Dictionary *object has over a collection are the* Exist *method, for checking if a particular item exists in the list, the* RemoveAll *method, for easily emptying all the items in the list, and the* CompareMode *property, which is handy if you are working with Jet databases in Microsoft Access or if you require a specific comparison mode.*

# Building Collections and Classes

Often, collections and classes are used together to only present methods that you want to expose, as well as providing a means of error checking. Recall from Lesson 13, "Understanding Classes," when you learned about the Class Builder Utility to assist in the creation of new class modules. When you wish to work with collections of classes or classes that contain collections, you can make use of the Class Builder Utility to save you creating all of the subroutines and functions yourself. Figure 27.6 shows the Collection Builder dialog that is part of the Class Builder Utility.

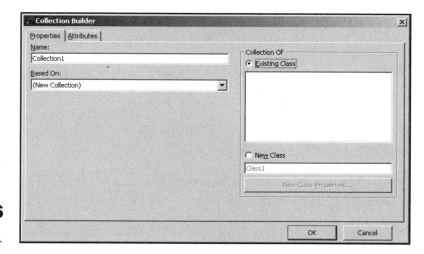

**Figure 27.6**

*The Collection Builder dialog.*

# What You Must Know

Arrays allow you to form a single reference to a group of related variables of the same type. You can create dynamic arrays using the *ReDim* statement, which allows your arrays to shrink and enlarge at runtime. Collections are a clean implementation of dynamic arrays that provide you with four basic methods for handling items within the collection. In Lesson 28, "Handling Program Errors," you will learn how to improve the quality of your programs by adding error handling techniques that will improve the robustness and stability of your programs and also prevent the user from accidentally causing errors to occur. Before you continue with Lesson 28, however, make sure you understand the following key concepts:

◆ Saving you a lot of time and code, arrays allow you to form a single reference to a group of related variables of the same type.

◆ Using the *Dim* statement, you can declare an array and place the array size directly after the variable name, inserting the size in parentheses.

◆ You can declare multi-dimensional arrays by specifying additional dimensions when declaring the array.

◆ You can use the *Array* function, which always uses type *Variant* to store different value types, such as integers and strings, in a single array.

◆ You can use the *LBound* and *UBound* functions to discover the upper or lower bounds of any particular dimension in an array.

◆ When you cannot say for certain how big an array must be, use dynamic arrays, which do not have a set size but grow and shrink as necessary during program runtime.

◆ To dynamically change the size or dimensions of an array at runtime, you can use the *ReDim* statement together with the *Erase* statement and *Preserve* keyword.

◆ Rather than using traditional loops, copying arrays to dynamic arrays can be done much more efficiently using array assignment.

◆ Unlike a standard array, collections provide a clean method of having a dynamic array of elements that do not impose the restriction of all elements having to be of the same type.

◆ You must declare a new instance of a collection when you create one in your programs, as a collection is really a class.

◆ To add new items to a collection, you can use the *Add* method with the option of specifying unique keys or inserting the new item before or after any existing item.

◆ Rather than trying to extract a particular item from an array using the *ReDim* statement, you can easily remove individual items from a collection using the *Remove* method.

◆ You can use the collection's *Item* method to retrieve the current value of any item within the collection, and you can use the collection's *Count* method to return the total number of items currently in the collection.

◆ When working with collections in classes, you can potentially save yourself a lot of time and effort by making use of the Class Builder Utility's Collection Builder.

# Lesson 28

# Handling Program Errors

Throughout this book so far, you have learned how to create Visual Basic programs with the intent on functionality. In this lesson, you will learn how to add error handling routines to your programs, which do not add any functionality to your programs but rather serve as preventative measures against possible misuse of controls or problems beyond the control of your program. By the time you finish this lesson, you will understand the following key concepts:

◆ Error handling is extremely important to ensure that a program is robust and stable even though users may never see any additional functionality in the program.

◆ When making use of external dependencies, such as files, folders, or drives from within your programs, always check first that the external dependency you are about to access exists, so you can prevent your program from crashing when a particular error occurs and handle it in a more elegant manner.

◆ The *Err* object provides properties and methods that allow you to easily work with errors by finding out information from the most recent error or raising your own errors.

◆ To create an error handling trap, you can use the *On Error Goto* statement with an error handler label or line number, which tells Visual Basic to jump to this code when an error occurs.

◆ Inline error handling checks for success after each error-potential object reference without resorting to discontinuous code execution.

◆ Centralized error handling is a practical method of writing functions that do all your error handling for you and that you can use from multiple places in your code.

◆ There are many common mathematical errors that can occur, but by writing safe functions that include explicit error handling of division by zero, overflow, and type mismatch errors, as well as making use of the *IsNumeric* function, you can avoid fatal errors caused by mathematical equations in your programs.

◆ Asserting code basically verifies that your assumption that a particular boolean expression is *True* is correct.

◆ You can disable error handling within your code for debugging purposes and also within the Visual Basic environment for the purpose of testing your own error handling routines.

# Understanding the Importance of Error Handling

Error handlers are preventative measures taken to ensure that a program is robust and stable, including when external factors do not meet your program's expectations. Error handling does not add any program functionality for your users and therefore, many programmers get lazy and neglect to include thorough error handling within their programs, as it is not a *feature* that they can stick in point form to advertise their product. Even though users may never see any additional functionality in the program, error handling is extremely important in your programs because what users will notice is the robustness and stability of the program.

The best time to add error handling is when you write the original code, not later. Later never comes, but more importantly, the programmer is most in tune with the code and can foresee problems better during the original coding time.

For instance, a simple calculator program may handle addition, subtraction, multiplication, and division. To add additional functionality to the program, you might add the ability to handle factorials, square roots, or exponential equations. These are features that the user would plainly see and can be thought of as additional functionality to the program. However, adding error handling to the simple calculator program might include such features as preventing division by zero occurring or only allowing numbers to be input by the user, as otherwise a letter or special character would cause an error to occur. If the user was careful about using the simple calculator program before the addition of error handling and only made use of number keys, she would not see any change in the functionality of the program after the addition of error handling.

# Checking for Existence

Often programs must make use of external dependencies, such as files, folders, or drives. If these external dependencies do not exist, then your program will give an error and probably crash, depending on the severity of the error. By checking for existence of whatever external dependency you are about to access first, you can prevent your program from crashing when a particular error occurs and handle it in a more elegant manner.

The following code comes from the program *ExistCrash*, which is at www.prima-tech.com/books/book/5250/945/. You can run the program yourself or look through the source code. The main idea is that you compare the two methods of opening a file, one without error handling and the other with error handling.

The first method does not use error handling and merely tries to open up a text file and then close it again. If the file actually exists, then no error would occur and the code would work perfectly well.

```
Private Sub cmdError_Click()
Dim fs As New FileSystemObject
Dim ts As TextStream
    Set ts = fs.OpenTextFile("c:\wgwjky.txt")
    Close ts
End Sub
```

Unfortunately, if the file does not exist, the program causes an error to occur, as shown in Figure 28.1, and then crashes.

**Figure 28.1**

*System error produced when file does not exist.*

However, by using error handling techniques, such as checking for the existence of the file first before you attempt to access the file, you can circumvent the critical error that crashes your program unnecessarily.

```
Private Sub cmdErrorHandle_Click()
Dim fs As New FileSystemObject
Dim ts As TextStream
Dim myFile As String
    myFile = "c:\wgwjky.txt"
    If fs.FileExists(myFile) = True Then
        Set ts = fs.OpenTextFile(myFile)
        Close ts
    Else
        MsgBox "The file " & Chr(34) & myFile & Chr(34) & _
        " does not exist.", vbExclamation, _
        App.EXEName & ": File not found"
    End If
End Sub
```

Although this code also produces an error dialog to the user, as shown in Figure 28.2, it can be more informative and meaningful than the system error so that the user is aware of the situation, yet does not cause the program to crash.

**Figure 28.2**

*A more informative error dialog box without crashing the program.*

You can check the existence of drives and folders too, just as easily, by using the *DriveExists* method and *FolderExists* method of the *FileSystemObject*. These are very handy if you are expecting a particular drive letter to be mapped by the user or expecting a folder to exist so that you can write a new file into it.

# Using the *Err* Object

To assist with error handling within your programs, Visual Basic provides you with the *Err* object. The *Err* object does not require any declaration and is available from anywhere in your program, having a global scope.

The *Number* property of the *Err* object is set by Visual Basic when an error occurs. You can use this error number to work out what has gone wrong and to determine what course of action to take, including what to say when informing the user.

The *Err* object's *Source* property is simply a string that lets you know the program that originally generates an error. If your program generates or raises an error, you can set this property to your application name and possibly add the name of the subroutine or function. The convention for the *Source* property is to use *project.class* when raising an error within a class module.

The *Err* object also has a *Description* property that gets set by Visual Basic when an error occurs. You can set the *Description* property to a string of your own choosing if you are unable to handle the error yourself.

The *LastDllError* property is a read-only property, which is useful if a call to a dynamic linked library fails for some reason. You will learn more about dynamic linked library calls in Lesson 31, "Declaring Application Programming Interfaces (APIs)."

To initialize the *Err* object you can use its *Clear* method, which will make all properties equal to 0, or if they are string values, equal to an empty string. When you explicitly use one of the following statements, *Exit Function*, *Exit Sub*, *Exit Property*, or *Resume Next*, Visual Basic automatically clears the *Err* object for you.

The *Err* object also has a *Raise* method, which you should use instead of the obsolete *Error* function to raise an error from within your code. You should be aware that the *Error* function does exist, as you may see it in another programmer's code; however, Microsoft does not advise using this anymore and suggests using the *Raise* method instead. Table 28.1 shows a list of some of the more common errors that you can raise.

**Table 28.1 Some common error numbers that you can raise and their meanings.**

| Error Number | Definition |
|---|---|
| 5 | Invalid procedure call |
| 6 | Overflow |
| 7 | Out of memory |
| 11 | Division by zero |
| 13 | Type mismatch |
| 48 | Error in loading DLL |
| 53 | File not found |
| 55 | File already open |
| 57 | Device I/O (Input/Output) error |
| 61 | Disk full |
| 70 | Permission denied |
| 71 | Disk not ready |
| 482 | Printer error |
| 521 | Cannot open Clipboard |
| 31001 | Out of memory (yes, again) |
| 31036 | Error saving to file |
| 31037 | Error loading from file |

The *Raise* method has the following syntax:

**Raise** *number, [source], [description], [helpfile], [helpcontext]*

Only the *number* argument is mandatory, although Visual Basic will automatically fill the other arguments if you use the *Clear* method immediately before raising an error. When raising your own errors, you should add the constant *vbObjectError* to the error number to distinguish the error as not being generated by Visual Basic, as shown:

```
Err.Clear
Err.Raise vbObjectError + 11, App.EXEName & ".Division", _
"You cannot divide by zero. Press F1 for help."
```

# Creating an Error Handling Trap

Although you know about the *Err* object, you need a means by which to catch the error at the moment it occurs so that you can evaluate the situation using the *Err* object and determine what you must do. When checking for existence of an external item, you are actually preventing a potential error from occurring. However, if an error that you are unable to prevent does occur, you can catch the error with an error handling trap.

There are a few different methods of implementing error handling traps, although the most common is to use the *On Error Goto* statement, which takes the name of an error handling label or a line number as its only argument. The following short example should make this clearer by showing you how to trap an error and provide a message box.

```
Private Sub Doh()
On Error GoTo ErrHandler
    'Create an error
    Err.Clear
    Err.Raise vbObjectError + 7
    Exit Sub

ErrHandler:
    MsgBox "Handling the error now."
End Sub
```

Notice the use of the *Exit Sub* statement to prevent the code for the error handler from executing when an error does not occur. This is important or else you can end up with some bizarre bugs in your programs. If you are creating an error handling trap in a function, then simply use the *Exit Function* statement rather than the *Exit Sub* statement.

The error label in the code above, *ErrHandler,* could have been any unique string, such as *myError, ErrorTrap, errhnd,* or whatever makes sense to you. The label must be within the procedure that references it with a *Goto* statement or else another error will occur from which you will be unable to recover, causing your program to crash.

Within the error handling trap you can have more than a simple message box. The code that you use for your error handling depends largely on the type of error, as well as the type of program that you have. Your error handling can be as simple or complex as you decide. You will see more complex error handling traps later in this lesson.

 **Using the *Resume* Statement**

*From within your error handler, you can use the* Resume *statement to have Visual Basic resume code execution at the line where the error occurred. This is extremely handy for giving the user a second chance in circumstances where a disk is full, a file was missing, a network drive was not mapped, or similar recoverable situations. All you have to do then is present the user with a meaningful message box with the Abort, Retry, and Ignore buttons, and then if the user remedies the situation and clicks her mouse on the Retry button, your program can use the* Resume *statement and the program carries on.*

# Understanding Inline Error Handling

Many programmers do not like to use the *Goto* statement, as it can lead to what is known as *spaghetti code,* where the code jumps about in a discontinuous and often highly confusing manner. Although using a single *Goto* statement for error handling purposes is not overly confusing, you can use a similar technique to what languages such as C and C++ programs use, known as *inline error handling.* Some books you read and some programmers you meet might also refer to this technique as *inline error trapping*.

Inline error handling does not jump code in a discontinuous manner, the way the *Goto* statement does. Rather, it aims at checking the validity of each object call immediately following the calling statement. To invoke inline error handling, use the following error handling trap in your subroutine or function:

```
On Error Resume Next
```

You can use the *Err* object to determine the nature of the error and how best to proceed gracefully. The following example shows how to use inline error handling to trap an error and offer the user a chance to remedy a situation where the drive is full. Note that even though the code is checking for the existence of a file before copying it, this is not always enough and you should not rely solely on existence checking for your error handling.

```
Private Sub MakeBackup(ByVal file As String)
Dim fs As New FileSystemObject
```

```
Dim result
On Error Resume Next
    'First check that the file exists.
    If fs.FileExists(file) = True Then
        fs.CopyFile file, file & ".bak"
        If Not Err.Number = 0 Then
            'There is a problem
            Select Case Err.Number
            Case 61: 'Disk is full
                result = MsgBox("The c: drive is full.", _
                vbAbortRetryIgnore & vbExclamation, _
                Err.Description)
                If result = vbRetry Then MakeBackup file
            Case Else: 'Any other error
                MsgBox "Unable to create the file " & _
                Chr(34) & "c:\myfile.txt" & Chr(34) & _
                ".", , Err.Description
            End Select
        End If
    End If
End Sub
```

# Centralizing Error Handling

If your program opens up files from 30 different places within your code, you would have to write practically identical error handling code in all of those places, which can lead to not only a lot of extra code, effort, and time but can also make troubleshooting more difficult because there is not one central place to look at.

Centralized error handling is a practical method of writing functions that do all your error handling for you and that you can use from multiple places in your code. For instance, you might create a module and declare a function as *SafeOpenTextFile*, which takes the same arguments as the *FileSystemObject*'s *OpenTextFile* method, yet handles all possible errors that might occur. Then you can easily call *SafeOpenTextFile* in any places within your code where you are opening a file and not have to worry about checking for existence of files, folders, or drives or any other errors that may occur.

You could easily make up error handling modules for many common tasks, such as *SafeFile.mod*, *Safe-Math.mod*, *SafePrint.mod*, and so on, and once you have written your error handling routines, reuse these modules in any of your new projects. You will see an example of creating a safe reusable function that includes error handling in the next section on handling math errors.

# Handling Math Errors

There are many functions available in mathematics that can potentially cause errors. Often, you must simply prevent non-numerical values being input by the user or checking that the value is numerical. There are many cases where you cannot accept numerical values only. Some examples would be negative numbers, fractions, numbers that require a decimal point, exponential and logarithmic numbers, monetary value using dollar signs, commas to separate thousands, and so on. In these cases you can use the function *IsNumeric* to determine if the input is numerical and avoid unnecessary errors. One point to note is that *IsNumeric* uses the regional settings of the computer, so although $527 would return *True* if you live in the United States, it would return *False* if you live in the United Kingdom.

```
result = IsNumeric($527)
```

Some other common mathematical errors to watch out for are the division of zero, overflow, and type mismatch. To write the sometimes exhausting but necessary error handling code after each mathematical operation would be extremely time- and code-intensive. A better method is to create error handling modules for all your mathematical operations and then simply call these from within your code. This is a practical use of centralized error handling seen earlier in this lesson. The following example shows you how to implement a safe function for division, although you could write similar functions for other mathematical functions and store them all within a *SafeMath* module:

```
'==================================================
' SafeDivide function with error handling
'==================================================
Public Function SafeDivide(ByVal numerator, _
ByVal denominator) As Variant
On Error GoTo ErrHandler
    SafeDivide = numerator / denominator
    Exit Function

ErrHandler:
    Select Case Err.Number
    Case 6: 'Overflow
        MsgBox "The numerator and denominator " & _
        "cannot both be zero.", _
```

```
        vbExclamation, Err.Description
    Case 11: 'Division by zero
        MsgBox "The denominator cannot be zero.", _
        vbExclamation, Err.Description
    Case 13: 'Type mismatch
        If IsNumeric(numerator) = False Then _
        MsgBox "Numerator is not numerical.", , _
        Err.Description
        If IsNumeric(denominator) = False Then _
        MsgBox "Denominator is not numerical.", , _
        Err.Description
    Case Else: 'Any other error that occurs
        MsgBox "An error occurred during division.", , _
        Err.Description
    End Select
    SafeDivide = Null
End Function
```

To call the *SafeDivision* function from anywhere in your code, you would use something similar to the following:

```
'=================================================
' Divide Button
'=================================================
Private Sub cmdDivide_Click()
Dim result
    'Divide the numbers safely
    result = SafeDivide(Text1, Text2)

    'Check the result for an error
    If IsNull(result) = True Then result = "Error"

    'Display the result to the user
    lblResult.Caption = CStr(result)
End Sub
```

Figure 28.3 shows an example of handling a mathematical error in a graceful and safe manner, supplying the user with a meaningful error message and without causing the program to crash.

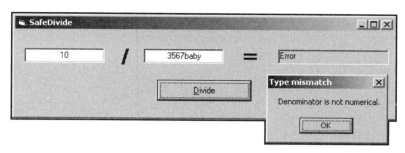

**Figure 28.3**

*Handling a mathematical error safely without crashing your program.*

 **Using Other Type Verifier Functions**

*You have seen the* IsNumeric *type verifier function, which returns* True *if the argument is of a numeric type and* False *otherwise. You may also have seen the use of the* IsNull *type verifier function in the example code of the* SafeDivide *program. Visual Basic has many useful type verifiers that you can use in your programs to assist with error handling, as shown in the list below:*

> *IsArray*
>
> *IsDate*
>
> *IsEmpty*
>
> *IsNull*
>
> *IsNumeric*
>
> *IsObject*

*One of the most important type verifiers, however, is the* VarType *function, which takes any variable as its argument and returns the type of variable rather than a boolean value. Some examples of using the* VarType *function are as follows:*

```
Private Sub Form_Load()
Dim s As String
Dim i As Integer
Dim l As Long
Dim result
```

```
      If VarType(s) = vbString Then MsgBox "A string!"
      result = VarType(i)  'result=vbInteger
      result = VarType(l)  'result=vbLong
End Sub
```

# Handling Printer Errors

Printers are notorious for causing unnecessary fatal errors in otherwise well-written programs. This is because there is an incredible range of different printers available and a vast difference in printer capabilities. Some of the main errors to watch out for are shown in Table 28.2.

*Table 28.2 Common printer errors.*

| Error Number | Description |
| --- | --- |
| 396 | **Property cannot be set within a page**—The *Height, Width,* or *PaperSize* properties of the *Printer* object were changed without first using the *NewPage* method. |
| 482 | **Printer error**—The printer might be jammed, out of paper, not online, or unable to print graphics. There may be no printer installed from the Control Panel. |
| 483 | **Printer driver does not support the property**—The printer is unable to handle a property of the *Printer* object that you are using. |
| 484 | **Printer driver unavailable**—The program cannot find the *Win.ini* file or information is missing from it. There may be no printer installed from the Control Panel. |
| 486 | **Can't print form image to this type of printer**—The printer is not able to handle printing raster graphics or failed to handle a *StartPage* command. |

You can trap these errors and handle them within your code using methods that you have already learned in this lesson; however, be aware that some printers can take a while to respond to your program and can cause your program to appear to have hung.

 **Simulating Errors and Quality Control**

*It is important that you test your error handling routines and do not simply assume that they will work. You can easily simulate any errors by using the* Err *object's* Raise *method to see how your program behaves. Some errors you can simulate simply by using the program in a specific way, such as loading a file from a drive that does not exist or dividing some number by zero.*

*Quality control in programs is where you purposefully try to break the program or cause it to crash to test the quality of a program's error handling. In any text box that expects a number, enter a letter or a special character. If your program requests a particular range of numbers, say 1 to 100, enter a number slightly greater than 100, enter a number that has 20 digits, enter a negative number, and so on, as shown in Figure 28.4.*

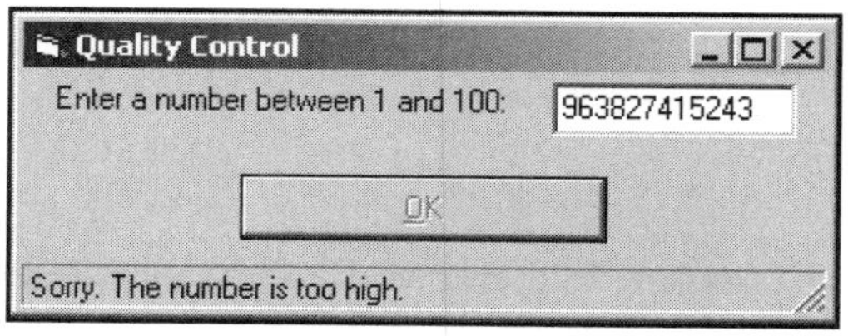

**Figure 28.4**

*Preventing invalid data from being input by the user.*

*When there are lots of buttons, press them out of order to see how the program handles it. If a particular button depends on a valid entry from the user it should be gray and the user should be unable to click her mouse on it until the valid entry has been input.*

*Resizing windows can also cause errors to occur, especially for certain controls that expect a certain size or when resizing routines have been written for the program hastily and work for practical resizing but not extremes.*

# Asserting Code

During development of your programs, you can save yourself a lot of work in tracking down errors that occur, yet may be syntactically correct and therefore difficult to spot, by using assertion in your code. Asserting code basically verifies that an expression is what you expect it to be. Assertion is only useful at development time, and you could classify it as error tracking rather than error handling, although the two concepts overlap and affect each other in parts.

When asserting boolean expressions in Visual Basic, you must use the *Debug* object. You do not have to declare this object explicitly, and you can use the *Debug* object from anywhere in your code. If the boolean argument given to *Assert* returns *True*, then code continues. However, if it returns *False*, then Visual Basic will highlight the line and break the code at that point, alerting you to the problem.

In the following example, you can see that if the variable *s2* is not equal to the string *Hippopotamus*, then Visual Basic will alert you that you are making an incorrect assumption at this point.

```
Private Sub Form_Load()
Dim s1 As String
Dim s2 As String
    s1 = "Hippopotamus"
    s2 = s1
    Debug.Assert s2 = "Hippopotamus"
    'continue on with code ...
End Sub
```

Basically, you should use code assertion wherever you are making assumptions. Remember the rule: Never assume!

# Disabling Error Handling

There are times when you have put in place extremely complex error handling code but now cannot test your programs properly. Perhaps you are trying to step through code in debug mode and the code keeps leaping off to your error handler because you are running from debug mode and not running from an executable. In these cases, you can disable your error handling by using the following statement:

```
On Error Goto 0
```

Another problem that occurs is that you cannot test your error handlers because Visual Basic breaks on all errors that occur regardless of whether you have written an error handler or not. To stop Visual Basic from breaking on all errors, click your mouse on the Tools menu Options menu item. Visual Basic will display the Options dialog box. Within the Options dialog box, select the General tab and look at the section containing error trapping options. Change the Break On All Errors option to Break on Unhandled Errors by selecting it with your mouse, as shown in Figure 28.5.

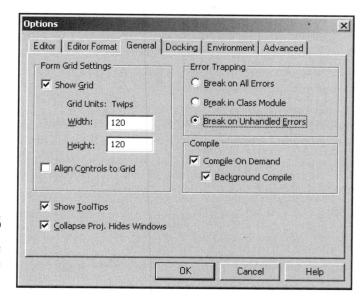

**Figure 28.5**

*Setting error trapping options in the Visual Basic environment.*

Click on the OK button and Visual Basic will close the Options dialog box and set the new error trapping option. You will now be able to test your error handling routines without interference.

**NOTE:** *Although this lesson has taught you all about error handling, you may notice that error handling has not been put to use in all of the example code seen throughout this book and at www.prima-tech.com/books/book/ 5250/945/. This is not an oversight or hypocritical act on the part of the author but a conscious decision to prevent confusion at the sight of complex error handling code detracting from the key concepts trying to be put across to the reader. In other words, error handling has purposefully been omitted to maintain code clarity. You are welcome to add error handling to any of the source code throughout this book and are strongly encouraged to use error handling in your own programs. Predicting errors so that your code can handle them is about 30% of a project, realistically.*

# What You Must Know

Error handling does not add visible functionality from the user's perspective; however, the user will see a noticeable improvement in program robustness and stability. The *Err* object provides a lot of information about the last error to occur, as well as giving you a method for raising your own errors. You can select whether you want to use discontinuous code routines for error handling or inline error handling, depending on your preference and programming background. In Lesson 29, "Using Help Files," you will move beyond the basic functionality aspect of your program and learn about various aspects of user support, which you can provide to users of your programs in many different ways. Before you continue with Lesson 29, however, make sure you understand the following key concepts:

◆ Even though users may never see any additional functionality in the program, error handling is extremely important to ensure that a program is robust and stable.

◆ To prevent your program from crashing when a particular error occurs and handle it in a more elegant manner, when making use of external dependencies, such as files, folders, or drives from within your programs, always check first that the external dependency you are about to access exists.

◆ By providing information from the most recent error or raising your own errors, the *Err* object gives you the properties and methods you need to easily work with errors.

◆ You can use the *On Error Goto* statement with an error handler label or line number to create an error handling trap, which tells Visual Basic to jump to this code when an error occurs.

◆ Without resorting to discontinuous code execution, inline error handling checks for success after each error-potential object reference.

◆ Centralized error handling saves repeatedly writing the same or similar error handlers by writing generic functions that do all your error handling for you and that you can use from multiple places in your code.

◆ You can avoid fatal errors caused by mathematical equations in your programs by writing safe functions that include explicit error handling of division by zero, overflow, and type mismatch errors, as well as making use of the *IsNumeric* function.

◆ The assumption that a particular boolean expression is *True* can be verified with certainty through code assertion.

◆ You can disable error handling within your code for debugging purposes and also within the Visual Basic environment for the purpose of testing your own error handling routines.

# Lesson 29

# Using Help Files

In Lesson 28, "Handling Program Errors," you learned about providing robustness and stability with your programs rather than focusing on raw functionality. In this lesson, you will again move beyond the basic functionality aspect of your program and learn about various aspects of user support in the form of Windows help files, HTML help files, and various other forms of program help. By the time you finish this lesson, you will understand the following key concepts:

♦ Help files are important to users, as a source of comfort and a place to turn if they run into difficulties with your program.

♦ WinHelp files consist of Rich Text Format files that have a special format which has been put into a single file using a utility such as Microsoft's Help Workshop tool.

♦ HTML Help is the newest form of help file and probably the most popular style at present, providing a split window with contents and topic links on one side and graphics and topic details on the other.

♦ The HTML Help Workshop program must be installed on your system from the Visual Basic CD and provides you with the ability to create new HTML help files or convert existing Win-Help files to the newer HTML Help style.

♦ Adding F1 Help to your Visual Basic programs allows your users to simply press F1 to get context-sensitive help depending on the current object that is active by making use of topic IDs and using the *App* object's *HelpFile* property.

♦ ToolTips are a very simple form of help you can add to your programs that result in a small yellow box displaying when you hover the mouse cursor over an object for a short length of time.

♦ You can add Tip of the Day help to your programs by adding the Tip of the Day form and providing a text file with a list of tips for your program.

◆ Adding WhatsThisHelp to your programs allows users to simply point to the object that they would like some help with, rather than having to guess what the technical name for that object is.

# Understanding the Importance of Providing Help

Many programmers are very keen on creating whiz-bang programs with flashy features that dazzle the user. Providing help for their programs is not one of those features and therefore, too often, an otherwise good program is let down by the sheer lack of user support or poorly written help files. Remember that many users may not be as competent and comfortable on a computer as you are. These users rely on friendly and intuitive help in different forms, such as ToolTips, F1 Help, Readme.txt files, and WinHelp or HTML Help. By providing all of the various forms of help to the user, you immediately make users of all levels comfortable.

In the same manner that error handling should be a part of your design and coding, so too should adding help support be an active part of your design and coding, and not merely an afterthought. Don't wait until you have finished the program to add help but make it part of the programming process.

# Adding WinHelp Files

WinHelp files, until recently, were probably the most common of all the available help file formats. The main part of WinHelp projects is made up of *topic pages* that describe various topics in detail or give help in achieving some effect with regard to a topic. Topic pages are made using Rich Text Format (*.RTF*) files that use a special format to structure the data properly. There are many options that you can use when constructing topic pages. However, by just learning the main options that you will require to create a topic page, you can easily create a WinHelp file. You will always be able to further embellish the topic pages later by using the Microsoft documentation for creating topic pages for WinHelp.

To begin making new topic pages for your program, you must use a Rich Text editor, such as Microsoft Word or even WordPad. You can start by typing in a general heading in bold, and then on subsequent lines type in some other topic headings that you would want the user to be able to link to. Do not worry too much about your content, but merely look at acquiring the skills to create a WinHelp file. When you have a better idea of how to create topic pages for your WinHelp file, you can plan the entire process and content much more thoroughly.

To define the start of a topic, you must click your mouse at the beginning of the topic heading and insert the # character as a footnote. For many programmers who are faced with the daunting task of creating a topic page for a WinHelp file, the first step of inserting a character as a footnote can be a frustrating one. Do not switch the view perspective to headers and footers and type in the # character. This is not the same as a footnote and will not work. In Microsoft Word you must select the Insert menu Footnote option to be able to insert a character as a footnote in the Footnote and Endnote dialog box, as shown in Figure 29.1.

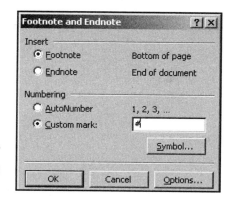

## Figure 29.1

*Inserting a character as a footnote using Microsoft Word.*

Inside the footnote, next to the # character you must type in the topic header.

There are many different footnote characters that you can use to customize your topic pages. For instance, to specify a particular window, you must insert the > character followed by the name of the window type that you want to use. You will use this window type name later during the creation of the WinHelp file.

To reference other topics from within the WinHelp file, you must mark each topic with a unique topic ID. To form topic IDs in your Rich Text file, you must insert a $ character as a footnote at the point where a topic starts. Topic IDs usually start with the characters IDH_, which you can then follow with some unique descriptive topic label.

To make a link to a topic ID, simply type in the topic ID immediately after the text that you would like to use to form the link and then double-underline the link text by highlighting the link text and selecting the Format menu Font option to select the double underline attribute. You should then make the topic ID text hidden, also using the Format menu Font option dialog box.

To indicate that you are about to start a new topic within the Rich Text file, you should use a hard page break. In Microsoft Word you can do this by selecting the Insert menu Break option, and then from the dialog box that displays select the Page break option. Figure 29.2 shows an example of using Microsoft Word to create a topic page in Rich Text Format (.RTF).

**Figure 29.2**

*Using Microsoft Word as a Rich Text editor to create topic files.*

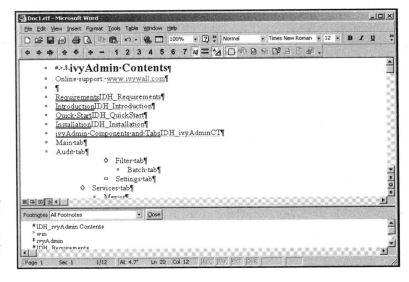

Microsoft provides a tool to assist you in the creation of WinHelp files, which is known as Help Workshop. If you are using Microsoft Visual Studio, you can access Help Workshop from your Start menu Programs sub-menu, as shown in Figure 29.3, although other installations may have a slightly different location.

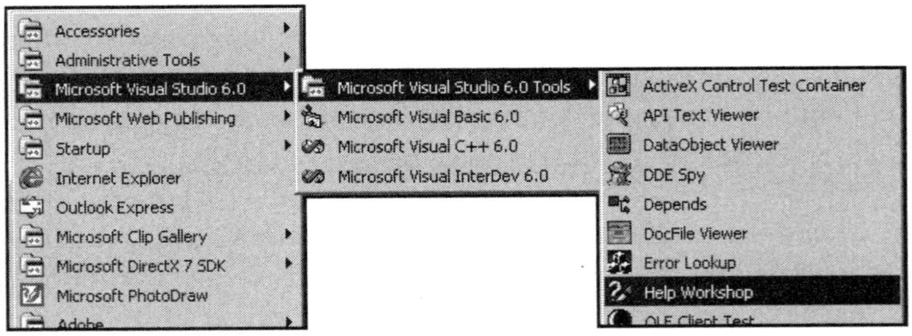

**Figure 29.3**

*Starting the Help Workshop program from menus.*

Start the Help Workshop program. Select the File menu New option. Help Workshop displays the New dialog box from which you must select Help Project to create a new help project. Type in a name for your new WinHelp project and give it an *.hpj* extension to identify it as a WinHelp project. To add your Rich Text Format file(s), start by clicking your mouse on the Files button. Help Workshop will present the Topic Files dialog box with which you can add your file(s) using the Add button. Click your mouse on the OK button to close the Topic Files dialog box.

To customize the look of the window that your WinHelp file will display in, click your mouse on the Windows button. Help Workshop will display the Window Properties in which you have five tabs: General, Position, Buttons, Color, and Macros. Each of the tabs contains settings for adjusting the help window to the specifications you want. You can have multiple windows but just make sure that you have one window with the name *main*, as your WinHelp project will use this.

Figure 29.4 shows the result of creating and configuring a new WinHelp project, although you may have different settings and files.

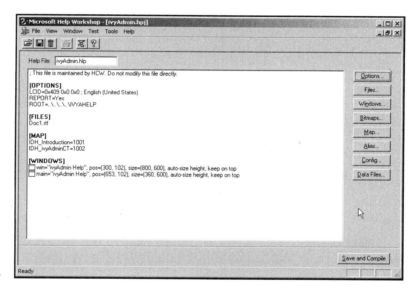

**Figure 29.4**

*The Help Workshop after creating a new project.*

To compile your project, you can select the File menu Compile option. Help Workshop will then display the Compile a Help File dialog box from which you can specify settings for the compiling process before clicking your mouse on the Compile button to actually compile the WinHelp file.

You can also view your WinHelp file by selecting the File menu Run WinHelp option. Microsoft Help Workshop will display the View Help File dialog box from which you can specify a particular topic and method of invoking the WinHelp file amongst other settings. Clicking your mouse on the View Help button will cause your WinHelp file to display, as shown in Figure 29.5.

# Lesson 30

---

# Building ActiveX and OLE Components

In Part II, "Interface—Look and Feel," you learned about providing the user with a look and feel that made using your programs as easy as possible, as well as attractive. In this lesson, you will cover a very useful feature known as Object Linking and Embedding (OLE), now more popularly known as ActiveX, which will enable you to provide the user with powerful features from other applications that support OLE and ActiveX. By the time you finish this lesson, you will understand the following key concepts:

♦ Object Linking and Embedding (OLE) is a technology that has been improved by Microsoft under the term ActiveX, of which OLE is just a part, to offer better safeguards and more features.

♦ The main idea of ActiveX and OLE is to make use of existing components for functionality in your programs rather than writing everything from scratch.

♦ The OLE container allows you to easily add the power and functionality of existing applications that have support for OLE into your own programs.

♦ Automation, or OLE Automation as it was originally known, allows you to tap into existing applications and make use of any functionality that they choose to expose.

♦ You can use the References dialog to add Object Libraries to your Visual Basic projects, to make use of the additional functionality that they offer.

♦ The Object Browser shows you all of the methods, properties, and constants that a project or object library exposes, allowing you to easily see what has been made available.

♦ ActiveX DLL projects run in the same thread as your Visual Basic programs, which means that they will usually run faster than ActiveX EXE projects, which run in a separate thread.

◆ To create your own ActiveX controls for use in your own projects or for other developers, you must first open a new ActiveX Control project before adding your own properties and methods for the control in a manner similar to class objects.

# Understanding ActiveX and OLE Basics

Before you start into the heavy material in this lesson, you should understand what the basic idea behind ActiveX and OLE is. Through separating functionality into components that other programs can make use of, you can tap into some of the power and features of existing programs without the need to rewrite from scratch all of the code that went into those features. ActiveX is a very object-oriented concept, and you will see that reusable code and routines are at its heart. The end result of making use of ActiveX and OLE is fast production times due to reusable components, as well as improvements in the interface for the user due to easy drag-and-drop functionality and immediate comfort with a familiar look and feel. ActiveX also works with many languages, not just Visual Basic, as well as online environments, making it useful to a broad range of programmers.

This lesson serves to introduce you to ActiveX and OLE technologies and gives you a solid foundation from which to branch off into more detailed studies, as you will discover that ActiveX is a very large and complex topic that you can spend a lot of time learning to harness the full range of functionality it offers.

**NOTE:** *In many books and online articles you will see the terms OLE and ActiveX made reference to almost interchangeably. This is because ActiveX is really just an enhancement to OLE or an improvement on the OLE concept and it might help you to think of OLE as a subset of what is now known as ActiveX.*

# Using the OLE Container Control

Visual Basic provides you with the OLE Container control to easily add OLE support to your programs. Adding OLE support to your programs means that users will be able to drag, for instance, a bitmap file onto your container and it will display either as an icon or as the content of the file. Users could drag other files too, such as Word documents or Excel charts, depending on the file formats that support OLE on a particular computer.

To add an OLE Container control, simply click your mouse on its icon, as shown in Figure 30.1, before dragging the size of the OLE Container that you require on your form.

### Figure 30.1

*The OLE Container control icon.*

When you add an OLE Container control to your form, Visual Basic displays the Insert Object dialog, as shown in Figure 30.2, which contains a list of object types that are available on the current computer.

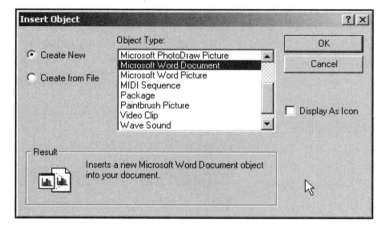

### Figure 30.2

*The Insert Object dialog for the OLE Container control.*

The Insert Object dialog allows you to either create a new instance of the object or to load in an existing instance of the object that is currently in the form of a file. For instance, you could create a new instance of a Microsoft Word document within your OLE container or you could load in an existing Microsoft Word document from file.

Using the *DisplayType* property, the OLE Container control allows you to work in two different modes: icon or content. Within the Insert Object dialog box the checkbox Display as Icon will set the *DisplayType* property to the constant *vbOLEDisplayIcon* when a check mark is present; otherwise, it will set the *DisplayType* property to the constant *vbOLEDisplayContent*. You cannot change the display of an OLE object after loading it, and so it is important for you to decide the mode you want the OLE Container object to use. Figure 30.3 shows clearly the diversity available using three OLE Container objects, the first two containing Microsoft Word documents and the third one containing an Adobe Photoshop document.

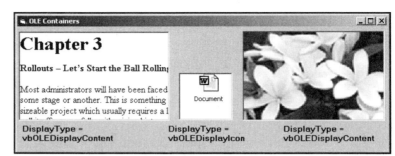

**Figure 30.3**

*Showing the diversity of the OLE Containers control.*

At runtime you can let the user add the OLE object of her choice using a variety of methods. One method is to use a file drag-and-drop technique. To try this technique simply set the *OLEDropAllowed* property to *True*. Alternatively, you could present your user with the Insert Object dialog box simply by using the OLE Container's *InsertObjDlg* method. Finally, you can also provide clipboard support by allowing your users to copy something into the clipboard and pasting it into the OLE Container object using the Paste Special dialog, as shown in Figure 30.4. You can display the Paste Special dialog to your users through the OLE Container object's *PasteSpecialDlg* method.

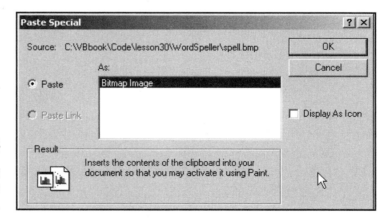

**Figure 30.4**

*The Paste Special dialog allows users to paste from the clipboard.*

The OLE Container control also has a *verb* menu that the user can display at runtime by right-clicking her mouse on the control to produce a pop-up menu containing available actions. You can turn this feature on or off using the *AutoVerbMenu* property. Within your code you can have the OLE Container perform any of these actions using the *DoVerb* method.

The OLE Container control is extremely powerful and has more properties and methods that you can use to customize its final behavior in your programs. By now you should have a good idea of what the OLE Container control is basically for, to be able to determine whether this functionality fits your program requirements. You have also seen a small preview of what the OLE Container control is capable of, and it is up to your ingenuity and imagination to try and harness this power tastefully into your own programs.

# Understanding Automation

Automation (formerly known as OLE Automation) allows you to tap into functionality that other applications have made readily available. The following example will show how to tap into Microsoft Word's spell checking functionality to check the spelling of text in your own programs. You can then apply this concept to other available applications or functions that support Automation using the same basic principles.

1. Open a new Visual Basic project and name it **WordSpeller**.

2. Add a TextBox control and a CommandButton control. Change the CommandButton's *Name* property to **cmdSpell** and its *Style* property to graphical and change its *ToolTip* property to **Check Spelling**.

3. Add an appropriate spelling picture to the CommandButton using the *Picture* property.

   You are welcome to use the bitmap for this example that is on the companion Web site for this book if you are not feeling graphically creative right now. (To locate all of the source code for this book, go to http://www.prima-tech.com/books/book/5250/945/.)

4. Select the Project menu References option. Visual Basic will present the References dialog from which you must scroll down and tick the checkbox for the item Microsoft Word 9.0 Object Library, as shown in Figure 30.5. Clicking your mouse on the OK button will close the References dialog box and load the reference for the Microsoft Word Object Library and all the methods and functionality that it exposes.

5. To see all the commands, methods, and general functionality that a reference to an object such as the Microsoft Word Object Library exposes, you can use the Object Browser in Visual Basic. To open the Object Browser, select the View menu Object Browser option. Visual Basic will display the Object Browser from which you must select the object library whose commands you wish to browse, as shown in Figure 30.6.

6. Select Word from the Project/Library combo box to see a list of all the commands that the Microsoft Word Object Library exposes for your use, including the *CheckSpelling* method, which you shall make use of shortly.

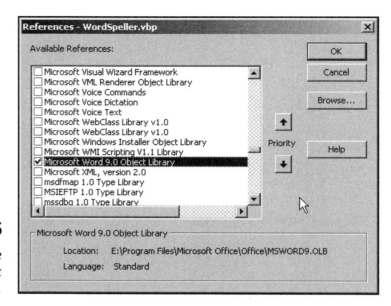

**Figure 30.5**

*Adding the reference for the Microsoft Word Object Library.*

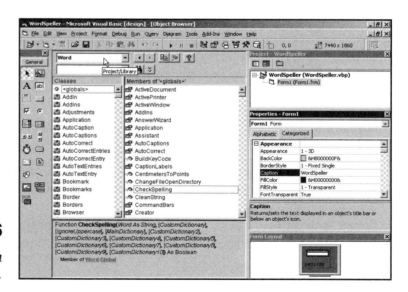

**Figure 30.6**

*Selecting an object library in the Object Browser.*

7. Add the following commented code to your code window, which shows clearly one method of using the *CheckSpelling* method of Microsoft Word to spell check text in your Visual Basic programs:

```
Private Sub cmdSpell_Click()
Dim myWord As New Application
    'Check that some text has been entered
    If Text1.Text = "" Then
        MsgBox "Enter some words in the text box and " & _
        "then click your mouse on the Check Spelling " & _
        "button.", vbInformation, "No text"
    Else
        'Create an invisible document
        myWord.Visible = False
        myWord.Documents.Add

        'Copy text to the document
        myWord.Selection.Text = Text1.Text

        'Check spelling with suggestions
        myWord.ActiveDocument.CheckSpelling , , True

        'If user did not select Cancel then copy text back
        If Not myWord.Selection.Text = "," Then _
            Text1.Text = myWord.Selection.Text

        'Close the document without saving changes
        myWord.ActiveDocument.Close wdDoNotSaveChanges
    End If

    'Free up resources used by Word object
    myWord.Quit
    Set myWord = Nothing
End Sub
```

8. Save the *WordSpeller* project and run the program, which should look something like Figure 30.7.

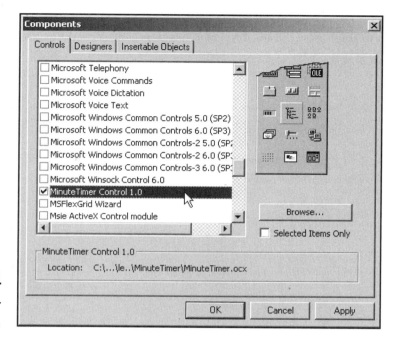

**Figure 30.11**

*Selecting the MinuteTimer component (ActiveX control).*

If you go to http://www.prima-tech.com/books/book/5250/945/, you will find a program with source code that you can use to test your MinuteTimer ActiveX control, as shown Figure 30.12.

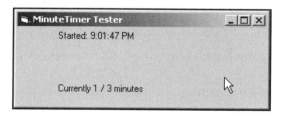

**Figure 30.12**

*The MinuteTimer Tester program putting your ActiveX control to the test.*

# What You Must Know

The OLE container allows you to easily add the functionality and features of other applications that support OLE into your own programs. By making use of Automation, you can tap into any properties or methods that an application exposes, using the Object Browser to assist in seeing what is available. Creating your own ActiveX controls allows you to add functionality with proper safeguards and error handling to your own Visual Basic programs in a clean, modular form rather than having to re-create the code for certain functionality each time you require it. In Lesson 31, "Declaring Application Programming Interfaces (APIs)," you will learn how to make use of the myriad Application Programming Interface (API) calls that are available in Windows, giving you access to some powerful low-level routines from your Visual Basic programs the same as C++ programmers have access to. Before you continue with Lesson 31, however, make sure you understand the following key concepts:

◆ To offer better safeguards and more features, Object Linking and Embedding (OLE) has been improved by Microsoft under the term ActiveX, of which OLE is now just a part.

◆ Rather than writing everything from scratch, the main idea of ActiveX and OLE is to make use of existing components for functionality in your programs.

◆ To easily add the power and functionality of existing applications that have support for OLE into your own programs, you can use the OLE Container control that Visual Basic provides.

◆ To tap into existing applications and make use of any functionality that they choose to expose, you can use Automation, or OLE Automation as it was originally known.

◆ To make use of the additional functionality that they offer, you can use the References dialog to add Object Libraries to your Visual Basic projects.

◆ To make it easier for you to see what is available for you to use in your programs, the Object Browser shows you all of the methods, properties, and constants that a project or object library exposes.

◆ ActiveX DLL projects run in the same thread as your Visual Basic programs, which means that they will usually run faster than ActiveX EXE projects, which run in a separate thread.

◆ Before adding your own properties and methods for the control in a manner similar to class objects, you must first open a new ActiveX Control project when creating ActiveX controls.

# Lesson 31

# Declaring Application Programming Interfaces (APIs)

In Lesson 30, "Building ActiveX and OLE Components," you learned how to add some powerful functionality to your Visual Basic programs, with little effort on your part, by making use of specially packaged code routines. In this lesson, you will learn how to make use of another type of specially packaged, powerful, low-level routine, the same as C++ programmers have access to, using the many Application Programming Interface (API) calls that are available in Windows. By the time you finish this lesson, you will understand the following key concepts:

◆ The Windows Application Programming Interface is not a single repository of routines, but rather, many various low-level routines that reside in multiple Dynamic Link Library files on the computer.

◆ You must use the *Declare* statement to declare an API call in your Visual Basic programs of which *Lib* is the part that determines the library to use.

◆ Windows core libraries such as GDI32, Kernel32, and User32 do not require you to use the DLL extension when specifying the library.

◆ The *Alias* keyword is optional and is for use mostly with text or string routines to avoid ambiguity between ANSI and Unicode formats.

◆ The API Text Viewer is a Microsoft tool that comes with Visual Basic, which you can use to easily copy and paste API calls that you require into your program modules without having to write the code yourself.

```
Declare Function StartService Lib "advapi32.dll" _
Alias "StartServiceA" (ByVal hService As Long, _
ByVal dwNumServiceArgs As Long, _
ByVal lpServiceArgVectors As Long) As Long
```

Finally, you create a subroutine within the module that shows a simple face to the developer.

**NOTE:** *Only Windows 2000 and Windows NT-based systems can run this code because Windows 9x and Windows ME operating systems don't offer the appropriate service handlers.*

```
Public Sub svcAction(ByVal computer As String, _
ByVal service As String, ByVal action1 As Action)
Dim SCManager As Long
Dim svcStatus As SERVICE_STATUS
Dim result As Long

    SCManager = OpenSCManager(computer, _
    SERVICES_ACTIVE_DATABASE, SC_MANAGER_ALL_ACCESS)

    If SCManager <> 0 Then
        service = OpenService(SCManager, service, _
        SERVICE_ALL_ACCESS)

        If service <> 0 Then
            Select Case action1
            Case svcStart
                result = StartService(service, 0, 0)
            Case svcStop
                result = ControlService(service, _
                SERVICE_CONTROL_STOP, svcStatus)
            End Select
            CloseServiceHandle service
        End If
        CloseServiceHandle SCManager
```

```
    End If

End Sub
```

When you complete all the details for working with a service inside the module, then the clarity of the resultant code in the form becomes obvious to the point of making working with services look simple. If you want to work with the services on the local computer, then you only need to supply an empty string; however, this could be the name of the local computer or the name of a remote computer. Be aware that you must be administrator or have administrative rights to start and stop services on a computer.

> **NOTE:** *All of the source code for this book can be found on the Web site that accompanies this book. You can access this at http://www.prima-tech.com/books/book/5250/945/.*

The following code you can place in a form's code window to start and stop a service, and Figure 31.5 shows the *ServiceStuff* program in action:

```
Private Sub cmdStart_Click()
    svcAction "", Text1, svcStart
End Sub

Private Sub cmdStop_Click()
    svcAction "", Text1, svcStop
End Sub
```

**Figure 31.5**

*The* ServiceStuff *program in action.*

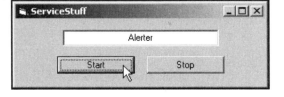

# What You Must Know

The Windows Application Programming Interface is made up of many various low-level routines residing in multiple Dynamic Link Library files on the computer. Use the *Declare* statement along with the *Lib* and *Alias* keywords to declare an API call in your Visual Basic programs. The API Text Viewer is a Microsoft tool that comes with Visual Basic, which you can use to easily copy and paste API calls that you require into your program modules without having to write the code yourself. In Lesson 32, "Using Active Directory," you will learn some of the basics of how to use Visual Basic with one of the major new technologies that has come from Microsoft recently, such as pulling up a list of all users or computers in a domain. Before you continue with Lesson 32, however, make sure you understand the following key concepts:

◆ Many various low-level routines that reside in multiple Dynamic Link Library files on the computer make up the Windows Application Programming Interface, which is not a single repository of routines.

◆ To declare an API call in your Visual Basic programs, you must use the *Declare* statement including the *Lib* keyword and a filename that determines the library to use.

◆ When specifying the library, Windows core libraries such as GDI32, Kernel32, and User32 do not require you to use the DLL extension.

◆ To avoid ambiguity between ANSI and Unicode formats in API calls with text or string routines, use the optional *Alias* keyword.

◆ To easily copy and paste API calls that you require into your program modules without having to write the code yourself you can use the API Text Viewer—a Microsoft tool that comes with Visual Basic.

**Using Schema to Find Class Properties**

*Learning how to access a particular class property in Active Directory is often very straightforward and intuitive. However, in practice, your program might have to retrieve information from properties that are unknown to them at design time, or perhaps you want to offer the users a list of all class properties for them to select from.*

*Each class or object in Active Directory has what is known as a schema. You can use this schema to see what properties are available for different objects or classes, almost in the same way that you would use an index in a book to discover where to go for information on a particular topic. The index does not contain a description of the topic but merely lets you know where you can go for more information. In the same way, the schema does not contain the actual property information but merely lets you know what properties are available, and then you can go and access the actual properties for the information that they contain.*

*The following code shows how to use the schema to discover all the mandatory and optional properties for the object robf, which is a class of type user. With a minor change to the initial GetObject call you could easily use this code for any variable making it suitable for users, groups, or computers.*

```
Option Explicit

Private Sub cmdGetUserProps_Click()
Dim obj As IADs
Dim cls As IADsClass
Dim property

    'Bind to the user class
    Set obj = GetObject("WinNT://" & _
        Environ("USERDOMAIN") & "/robf")

    'Set the class to the object schema
    Set cls = GetObject(obj.Schema)

    'Add all the mandatory properties
    List1.Clear
```

```
    For Each property In cls.MandatoryProperties
        List1.AddItem property
    Next


    'Add all the optional properties
    List2.Clear
    For Each property In cls.OptionalProperties
        List2.AddItem property
    Next
End Sub
```

*Figure 32.3 shows the result of running this code at a point when it is displaying
the properties of the* user *class using schema.*

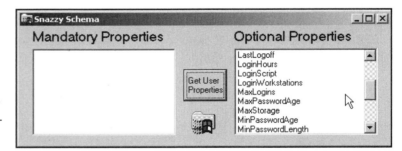

**Figure 32.3**

*Displaying the properties of
the* user *class using schema.*

# Accessing Microsoft Exchange with Active Directory

Microsoft Exchange is the most widely used e-mail server in use today. You can use Active Directory to easily
tap into Microsoft Exchange from your Visual Basic programs to list all the mailbox recipients and display data
about individual accounts, such as their home server or full name. There are far too many options available to
you to be able to cover them all here; however, so long as you are aware that such ability is available to you
through Active Directory, you can always experiment on your own or learn more from Microsoft references and
books.

The following example shows you the basics of how to tap into Microsoft Exchange to produce a list of mailbox
recipients:

```
Private Sub Form_Load()
Dim myIADs As IADs
Dim child As IADs

    Set myIADs = GetObject( _
    "LDAP://bwcpo002/cn=recipients, ou=ilbwc, o=Bahai")

    For Each child In myIADs
        List1.AddItem Mid(child.Name, 4)
    Next
End Sub
```

You should notice that the *GetObject* function is not using the *WinNT://* method but rather the *LDAP://* method.

You could have used another property of the child variable to retrieve the display name of the recipient rather than using the *Mid* function to strip the first few characters from the *Name* property. However, in practice, you will find that there is a noticeable delay when comparing the two methods, especially if you try this on a production Microsoft Exchange server with over a thousand recipients in its database. The results are similar but not necessarily the same in both cases. The following code shows this alternative method:

```
For Each child In oIADs
    List1.AddItem child.cn
Next
```

# What You Must Know

You can think of Active Directory as a hierarchical directory database that stores information relating to a particular network. You must add a reference to Microsoft's Active DS Type Library component before you can start using Active Directory from within your Visual Basic programs. You can easily obtain lists of computers, users, groups, and more, as well as retrieve many details concerning those objects by binding to different objects within Active Directory. In Lesson 33, "Winsock and Networking," you will learn how to communicate with other computers from within your Visual Basic programs to create much more interesting and powerful tools that can either integrate with existing programs or work in a server-client role. Before you continue with Lesson 33, however, make sure you understand the following key concepts:

◆ Active Directory is a hierarchical directory database that stores information relating to a particular network, such as computers, users, groups, policies, and more.

◆ Before you can start using Active Directory from within your Visual Basic programs, you must add a reference to Microsoft's Active DS Type Library component.

◆ You must declare a variable of type *IADS* and then bind it to an *Active Directory* object using the *GetObject* function, passing as an argument, the path of the object.

◆ Using Active Directory you can easily retrieve the list of computers after binding to a domain and iterating through the child objects extracting those of class *Computer*.

◆ You can obtain the list of users in a domain or on the local computer and then retrieve further properties and methods pertaining to the user by binding to the user object itself.

◆ You can use Active Directory to find a list of all the groups on a domain or a local computer and then simply bind to a particular group to find out more information, such as discovering who the members of that group are.

◆ To access Microsoft Exchange Server and recover lists of all the recipient mailboxes or find out specific details from within your Visual Basic programs, you can use Active Directory.

# Lesson 33

# Winsock and Networking

In Lesson 32, "Using Active Directory," you learned how to retrieve a list of all the computers on a network. In this lesson, you will learn how to communicate with those computers from within your Visual Basic programs, by making use of the Winsock control using Transmission Control Protocol (TCP) and User Datagram Protocol (UDP). By the time you finish this lesson, you will understand the following key concepts:

- ◆ The Winsock control allows your programs to communicate with other computers using either TCP or UDP as its communication protocol.

- ◆ To use the Winsock control, you must first add the Microsoft Winsock Control 6.0 component to your Visual Basic project.

- ◆ UDP is a connectionless protocol with no built-in error checking or redundancy but is very simple to implement.

- ◆ The three main steps for a UDP connection using the Winsock control are setting the *RemoteHost* property, setting the *RemotePort* property, and binding the local port that you wish to use.

- ◆ The *DataArrival()* event fires when data arrives at the port your Winsock control is bound to.

- ◆ To get the data when it arrives, you must use the *GetData* method to assign the data to a variable.

- ◆ To send data you simply use the *SendData* method and pass it the string that you want to send as its only argument.

- ◆ TCP is a connection-oriented protocol that uses error checking and is slightly more difficult than UDP to configure.

◆ The four main steps for a TCP connection using the Winsock control are setting the *Remote-Host* property, setting the *RemotePort* property, setting the *LocalPort* property, and then calling the *Connect* method.

◆ The *LocalPort* property must be set and the *Listen* method used by the program that is receiving the connection request rather than binding.

# Understanding Basic Network Communication Concepts

After having seen all the great things that you can do with Visual Basic, you may be wondering why you would ever want to write networking programs. Having network communication between computers allows programs to exchange data with each other, which opens up a whole range of possibilities for you.

You can write client-server applications, where one program sits on one computer and listens for a connection and another program on another computer communicates with it. The server is always the program that is listening for someone trying to connect, and the client is always the program that initiates communication. Therefore, if you have a small program on one hundred computers and one main program that sits on one computer from which you can initiate communication with any of the others to retrieve some data, the server piece is actually on the hundred computers and the client piece is on the single computer. Many people find this concept confusing and always call the program that goes out to many computers the client piece, although this is not correct.

You can also write what are known as peer-to-peer applications, which are really both client and server rolled into one program. In a peer-to-peer application, each program is both listening for connections and also capable of initiating communication with others.

Another possibility is to write programs that simply communicate with other existing programs. For instance, you might make use of some of the well-known ports, typically in the range 0–1023, for which there are many programs already written that are either set to listen for connections or able to communicate.

# Adding a Winsock Control

Visual Basic has a handy control that you can use to make communication with other computers very easy. It uses Windows Sockets, known as Winsock, which was originally made for Unix systems, where it was known as BSD Sockets.

Before you can use the Microsoft Winsock control in your Visual Basic programs you must first add the right component to your project. Within the Visual Basic environment, click your mouse on the Project menu

Components option. Visual Basic presents the Components dialog box, with which you are probably now quite familiar. Select the Microsoft Winsock Control 6.0 item by placing a check mark in the corresponding checkbox, as shown in Figure 33.1.

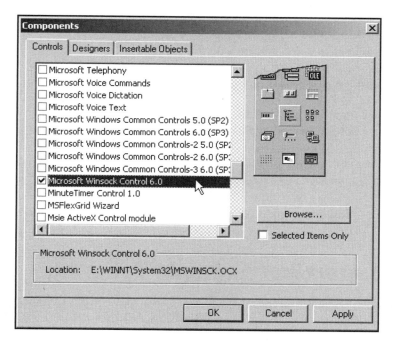

**Figure 33.1**

*Adding the Microsoft Winsock Control 6.0 component.*

Click your mouse on the OK button to close the Components dialog box. The Winsock control icon as it appears on the control panel is shown in Figure 33.2.

**Figure 33.2**

*The Winsock control icon.*

# Using the User Datagram Protocol (UDP)

You may already be aware that the User Datagram Protocol (UDP) is part of the TCP/IP family of protocols. UDP is a connectionless protocol with no built-in error checking or redundancy that is simple to implement. Sending a UDP signal is similar to sending out a radio signal. If nobody receives the signal because they were not listening for it at the time, you really do not want to know, and therefore Visual Basic generates no error.

There are three steps that you must take to have your program send data, as shown below:

1. Set the *RemoteHost* property to the name or IP number of the computer you want to send data to.

2. Set the *RemotePort* property to the number of the port that the remote computer is listening to.

3. Bind the local port that you wish to use.

To have your program receive data, you only require step 3, binding to a local port. When you are writing programs where both computers will send and receive data, then both programs will require all three steps.

You can change the *RemoteHost* or *RemotePort* properties whenever you require without having to bind the local port again. In this manner, you can bind a local port and keep it for your program while switching between different remote hosts or remote ports. As you shall see later in this lesson, you cannot do this with TCP but must actually close any current connection before you can change the *RemoteHost* or *RemotePort* properties.

# The *SuperChat* Example Program

The *SuperChat* example program shows you clearly how to use the Winsock control with UDP to create a peer-to-peer chat program. When you finish creating the *SuperChat* program you can run the program on multiple, networked computers and chat with your friends. The program is relatively simple, as the idea is to show you how to use UDP with the Winsock control, but you can easily enhance the *SuperChat* program to send data to a list of computers, to have better error handling, to use preformatted comments, or any other popular features.

1. Create a new project and name it **SuperChat**.

2. Add two TextBox controls and name them **txtHistory** and **txtSay**. Add a smaller TextBox control and name it **txtPC**. Add a CommandButton below *txtPC* and name it **cmd RemotePC** and change its *Caption* property to **&Remote PC**.

   Optionally, you can enhance the user interface with graphics, colored text, scrollbars, etc. Figure 33.3 shows the *SuperChat* program in action and gives you an idea of the layout of the controls.

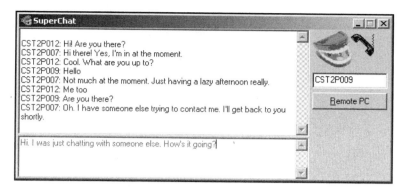

## Figure 33.3

*The* SuperChat *program in action.*

3. In the Visual Basic code window, you must now add the following code, which will be broken up with an explanation of what is going on to make the code clearer.

   The first section declares a constant to clearly show the port that the program will use. This makes it easy to change the port in one place with no hunting through code for binding calls or port setting calls. In the *Form_Load()* event, set the protocol for the Winsock control to *sckUDPProtocol* before binding a local port.

```
Option Explicit
Private Const port = 3001


'============================================================
'Initialize the Winsock control
'============================================================
Private Sub Form_Load()
sckChat.Protocol = sckUDPProtocol
sckChat.Bind port
End Sub
```

4. When the user enters the name of a remote computer to chat with in *txtPC* and then clicks her mouse on the *Remote PC* button, your program must set the *RemoteHost* property. Inform the user if the computer to chat with is an empty field.

```
'============================================================
'Change the remote PC that data is being sent to
'============================================================
```

```
Private Sub cmdRemotePC_Click()
sckChat.RemoteHost = txtPC.Text
sckChat.RemotePort = port
If sckChat.RemoteHost = "" Then
MsgBox "Enter a computer to chat with.", _
vbInformation, "No computer name!"
End If
End Sub
```

5. You must use the Winsock control's *DataArrival()* event to receive the data that arrives on the port your program is listening to. If data arrives on a port other than the one to which your Winsock control is bound, the *DataArrival()* event will not fire, saving you a lot of unnecessary error handling and confusion. You must save the data into a variable before assigning it elsewhere using the Winsock control's *GetData* method, which takes the variable as its only argument. In the case of the *SuperChat* program, you can append any incoming data to the *txtHistory* textbox, giving the user the chance to read messages at her own pace.

**NOTE:** *An important point to note is the error handling. Although you do not require this normally, there is a known bug that causes problems with the Winsock control when using UDP on Windows 2000 that sends a single byte of data and fires the* DataArrival() *event. Microsoft has put a fix in SP-1 (Service Pack 1), although you cannot guarantee that all users of your software will have this installed. Adding explicit error handling, as shown below, fixes this problem in your code.*

```
'==========================================================
'Data has arrived so add it to the chat history
'==========================================================
Private Sub sckChat_DataArrival(ByVal bytesTotal As Long)
Dim data As String
On Error GoTo ErrHnd
sckChat.GetData data
txtHistory.Text = txtHistory.Text & vbCrLf & data
ErrHnd:
End Sub
```

6. Finally, to actually send data whenever the user presses the return or enter key, you can use the *KeyPress()* event, that you learned about in Lesson 17, "Working with the Mouse and Keyboard." Alternatively, you might want to send data as the user types each character in the *txtSay* textbox, in which case you might opt for the *txtSay_Change()* event instead.

Add the data that you want to send into a variable of type *String*, and then simply use the Winsock control's *SendData* method with the string variable as its only argument. In the case of the *SuperChat* program, you might want to clear the *txtSay* textbox to both prepare it for their next message as well as giving them feedback that their message has been sent. To stop the actual return character being put into *txtSay*, simply assign 0 to *KeyAscii*.

```
'==========================================================
'Send the data when the user presses the return (enter) key
'==========================================================
Private Sub txtSay_KeyPress(KeyAscii As Integer)
Dim s As String
If KeyAscii = vbKeyReturn Then
s = sckChat.LocalHostName & ": " & txtSay.Text
txtHistory.Text = txtHistory & vbCrLf & s
sckChat.SendData s
txtSay.Text = ""
KeyAscii = 0
End If
End Sub
```

7. Save the project and run the *SuperChat* program on two different computers that are on the same network. Type in the name of the remote computer for each instance of the program before clicking your mouse on the Remote PC button, and then simply type messages in the *txtSay* textbox.

Feel free to enhance this program or modify it if you would like to actually write a chat program and refer to http://www.prima-tech.com/books/book/5250/945/ for the *SuperChat* source code and executable.

**Enhancing Your Winsock Programs**

*Although you have not yet learned everything in this lesson, you may want to write some serious programs that use Winsock controls and then find yourself coming up against difficulties in implementation.*

*One area that you may have difficulty with is being able to handle multiple connections simultaneously. The Winsock control can handle this advanced feature and provides the* Index *property for this purpose. You must set the* Index *property to 0, and then when you use the* Accept *method, which you shall see later in this lesson, you can use a new instance of the Winsock control to actually make the connection, leaving the initial instance of the Winsock control, index 0, in a listening state. In this manner you can handle multiple connections simultaneously, without the need for code repetition.*

*The other area that can cause difficulties is trying to achieve more control of the Winsock control's features or functionality. For this reason, if you wish to use Winsock at a low level for additional control or functionality, Visual Basic provides you with the* SocketHandle *property, which is only available at runtime and even then it is read-only and cannot be set. You can use this low-level handle to the Winsock control together with API calls for handling Winsock.*

# Using the Transmission Control Protocol (TCP)

Unlike the User Datagram Protocol (UDP), the Transmission Control Protocol (TCP) is a connection-oriented protocol that uses error checking. TCP is the most widely seen network connectivity protocol in use today. To use TCP with the Winsock control is more complex than its UDP cousin; however, as with many controls in Visual Basic, it is not too difficult with much of the complexity taken out by the control itself.

To receive data you must set the Winsock control's *LocalPort* property to the port your program will listen to and then you use the Winsock control's *Listen* method. A TCP port can be thought of as a specific location, almost like a mailbox at the postal office, to send and receive TCP packets. Port numbers below 1024 are well-known ports and are assigned by the Internet Assigned Numbers Authority (IANA), so you are often using port numbers higher than 1024 for your own programs to communicate. You do not use the *Bind* method with TCP.

There are four steps that you must take to have your program send data, of which the latter two steps differ from the UDP method, as shown on the following page:

1. Set the *RemoteHost* property to the name or IP number of the computer you want to send data to.

2. Set the *RemotePort* property to the number of the port that the remote computer is listening to.

3. Set the *LocalPort* property to the port number your program on the local computer will listen to.

4. Use the Winsock control's *Connect* method to request a connection.

When the remote computer accepts the connection request, you can send data using the *SendData* method, in the same manner as you did when using UDP.

# Using the *SystemInfo Agent* Example Program (Server)

The *SystemInfo Agent* example is really made up of two programs and demonstrates a client-server application that uses the Transmission Control Protocol (TCP) to report back information pertaining to the local system. The agent piece would typically be put on all of the computers on a Local Area Network (LAN) and the controller piece only given to administrators or IT staff who manage the computers. The *SystemInfo Agent* does not require anything to be shown to the user, as you can see in Figure 33.4, and you can easily make the form invisible and set the following line of code if you were writing a professional agent piece:

```
App.TaskVisible = False
```

**Figure 33.4**

*The* SystemInfo Agent *(server) form at design time.*

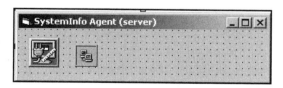

1. Open a new project and name it **SIserver**. Add a Winsock control and name it **sckSvr**. Add the component Microsoft SysInfo Control 6.0, and then add a SysInfo control to your form and leave it with the default name.

2. To start with, you must set the *Protocol* property to **sckTCPProtocol** and then set the local port to use. Although you can use a constant to define the port, it is possible to simply assign the port number directly, as the following code shows, which is acceptable when there is only a single reference to this value in the entire program.

3. After setting the *LocalPort* property, you use the *Listen* method to start listening to the port for incoming data.

```
Option Explicit
'============================================================
'Program starts here
'============================================================
Private Sub Form_Load()
'Initialize Winsock control and start listening
sckSvr.Protocol = sckTCPProtocol
sckSvr.LocalPort = 5000
sckSvr.Listen
End Sub
```

4. When another program, usually from a remote computer, tries to connect to the port your Winsock control is listening to, the *ConnectionRequest()* event fires. First, you should check that your Winsock control is in a state that is able to accept the request. You will see more about Winsock states later in this lesson. To accept the connect, simply use the *Accept* method with the *requestID* argument. In the case of the *SystemInfo Agent* program, you can simply use the *SendData* method to send back the system information. However, in an actual situation you can use handshaking methods and encrypted passwords before handing out information.

```
'============================================================
'A new connection request has come in
'============================================================
Private Sub sckSvr_ConnectionRequest _
(ByVal requestID As Long)
'Close the connection if necessary
If sckSvr.State <> sckClosed Then sckSvr.Close
'Accept the connection request
```

## Figure 34.2

*The MSChart control icon as it appears in the control panel.*

To add an MSChart control to your form, simply click your mouse on its control icon and then drag out the size of the object that you want on the form. The MSChart control has many properties and methods, many of which take specific constants. You may find the number of options in the MSChart control rather overwhelming, but you should focus on the basics first and simply view all of the other properties, methods, and events as extra functionality should you require something specific. Taking this approach, you will soon master the MSChart control and be able to provide professional and powerful charting and graphing capabilities to users of your Visual Basic programs.

# Understanding Chart Type Variations

One of the easiest methods to see the type of chart that you can produce with each of the various constants for the *ChartType* property is to change the value of the *ChartType* property at design time, and Visual Basic will automatically update the MSChart control showing you a default view for that style. For use within your Visual Basic programs, however, you can use the list of constants that are available for the *ChartType* property, as shown in Table 34.1.

*Table 34.1 Possible constants for use with the ChartType property.*

| Constant | Description |
|---|---|
| VtChChartType2dArea | 2-D Area |
| VtChChartType2dBar | 2-D Bar |
| VtChChartType2dCombination | 2-D Combination |
| VtChChartType2dLine | 2-D Line |
| VtChChartType2dPie | 2-D Pie |
| VtChChartType2dStep | 2-D Step |
| VtChChartType2dXY | 2-D XY |
| VtChChartType3dArea | 3-D Area |
| VtChChartType3dBar | 3-D Bar |
| VtChChartType3dCombination | 3-D Combination |
| VtChChartType3dLine | 3-D Line |
| VtChChartType3dStep | 3-D Step |

# Using the Property Pages Dialog

To work with the MSChart control at design time, the easiest method to customize the control to achieve a particular effect is to use the Property Pages dialog. To open the Property Pages dialog, click your mouse on the MSChart object on your form and then select View menu Property Pages option.

The tabs in the Property Pages dialog are fairly intuitive, and at this stage of your Visual Basic knowledge you should be comfortable with experimenting with new control options. You can use the Property Pages dialog to modify or set titles, axes, borders, backdrops, legends, colors, fonts, and more, as shown in Figure 34.3. The nice thing about using the Property Pages dialog is that it updates the MSChart control at design time so you can see the result of making a change without having to save and run the program.

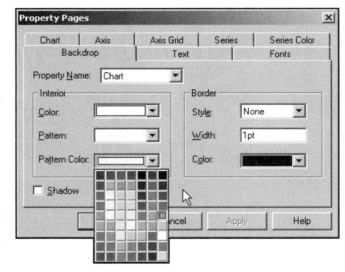

**Figure 34.3**

*The Property Pages dialog.*

 **Alternative Methods to Open Property Pages**

*Due to the complexity of the MSChart control and the fact that the Property Pages dialog makes using the control much easier, you will find that you want to access the Property Pages dialog quite often when working with MSChart controls. Rather than having to move your mouse up to the View menu and then select the Property Pages option, there are some alternatives that you may find suit your work style better.*

*One method is to click your mouse on the MSChart object and then press the keys Shift-F4. Another method that can save time is simply right-clicking your mouse on the MSChart object and selecting the Properties option from the pop-up menu that appears.*

# Working with Rows and Columns

When using the MSChart control, some of the key properties that you should become comfortable with are those dealing with rows and columns.

To get the number of rows or columns in a chart, simply use the *RowCount* and *ColumnCount* properties. You can use these same properties to set the number of rows or columns in a chart, as shown in the following code:

```
totalrows = MSChart1.RowCount      'Gets the number of rows
MSChart1.RowCount = 5              'Sets the number of rows
```

To work with a particular row or column element, you must assign the value of that element to the *Row* or *Column* properties, respectively. For instance, when you assign the value 3 to the *Row* property, you are making row 3 the current row. You can use the *Row* and *Column* properties to get the current row and column, as well as set them.

You can assign a label to each row or column by using the *RowLabel* and *ColumnLabel* properties. Both of these properties work with the current row or column, respectively. In the same manner, working with the current row and column, you can get or set the data value for a particular row and column, using the *Data* property. The following code sets the current working row and column and then proceeds to set labels and data for them:

```
MSChart1.Row = 3
MSChart1.Column = 2
MSChart1.Data = 5
MSChart1.ColumnLabel = "Green"
MSChart1.RowLabel = "1998"
```

# Using a Legend

A legend displays the key to the chart in a graphical form. You can easily generate a legend for your charts by setting the *ShowLegend* property to *True*, either in the *Properties* section or in your code, as follows:

```
MSChart1.ShowLegend = True
```

The legend will make use of the *ColumnLabel* property, which you can set for each column. You can modify the legend extensively through the Property Pages dialog at design time or through code at runtime. Figure 34.4 shows an example of a legend.

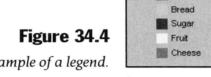

**Figure 34.4**

*An example of a legend.*

# Setting a Chart Title

Set the title of your chart by assigning text to the *TitleText* property. You can modify the font of the title, as well as the color, orientation, alignment, and other factors through the Property Pages dialog at design time or through code at runtime.

You can also make use of the *Title* property to set the backdrop, font, location, or actual text, although you should use the *TitleText* property. You will see some example code for setting a chart title later in this lesson in the pie chart example code.

# Copying Charts

You can easily copy the chart data or the graphical picture of the chart itself by using the MSChart control's *EditCopy* method, which places data into the Clipboard. To paste the data into an Excel spreadsheet, use the Edit menu, Paste option from within Excel. To paste the picture of the chart, use the Edit menu Paste Special option from within Excel.

You can also paste charts and data into an MSChart control by using the *EditPaste* method, which will use the data or graphic in the clipboard if it can. To paste data into an MSChart control, you must make sure that the currently selected chart element is the entire chart and not a label, title, legend, point, or some other element. To paste graphics into an MSChart control, you must similarly make sure that the currently selected chart element is an element which accepts a metafile.

# Working with Manual Data

To actually put some of the key concepts that have been seen so far into practice, you will now create a new program that uses the MSChart control and assigns multiple rows and columns to a three dimensional (3-D) bar chart. The source code for this example is on the companion Web site for this book if you do not want to type this in yourself or if you wish to reference it for comparison reasons. To access the Web site, go to http://www.prima-tech.com/books/book/5250/945/.

1. Start a new Visual Basic project and name it **ManualChart3D**. Add a Timer control, with an *Interval* property of **50**, and an MSChart control to the form, and add the following code to the code window:

```
Option Explicit

'===========================================================
'Declare constants
'===========================================================
Private Const colnum = 5
Private Const rownum = 4


'===========================================================
'Draw the 3d chart when program starts but after form loads
'===========================================================
Private Sub Timer1_Timer()
Dim intCol As Integer
Dim intRow As Integer

    Timer1.Enabled = False
    With MSChart1
        'Use the 3d Bar style for the chart
        .chartType = VtChChartType3dBar

        'Set the number of columns and rows using constants
        .ColumnCount = colnum
        .RowCount = rownum

        'Set some manual data for each column and each row
```

```
For intCol = 1 To colnum
    For intRow = 1 To rownum
        .Column = intCol
        .Row = intRow
        .Data = (intRow + intCol) * 10
    Next intRow
Next intCol

    'Show a legend for the chart
    .ShowLegend = True
    End With
End Sub
```

2. Save the *ManualChart3D* project and run the program. The program should look similar to Figure 34.5.

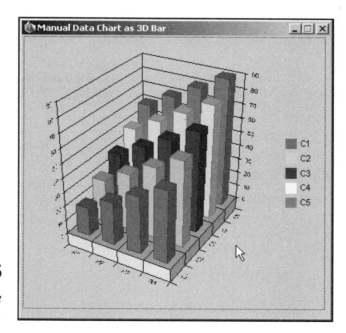

**Figure 34.5**

*The result of running the ManualChart3D program.*

# Dynamic Rotation of Graphs and Charts

When the control key is held down and an MSChart control is active, Visual Basic changes the mouse cursor from a standard arrow to a curvy multi-directional cross, as shown in Figure 34.6. By holding down the control key and moving his mouse while depressing the left mouse button, the user is able to actually change the perspective of the chart to suit his own preferences. A group of dotted lines indicates the shape and perspective of the chart prior to releasing the left mouse button. You can turn this feature off by setting the MSChart control's *AllowDynamicRotation* property to *False*.

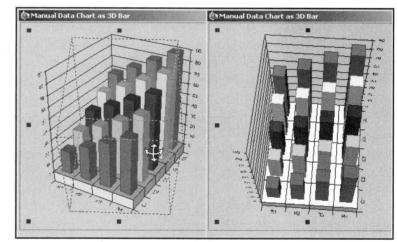

**Figure 34.6**

*Changing the perspective of an MSChart object at runtime— during and after.*

# Using Arrays for Chart Data

You have already seen how useful arrays are in your Visual Basic programs. Many programs store information in arrays, and so the MSChart control allows you to simply assign an array to the *ChartData* property.

```
Private Sub MSChart1_Click()
Dim profit(11) As Long
Dim i As Integer

    'Initialize profit array
    For i = 0 To 11
        profit(i) = Rnd * 100
    Next
```

```
    'Set chart properties
    With MSChart1
        .chartType = VtChChartType2dLine
        .TitleText = "Sales for 2000"
        .ChartData = profit
        .ColumnCount = 1
        .RowCount = 12
        .Refresh
    End With
End Sub
```

Figure 34.7 shows the result of running the code above. Notice that each time you click on the chart, a random set of new values will be created and displayed.

**Figure 34.7**

*A two-dimensional (2-D) line chart showing sales figures for the year.*

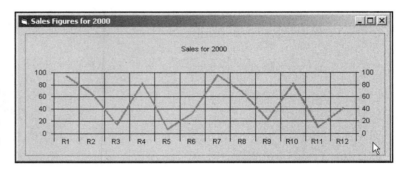

## Working with Pie Charts

Quite often, users who work with charts will require a pie chart, especially when portraying proportions. An example of using a pie chart might be to show various departments of a university and the proportion of the overall budget that each department spends. You can provide support for pie charts from your Visual Basic programs using the MSChart control. To work with a single pie chart and provide data concerning each slice of the pie, set the *RowCount* property to *1* and the *ColumnCount* property to the number of slices.

```
Private Sub Form_Load()
Dim i As Integer
    With MSChart1
        'Assign general settings
```

```
.chartType = VtChChartType2dPie
.RowCount = 1
.ColumnCount = 5
.ShowLegend = True
.RowLabel = ""
.TitleText = "Grocery breakdown"
.Title.VtFont.Style = VtFontStyleBold
.Title.VtFont.Size = 14
.Title.VtFont.Effect = VtFontEffectUnderline

'Assign specific data settings
.Column = 1
.Data = 10
.ColumnLabel = "Milk"
.Column = 2
.Data = 10
.ColumnLabel = "Bread"
.Column = 3
.Data = 25
.ColumnLabel = "Sugar"
.Column = 4
.Data = 40
.ColumnLabel = "Fruit"
.Column = 5
.Data = 15
.ColumnLabel = "Cheese"

'Make the pie labels show as a percentage
For i = 1 To .Plot.SeriesCollection.Count
    With .Plot.SeriesCollection(i).DataPoints(-1).DataPointLabel
        .LocationType = _
        VtChLabelLocationTypeOutside
        .Component = VtChLabelComponentPercent
        .VtFont.Style = VtFontStyleBold + _
        VtFontStyleItalic
        .PercentFormat = "0%"
```

```
          End With
      Next
   End With
End Sub
```

First, the code sets general properties, such as *ChartType* and *TitleText*. Next, it assigns data to the five portions of the pie by assigning values to the *Column* property. Finally, the code illustrates for you how to set the pie labels so that the labels appear as a percentage. The code for the pie chart example may be short, but it is not entirely simple. Some of the lines of code show you how to do some complex changes but should also lead you to experiment further with the myriad properties and features that the MSChart control contains. Figure 34.8 shows the result of running the *Pie Chart* example code.

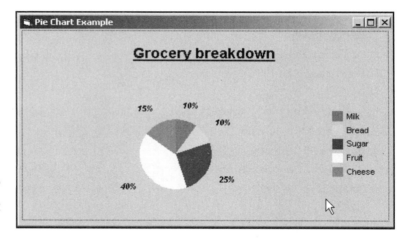

**Figure 34.8**

*The result of the* Pie Chart *example code.*

# What You Must Know

To produce charts and graphs in Visual Basic, you should use the Microsoft Chart control, which is also known as the MSChart control. There are many properties, methods, and events in the MSChart control, which show the level of control that you have for chart customization and functionality. The *ChartType* property is where you can choose one of twelve various chart styles ranging from 3-D bar charts to pie charts. In Lesson 35, "Packaging the Program," you will learn how to package your programs so that you can install them for use on other computers using both the Package and Deployment wizard that comes with Visual Basic, as well as the newer Visual Studio Installer, which creates *.msi* files that are used with Active Directory and Windows Installer. Before you continue with Lesson 35, however, make sure you understand the following key concepts:

◆ The Microsoft Chart control, which is also known as the MSChart control, is the easiest method to produce charts and graphs in Visual Basic and requires the component Microsoft Chart Control 6.0 to be added to your Visual Basic project.

◆ The MSChart control has many properties, methods, and events that may seem overwhelming but really just show the level of control that you have with this comprehensive chart creation tool.

◆ 3-D bar charts, 2-D line charts, pie charts, and more, can all be chosen from the *ChartType* property, where you can choose one of twelve various chart styles.

◆ Allowing you to easily set up the chart at design time, the Property Pages dialog also lets you see the results of modifications without the need to recompile and run the program.

◆ You can set the current working element using the *Row* and *Column* properties and then modify its data value or labels.

◆ Using the MSChart control's *ShowLegend* property you can easily have legends for your charts, which make use of the column labels for identification.

◆ To customize the chart title's text, font, backdrop, and location, you can use the *TitleText* property and the *Title* property.

◆ Working with the Clipboard, the *EditCopy* and *EditPaste* methods let you copy chart data and pictures into and out of charts.

◆ A very valuable and attractive feature for your Visual Basic programs, the MSChart control can be dynamically rotated at runtime by the user using the control key and the mouse.

The next window is the Shared Files window, as shown in Figure 35.9. Only check the box for any file that appears in the Shared Files window if it is actually used by another program. Often this is not the case, and no files in your project are shared besides system files. Click your mouse on the Next button to continue.

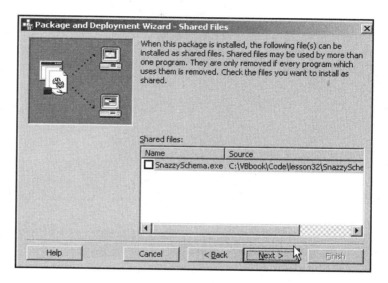

**Figure 35.9**

*The Shared Files window.*

The last window is the Finished! window. Change the name of the installation script, which will store all of the information that you have just input, as well as the options that you have chosen. Later, you can simply edit your script to make modifications to some of your choices without having to go through the entire process again. You should use a different script name for each project that you create an installation package for. Click your mouse on the Finish button, as shown in Figure 35.10, to actually create your installation package.

Finally, you will see a small Packaging Report window that basically gives you a summary of the package creation process that you have just completed. Click your mouse on the Save Report button if you would like to keep a record of the report, or simply click your mouse on the Close button to close the window.

That is all there is to creating a setup package for your Visual Basic programs. You can now burn that setup package to a CD, upload it to an Internet site for others, or make use of some other method of distributing your program.

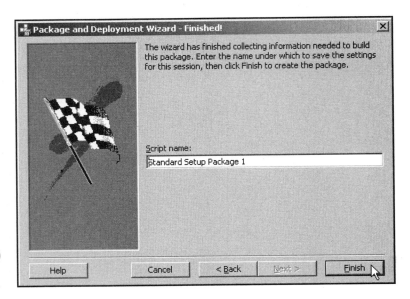

**Figure 35.10**

*The Finished! window.*

# Using the Visual Studio Installer 1.1

The Visual Studio Installer 1.1 is Microsoft's latest package creation utility and, at the time of writing, is available to licensed Visual Basic users at the following URL for downloading:

http://msdn.microsoft.com/vstudio/downloads/updates.asp

This URL may change, as the Microsoft site is continually changing and updating.

There is good news and bad news with this installer depending on what software you have. The good news is that this installer allows you to create native Windows Installer Package (*.msi*) files, which administrators can install through Active Directory and Group Policies. The *.msi* packages will become the installation of choice for any networks running Windows 2000 or higher and offer such capabilities as *side-by-side versioned installs*, *self-healing*, and *install on demand*, making this method of packaging something that every serious Visual Basic programmer will not want to ignore.

The bad news for some developers is that this very nice utility, Microsoft Visual Studio Installer 1.1, requires Visual InterDev to create your packages. In the next release of Visual Basic, Visual Basic .NET, Visual InterDev has been made a part of the Integrated Developer Environment (IDE).

After obtaining Microsoft Visual Studio Installer 1.1 and running the setup program, you must then start Visual InterDev. Visual InterDev will present you with the New Project dialog, as shown in Figure 35.11.

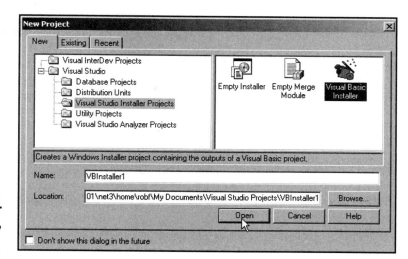

**Figure 35.11**

*The Visual InterDev New Project dialog.*

Within the New Project dialog beneath the New tab, click your mouse on the small plus sign to the left of the Visual Studio folder. Visual InterDev will display the various project types that it currently supports, from which you must choose Visual Studio Installer Projects. When you choose this, the right hand pane displays icons for three different types of installers, of which you must select the Visual Basic Installer icon, as shown earlier in Figure 35.11. In the Name field you can enter the name that you want to give your project. In the Location field you can enter the drive location that you want to save the project to.

When you have made the necessary changes, click your mouse on the Open button. Visual InterDev closes the New Project dialog and opens a new dialog from which you must select the Visual Basic project that you would like to create an installer file for. Select the option for creating an installer file rather than a Merge Module, as shown in Figure 35.12. A Merge Module is very useful for other purposes, such as when you have a development team that wants to synchronize the set of *.dll* files that it distributes with its in-house programs, for instance.

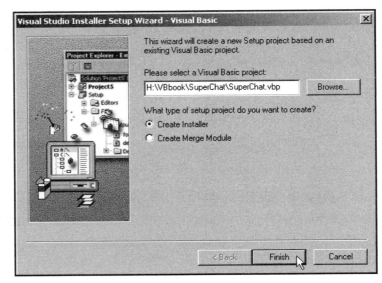

**Figure 35.12**

*Selecting the Visual Basic project to make an Installer file for.*

When you finish selecting the Visual Basic project that you want to make an Installer file for, click your mouse on the Finish button. Visual InterDev will close the Visual Studio Installer Setup Wizard dialog box and open up the Microsoft Developer Environment window. Within the Microsoft Developer Environment window you can customize the installer project in fine detail. There are many options for which you can make changes and alterations, although this is not necessary to successfully create your installer file.

One area that you may want to customize is the setup interface that the installer will present to users. By double-clicking your mouse on the User Interface option beneath the Target Machine folder, you will see a list of all the various steps and screens that the user will see. By selecting any of these items, you can easily customize its various properties, as shown in Figure 35.13.

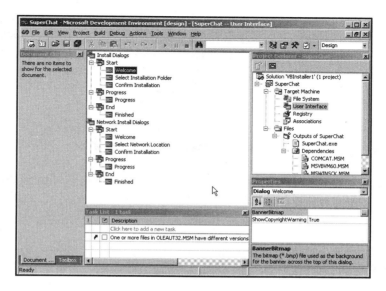

**Figure 35.13**

*Customizing the user interface of the installer.*

Another area that you may want to customize is under the Properties of your project. When you right-click your mouse on your project and select Properties from the pop-up menu that appears as a result, Visual InterDev will present the Project Properties dialog where you can make all sorts of modifications and tweaks to the setup, as shown in Figure 35.14. For instance, if you were developing for the Internet, you might want compression to be optimized for size rather than speed.

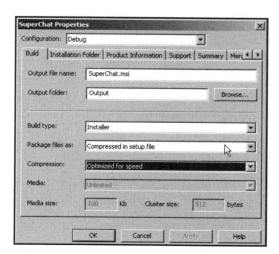

**Figure 35.14**

*The Project Properties dialog allows you to make many fine setup alterations.*

When you have made all the changes to the setup in the Project Properties dialog box, click your mouse on the OK button. Visual InterDev will close the dialog box and return to the Microsoft Developer Environment window. From the Build menu select the Build option. The Microsoft Visual Installer 1.1 builds the actual Windows Installer Package (*.msi*) file for you, which you can then distribute by CD, Internet, or various other means for others to install your Visual Basic programs.

# Where Do You Go From Here?

There are still many other areas of Visual Basic that you may want to explore. The following few paragraphs will introduce you to some of these areas, which you can, if something particularly interests you, research in greater detail.

**ActiveX**—You saw something of ActiveX in this book, but you should have picked up on the fact that there is so much more to ActiveX than what you have seen so far. You have only scratched the surface of a technology for which there is a wealth of material and seemingly endless potential possibilities. In fact, even within ActiveX you will be able to learn about specific areas in greater detail without having to cover every section in depth. There are many books on this very useful technology and even books on subsections of this technology, which you would do well to learn more about.

**DirectX**—Although you already know how to produce graphics and sound in Visual Basic, there is a technology known as DirectX, which comes from Microsoft, which allows your programs to directly work with the underlying hardware of a computer without having to know exactly what you are supporting. This means that you get the benefit of additional speed with less overhead without having to directly support a myriad of variations of hardware. If you are planning to write programs for games, music and synthesizers, or special devices, such as joysticks, you may want to seriously consider learning more about DirectX for Visual Basic.

**API**—There are so many things that you can achieve through use of API calls that it almost goes without saying that this is an area where you would do well if you wanted to advance your Visual Basic skills. API calls will also give you a better understanding of the underlying manner in which Microsoft Windows works, as well as providing your Visual Basic programs with some low-level power that can really boost program performance.

**Active Directory**—Many possibilities exist by learning further Visual Basic skills that deal with Active Directory. You can tap into so much information and add so much power to your Visual Basic programs that, for this reason alone, furthering your knowledge of this subject becomes worthwhile. If you are thinking of working on any tools for networks, whether administrative or otherwise, learning Active Directory is an important technology that you will want to cover in greater detail.

**Active Server Pages (ASP)**—When browsing the Internet, many pages that once had a suffix of *.htm* now contain a suffix of *.asp*. These Active Server Pages are actually just Visual Basic with a few rules here and there, which you would find very easy to learn and which would allow you to expand your Visual Basic skills to the Internet. There is a lot of material on this subject and also a lot of work for people that know how to write Active Server Pages.

**VBScript**—VBScript is seen both in dynamic HTML pages and also as stand-alone scripts for performing tasks on local computers. The beauty of VBScript is that you can edit this simply with Notepad or some other text editor and do not require a compiler to make any changes. This makes learning VBScript perfect for administrators or IT personnel that must be able to make rapid changes. A high turnover of staff or a shared environment lends itself to using VBScript so that other people can see clearly what is happening. VBScript is almost like a subset of Visual Basic, although this is not strictly true; however, thinking of it in this light shows you that you practically already know VBScript with the knowledge you have now.

**SQL**—If you are looking at getting into database work, then you can do quite well by advancing your Visual Basic skills with SQL programming skills, which tie in together to give your programs tremendous power when dealing with vast volumes of data. Having Visual Basic and SQL programming skills is another area that is in high demand in the workforce. Although purely for the additional database power that this could give your programs, you might want to look into this area in more detail.

# What You Must Know

Congratulations! You have completed the *Starting with Visual Basic* book and can now look at advancing and consolidating your Visual Basic skills. Hopefully, this book will have shown you that you can achieve even seemingly daunting programming tasks in Visual Basic by breaking down the project into smaller, manageable sections and using good coding practices. Remember that programming in Visual Basic should be a rewarding and enjoyable experience, not a chore—so get out there and start getting creative! Before you continue your Visual Basic programming, make sure you understand the following key concepts:

- ◆ You can use Microsoft's Package and Deployment Wizard to create standard setup programs that you can use for distributing your programs to other people.

- ◆ The new Microsoft Visual Studio Installer 1.1 allows you to create Windows Installer Package files (*.msi*) that let your Visual Basic programs install using Active Directory and Windows Installer, giving your packages many advantages over traditional installation methods.

- ◆ There are still many areas of Visual Basic that remain for you to explore and an idea of where to go from here will be useful to you to get even more out of the Visual Basic language.

# License Agreement/Notice of Limited Warranty